for being under the ice
das Eismeer, das sich unter dem Eis befindet
la mer de glace pour être sous la glace

for having provided the elegance of engineering
der der Technik Eleganz verlieh
pour avoir apporté l'élégance de l'ingénierie

for being so much himself
der so sehr er selbst ist
pour être tellement lui-même

rte
Amérique

e Chareau

The frozen sea

Denis Santachiara

Alberto Meda

Frank O. Gehry

Francesco Clemente

oir inventé la maison intelligente
intelligente Haus erfand
ng invented the smart house

pour être un inventeur et non un styliste
der ein Erfinder und kein Stilist ist
for being an inventor and not a stylist

pour être libre dans un pays qui ne l'est plus
freier Mann in einem unfrei gewordenen Land
for being free in a country which is no longer so

Ph.S. 1987

TASCHEN

KÖLN LONDON MADRID NEW YORK PARIS TOKYO

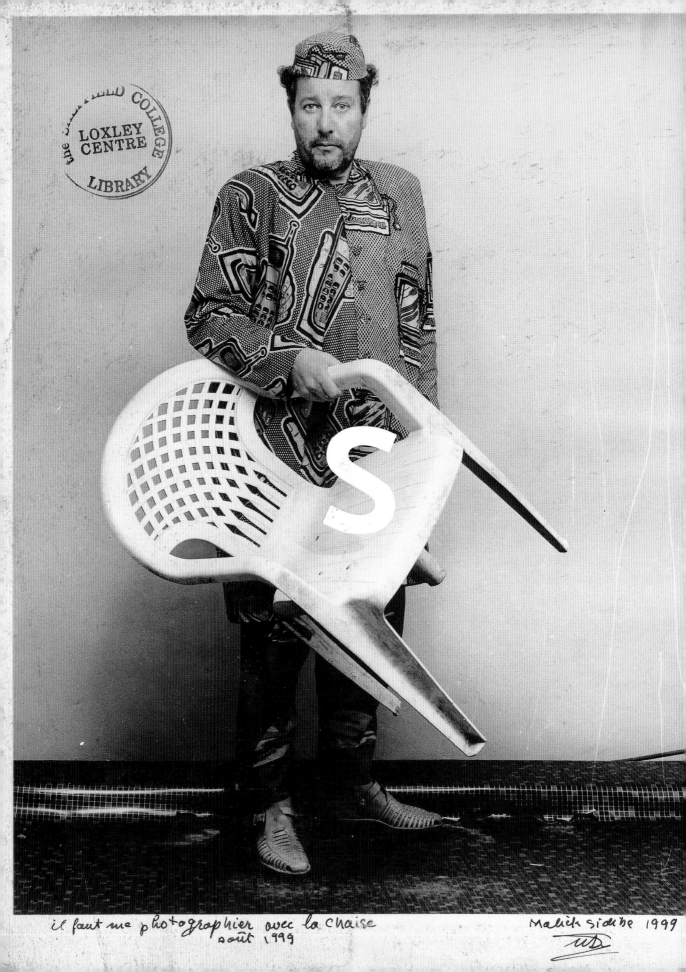

il faut me photographier avec la chaise
août 1999

Malick Sidibé 1999

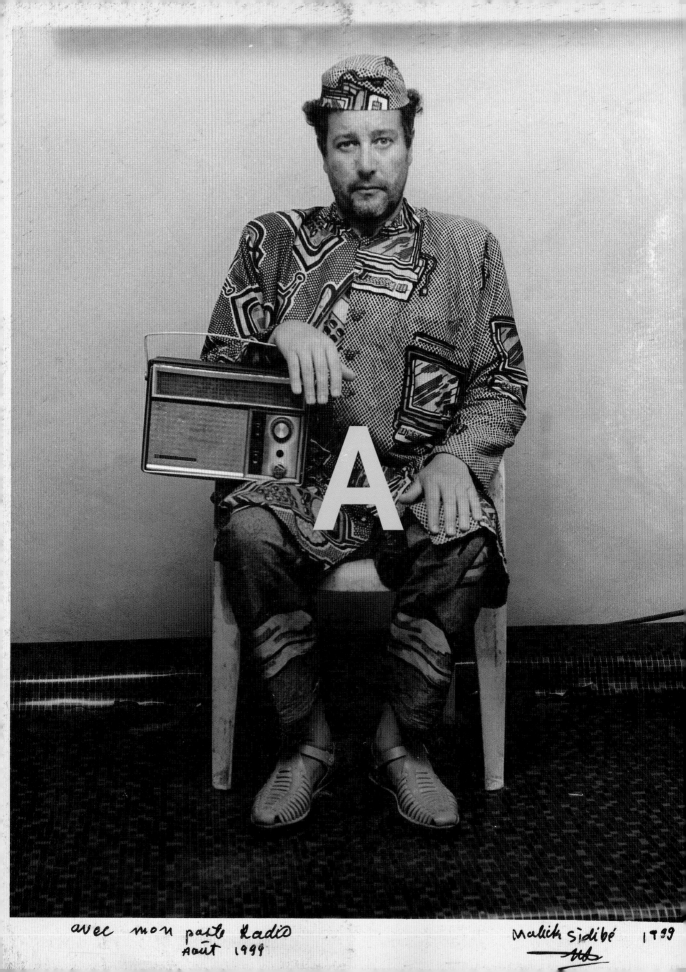

avec mon parle radio
août 1999

Malick Sidibé 1999

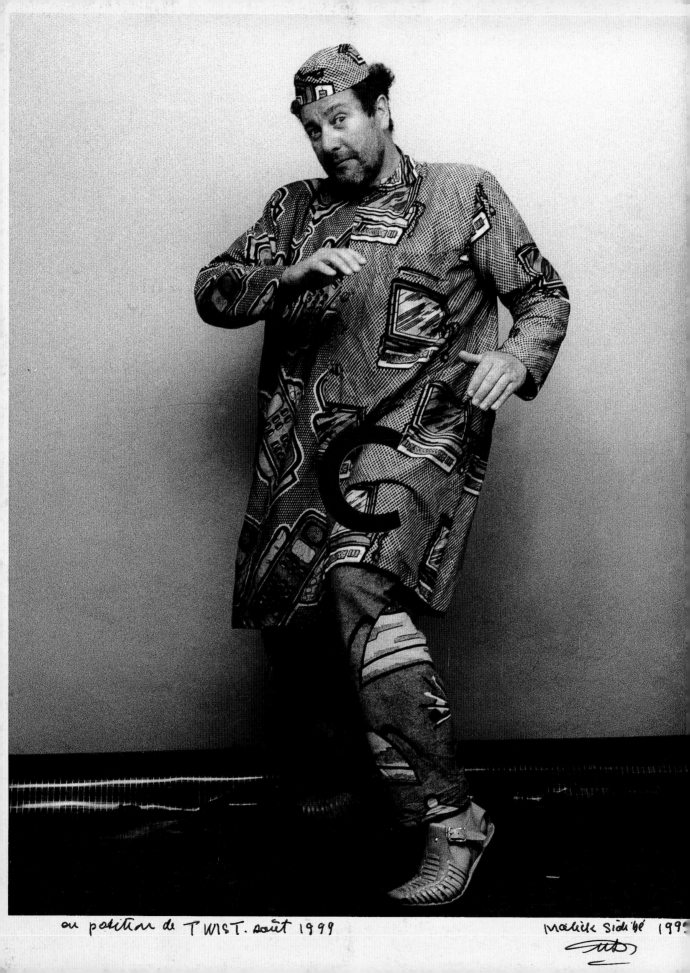

en position de TWIST. août 1999

Malick Sidibé 199

STARCK
Benedikt Taschen Verlag GmbH
ISBN 3–8228–6397–1

Edited by Simone Philippi, Cologne
Designed by Mark Thomson, London, and Catinka Keul, Cologne
Captions and index by Susanne Husemann and Anja Lenze, Cologne
Production by Ute Wachendorf, Cologne
German translations by Sylvia Gehlert, Cachan, and Stefan Barmann, Cologne
English translations by Terry Hale, Norwich, and Peter Snowdon, Newcastle upon Tyne
Printed in Italy

Kominform (1947) et engage contre l'Occident la « guerre froide ». Objet d'un culte, célébré tant en U. R. S. S. que dans les partis communistes des démocraties populaires et des pays occidentaux, il fait procéder à de nouvelles purges (« procès de Prague », « complot des blouses blanches ») avant de mourir en mars 1953. Le XX⁰ Congrès du parti communiste (1956) amorça la « déstalinisation » et en 1961 le corps de Staline fut retiré du mausolée de Lénine dans lequel il avait été placé.

Stalingrad *(bataille de)* [sept. 1942 - févr. 1943], victoire décisive remportée après de durs combats — qui se sont déroulés autour de Stalingrad (auj. Volgograd) — par les Soviétiques sur la VI⁰ armée allemande (Paulus), qui capitula le 2 février 1943. Elle marqua le tournant de la guerre sur le front russe.

STAMBOLIJSKI (Aleksandăr), homme politique bulgare (Slavovica 1879 - *id.* 1923). Chef de l'Union agrarienne depuis 1905, il fut Premier ministre en 1919-20 puis en 1920-1923. Il fut fusillé lors du coup d'État de 1923.

STAMFORD, port des États-Unis (Connecticut) ; 102 000 h.

STAMITZ (Johann Wenzel) ou **STAMIC** (Jan Václav), compositeur tchèque (Německý Brod, Bohême, 1717 - Mannheim 1757), chef de l'école de Mannheim, un des foyers de l'art symphonique en Europe, à l'origine du style galant.

Stampa (la), quotidien italien de tendance libérale progressiste, créé à Turin en 1894.

Stamp Act (1765), loi britannique, qui frappa d'un droit de timbre les actes publics dans les colonies de l'Amérique du Nord. Très impopulaire, elle fut à l'origine de la guerre de l'Indépendance.

Standaard (De), quotidien belge de tendance catholique, créé en 1914 à Anvers.

STANHOPE (James, 1ᵉʳ *comte* **de**), homme politique britannique (Paris 1673 - Londres 1721). L'un des chefs du parti whig, secrétaire d'État (1714-1721), il dirigea la politique étrangère, privilégiant l'alliance avec la France.

STANISLAS *(saint)*, martyr polonais (Szczepanow, près de Tarnów, 1030 - Cracovie 1079). Évêque de Cracovie (1072), il fut tué par le roi Boleslas II, qu'il avait excommunié. — Il est le patron de la Pologne.

STANISLAS Iᵉʳ LESZCZYŃSKI (Lwów 1677 - Lunéville 1766), roi de Pologne en titre de 1704 à 1766, en fait de 1704 à 1709 et de

STANLEY POOL → *Malebo Pool.*

STANLEYVILLE → *Kisangani.*

STANOVOÏ *(monts),* chaîne de montagnes la Sibérie orientale ; 2 412 m.

STANS, comm. de la Suisse, ch.-l. du de canton de Nidwald (Unterwald) ; 6 000 h.

STARA PLANINA, nom bulgare du Balk

STARA ZAGORA, v. de Bulgarie ; 142 000

STARCK (Philippe), designer et archit d'intérieur français (Paris 1949). Créateur séries de meubles et d'objets d'une struc simple, mais inventive, il est attaché à l'exp sion symbolique des formes comme de l'esp

STARK (Johannes), physicien allemand (S ckenhof 1874 - Traunstein 1957). Il a décou le dédoublement des raies spectrales s l'influence d'un champ électrique. (Prix N 1919.)

STAROBINSKI (Jean), critique suisse de l gue française (Genève 1920). Une formatio psychiatre et une vision philosophique, fon sur la « sympathie » pour l'auteur, sous-ten sa méthode critique *(Jean-Jacques Rousseau, transparence et l'obstacle).*

STASSFURT, v. de l'Allemagne démocr que ; 26 000 h. Mines de potasse et de

STATEN ISLAND, île des États-Unis, cor tuant un borough de New York, au S.-O. Manhattan.

STAUDINGER (Hermann), chimiste allem (Worms 1881 - Fribourg-en-Brisgau 1965), Nobel en 1953 pour ses recherches sur macromolécules.

STAUDT (Karl Georg Christian **von**), mat maticien allemand (Rothenburg ob der Tau 1798 - Erlangen 1867). Il essaya de reconsti l'ensemble de la géométrie projective, indép damment de toute relation métrique.

STAUFFENBERG (Claus **Schenk**, *comte* v officier allemand (Jettingen 1907 - Berlin 19 Il prépara et exécuta l'attentat du 20 juill. 19 auquel échappa Hitler. Il fut fusillé.

STAVANGER, port de Norvège, sur l'Atla que ; 93 000 h. Port de pêche, de comme de voyageurs et pétrolier. Centre indust Cathédrale romane et gothique.

STAVELOT, v. de Belgique (Liège) ; 6 00 Restes d'une ancienne abbaye (musées).

Stavisky *(affaire)* [1933-34], scandale finan au Crédit municipal de Bayonne, dévoilé en 1933. Elle contribua à la chute du minis

TEINBECK (John), écrivain américain (Sali-
s, Californie, 1902 - New York 1968). Ses
mans peignent les milieux populaires califor-
ns (*Tortilla Flat*, 1935 ; *Des souris et des hommes*,
37 ; *les Raisins de la colère*, 1939 ; *À l'est d'Éden*,
52). [Prix Nobel 1962.]

TEINBERG (Saul), dessinateur américain
rigine roumaine (Rîmnicu Sărat, Munténie,
14). Il a renouvelé l'humour et la satire par
exceptionnelle invention plastique, nourrie
si bien d'anciennes traditions calligraphiques
e de l'influence du cubisme.

TEINER (Jakob), mathématicien suisse (Ut-
storf 1796 - Berne 1863), l'un des plus
nds spécialistes de la géométrie.

TEINER (Rudolf), philosophe et pédagogue
richien (Kraljević, Croatie, 1861 - Dornach,
s de Bâle, 1925), auteur d'un système,
throposophie, et d'une pédagogie qui décloi-
ne les matières traditionnelles et intègre
tivité artisanale.

TEINERT (Otto), photographe allemand (Sar-
ruck 1915 - Essen 1978). Ses théories sur la
tographie subjective (objectivité illusoire, irréalité
tout présente et perceptible) sont à l'origine
renouveau de la photographie abstraite.

EINITZ (Ernst), mathématicien allemand
urahütte 1871 - Kiel 1928), fondateur de la
orie algébrique des corps.

EINKERQUE, auj. **Steenkerque,** anc. comm.
Belgique, auj. rattachée à Braine-le-Comte.
maréchal de Luxembourg y vainquit Guil-
me III le 3 août 1692.

EINLEN (Théophile Alexandre), dessinateur,
veur et peintre français d'origine suisse
usanne 1859 - Paris 1923). Il a représenté,
s un esprit libertaire, le peuple de Montmar-
et la vie ouvrière.

inway, manufacture américaine de pianos
dée à New York en 1853 par le facteur
mand Heinrich Engelhard Steinweg (Wolfs-
en 1797 - New York 1871).

EKEL (Wilhelm), médecin et psychanalyste
richien (Boian, Bucovine, 1868 - Londres
0). Il se sépara de Freud et préconisa une
e plus courte où le thérapeute intervient plus
vement.

EKENE, comm. de Belgique (Flandre-Orien-
) ; 15 000 h.

le du roi serpent (musée du Louvre),
nument comportant, sculpté dans le calcaire

la musique, la peinture et un récit de v
Rome, Naples et Florence (1817-1826) qu'il si
nom de « Stendhal ». Il publie ensuite *De l'.*
(1822) et un essai sur le romantisme (*Ra
Shakespeare*, 1823-1825). Méconnu, il fait pa
Armance (1827), *le Rouge* et le Noir* (1830).
il retourne en Italie comme consul à Civit
chia, persuadé que son œuvre ne peut
immédiatement comprise. Pendant un co
Paris, il publie *les Mémoires d'un touriste* (18
Chartreuse* de Parme (1839) et les *Chro
italiennes* (1839). Son œuvre posthume a dé
vement consacré sa gloire (*Lamiel*, 1889 ;
Henry Brulard, 1890 ; *Lucien Leuwen*, 1894
style nerveux fait vivre dans une action
des héros lyriques qui dissimulent une s
sensibilité sous un apparent cynisme.

STENTOR. *Myth. gr.* Héros de la gue
Troie, célèbre par la force de sa voix.

STEPHENSON (George), ingénieur bri
que (Wylam, près de Newcastle, 1781 -
House, Chesterfield, 1848). Il est con
comme le véritable créateur de la trac
vapeur sur voie ferrée (locomotive *Rocket*,
Son œuvre principale fut l'établisseme
chemin de fer de Liverpool à Manc
(1826-1830).

STERLITAMAK, v. de l'U. R. S. S., a
d'Oufa ; 240 000 h. Centre industriel.

STERN (Isaac), violoniste russe nat
américain (Kremenets, Ukraine, 1920)
fondé, avec Eugene Istomin et Leonard
un trio pour défendre le répertoire roma

STERN (Otto), physicien américain d'
allemande (Sohrau, auj. Żory, 1888 - B
1969). Il a découvert, avec W. Gerla
propriétés magnétiques des atomes et v
concept, introduit par de Broglie, d'ond
ciée à une particule. (Prix Nobel 1943.

STERNBERG (Josef von), cinéaste am
d'origine autrichienne (Vienne 1894 - L
geles 1969). Peintre des passions violente
atmosphères troubles, magicien de l'ima
la lumière, il a fait de Marlène
l'archétype de la femme fatale : *l'A
(1930), *Cœurs brûlés* (id.), *Shanghai Express
l'Impératrice rouge* (1934), *la Femme et l*
(1935).

STERNE (Laurence), écrivain brita
(Clonmel, Irlande, 1713 - Londres 1768)
de *la Vie et les opinions de Tristram Shandy,*

Asahi Beer Hall, Tokyo 1990

Asahi Beer Hall, Tokyo 1990

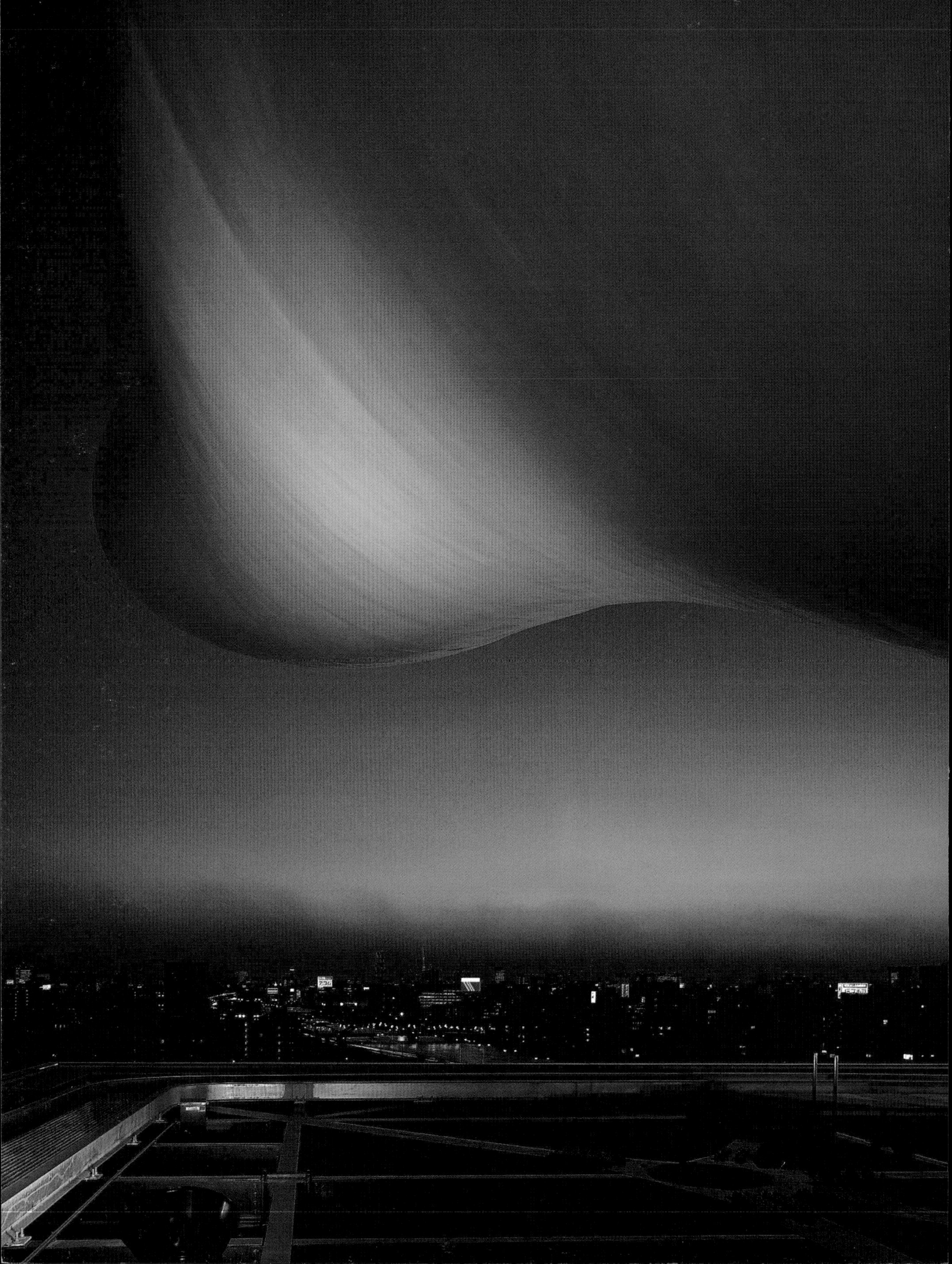

Nani Nani, Tokyo 1989

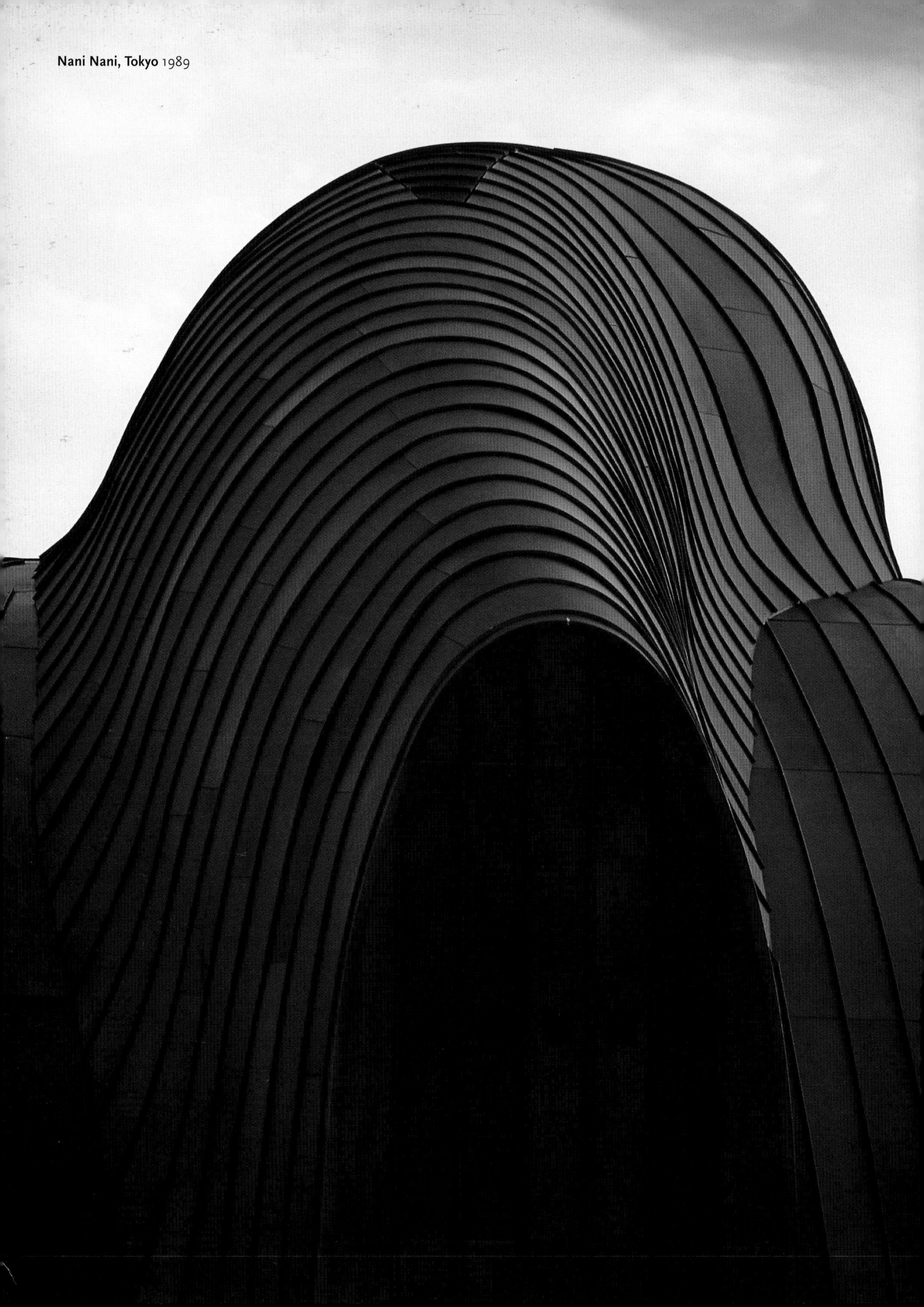

Formentera House 1995

Starck House (3 Suisses) 1994

Starck House (3 Suisses) 1994

Starck House (3 Suisses) 1994

Le civisme est d'avant-garde

Groningen Museum 1993
(with Alessandro Mendini)

1982

CITIES WILL DIE
ROADS WILL DISAPEAR
SCHIZOPHRENIA WILL REIGN
ARCHAIC FAMILY TRIBES RETIRED
IN FAR-AWAY FORESTS
WILL PARTICIPATE IN THE BIG RACE
THANKS TO THEIR VIBRATING ANTENAE
THE SATTELITES WILL BE THE
ONLY MEANS OF EXCHANGE
STARCK FUTURE.

Groningen Museum 1993
(with Alessandro Mendini)

Laguiole factory, Laguiole 1987

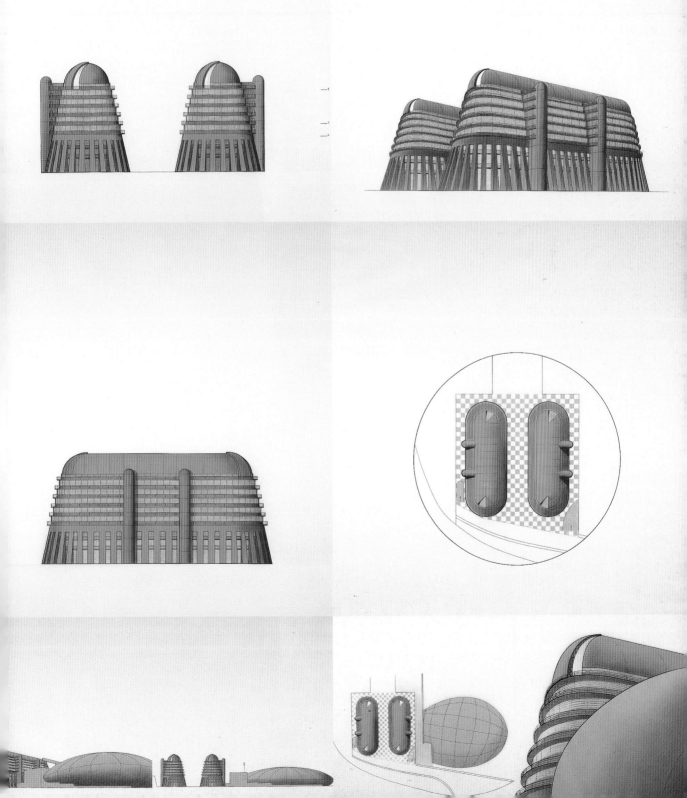

Mutons

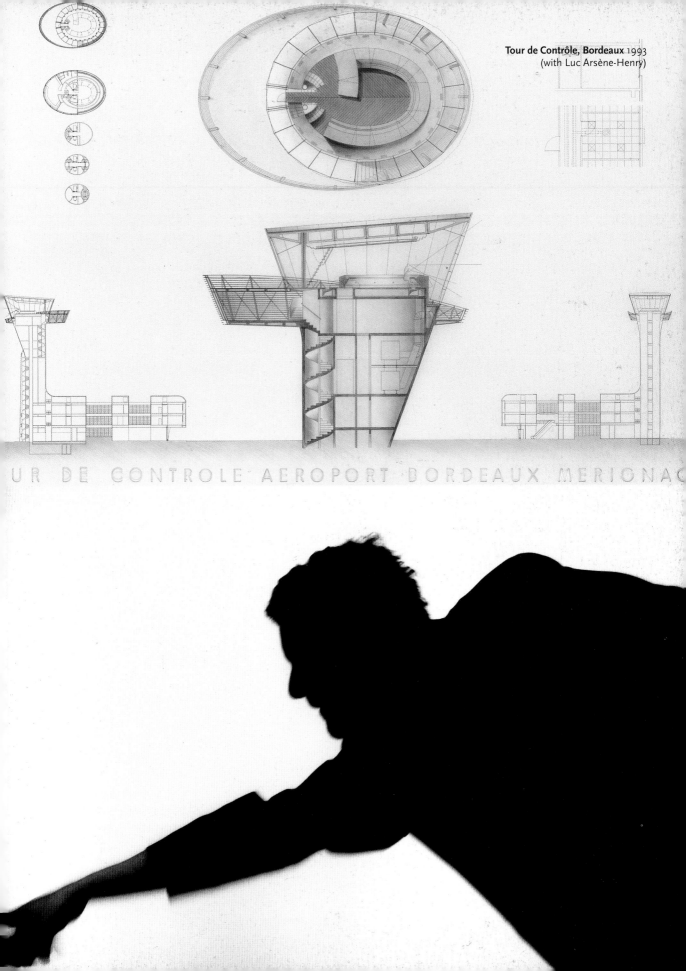

Tour de Contrôle, Bordeaux 1993
(with Luc Arsène-Henry)

UR DE CONTROLE AEROPORT BORDEAUX MERIGNAC

Moondog (project), Tokyo 1990

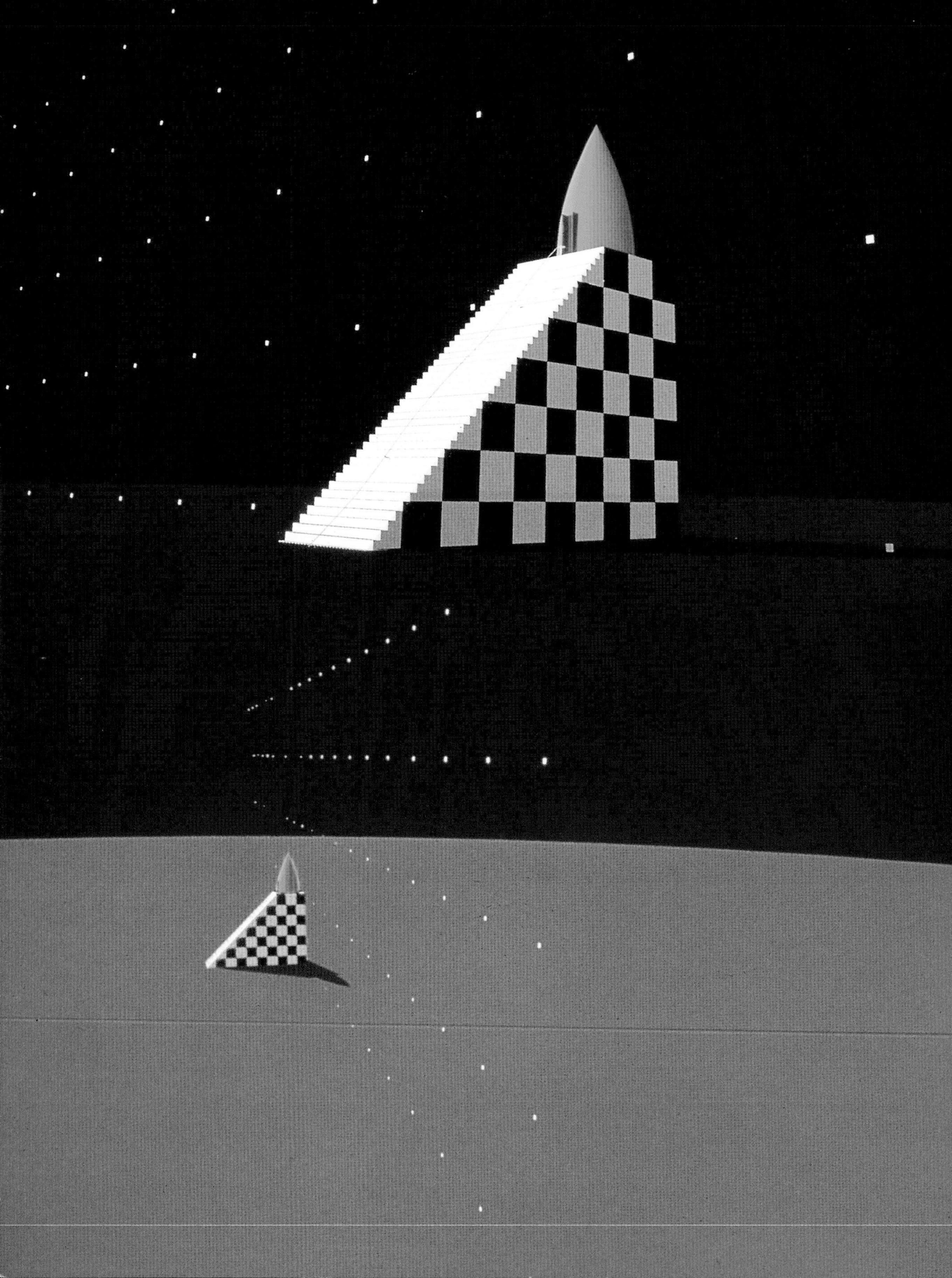

ONAVAITREMPLICETTEBOITEDE
TANTD'ESPRITFRANÇAISQU'ALAFIN
ELLES'INCLINAETDEVINTVENITIENNE

Vitry 2001
(with Luc Arsène-Henry)

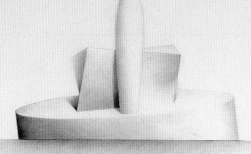

FACADE SUR LE QUAI JULES GUESDE ECHELLE 1/500°

FACADE SUR LA RUE LEON MAUVAIS ECHELLE 1/500°

Ecole des Beaux-Arts, Paris 1991
(with Luc Arsène-Henry)

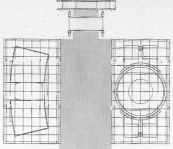

PLAN D'ENSEMBLE DES TOITURES

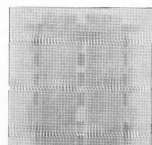

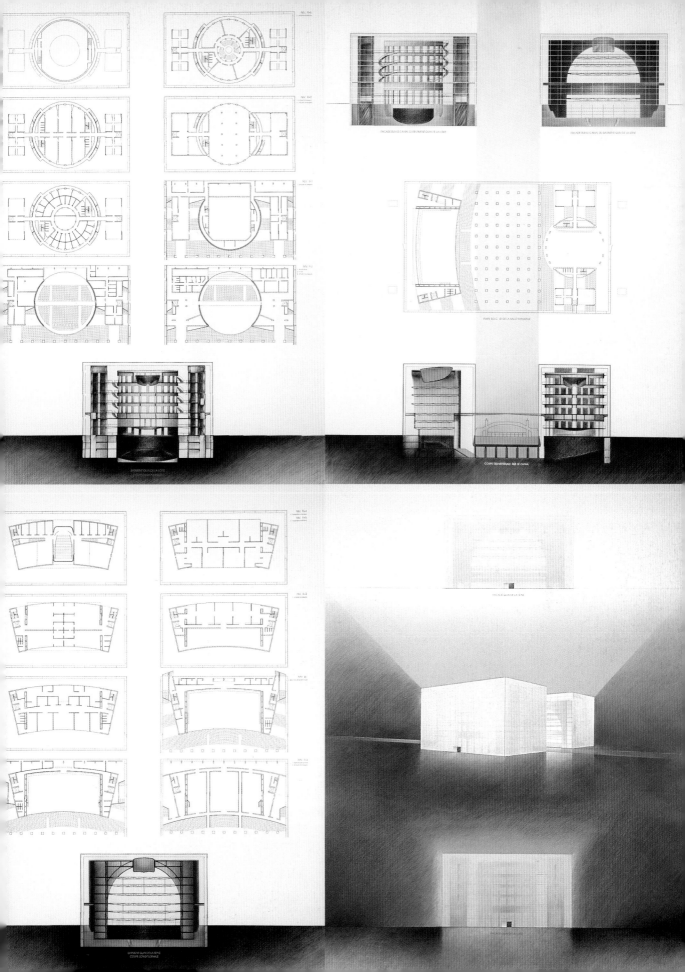

L'obscurité

s'épaissit

ENSAD, Paris 1998
(with Luc Arsène-Henry)

ENSAD, Paris 1998
(with Luc Arsène-Henry)

Rue Starck (project), Issy-les-Moulineaux 1991

Starck House (project), Issy-les-Moulineaux 1991

Condominiums (project), Los Angeles 1992

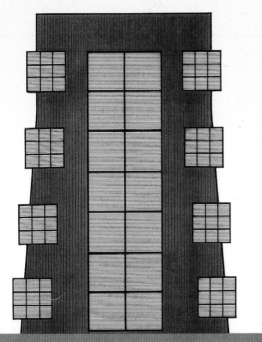

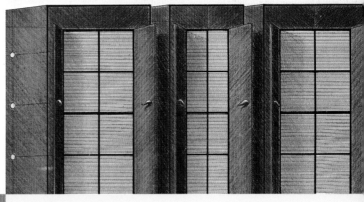

Condominiums (project), Los Angeles 1992

Angle (project), Antwerp 1991

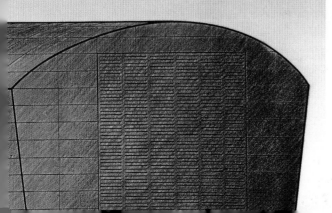

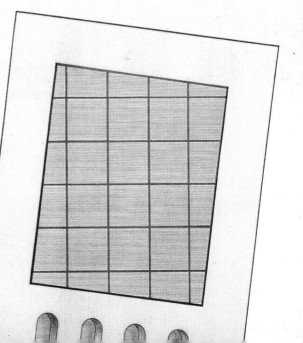

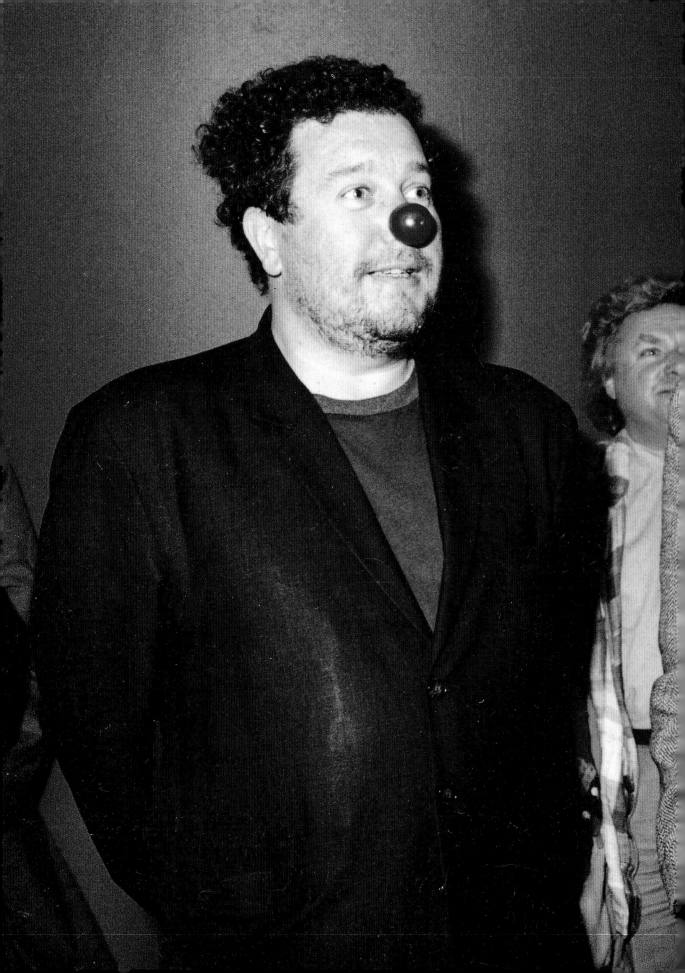

12   Architecture

68   Interiors

152   Furniture

228   Industrial Design

392   Magma

400   Words

422   Overview

446   A–Z

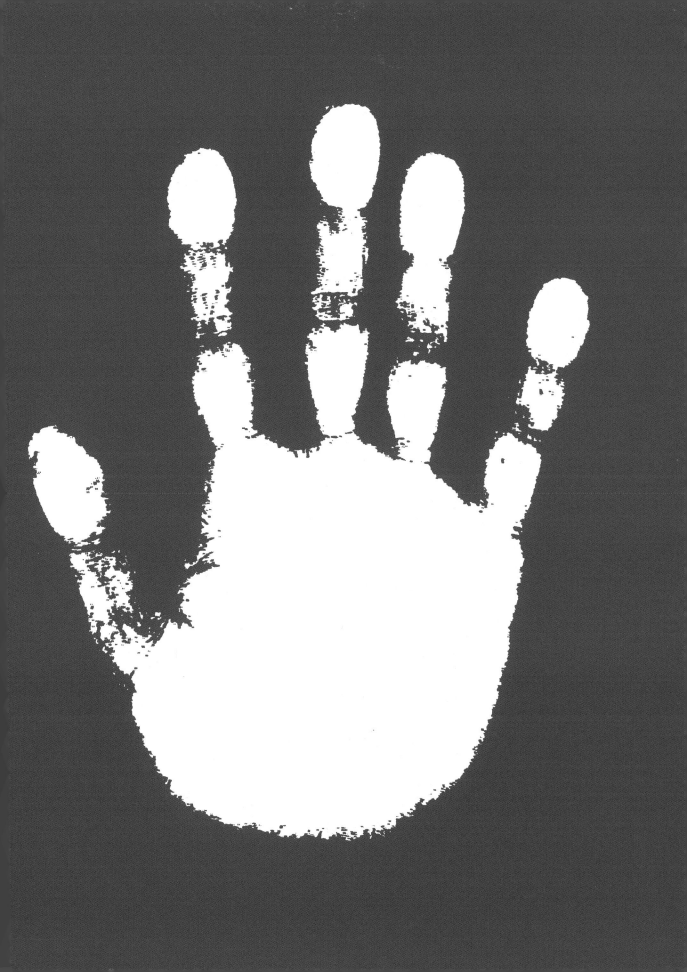

S

Cafe Costes, Paris 1984

Royalton Hotel, New York 1988

Royalton Hotel, New York 1988

Paramount Hotel, New York 1990

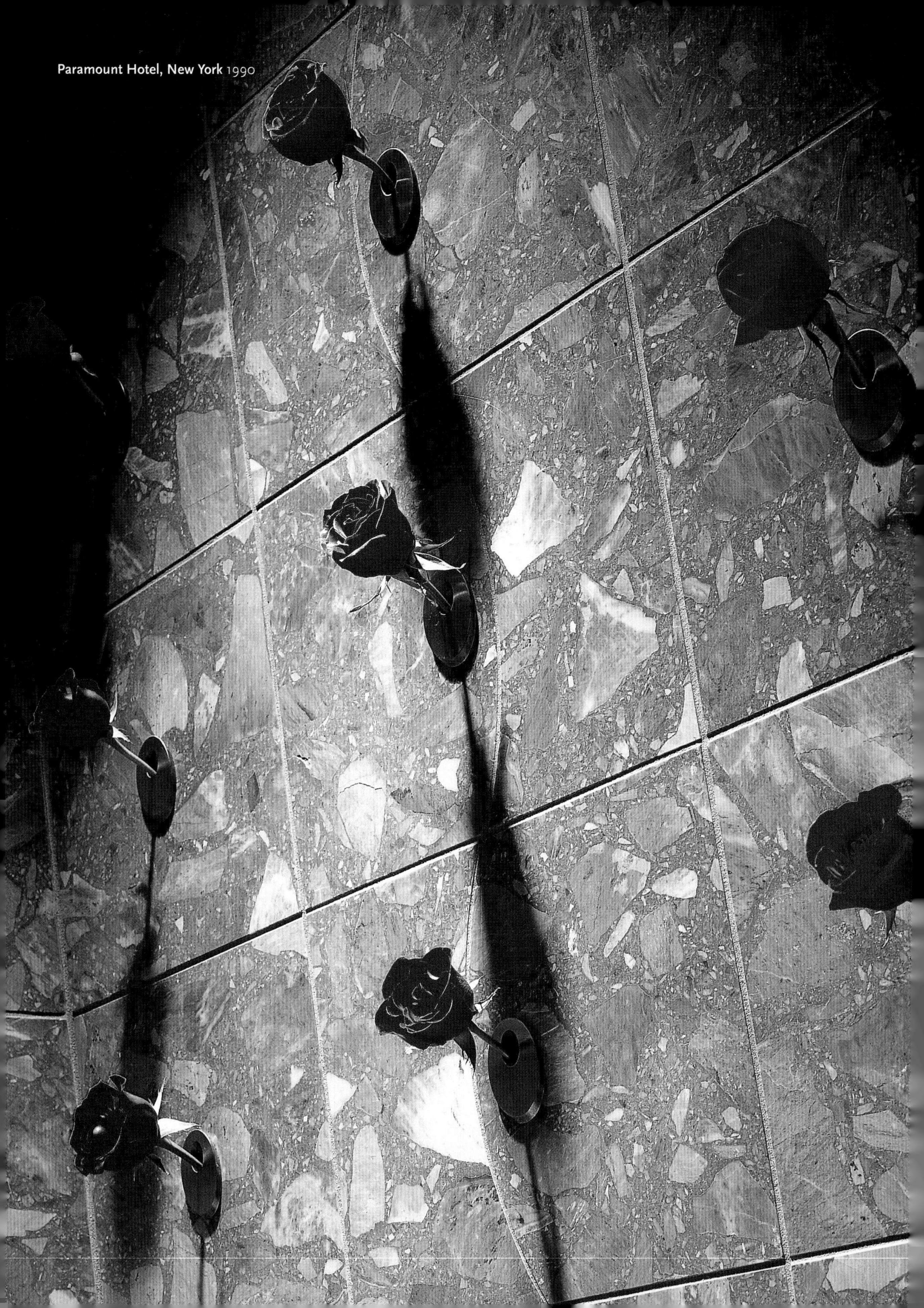

Paramount Hotel, New York 1990

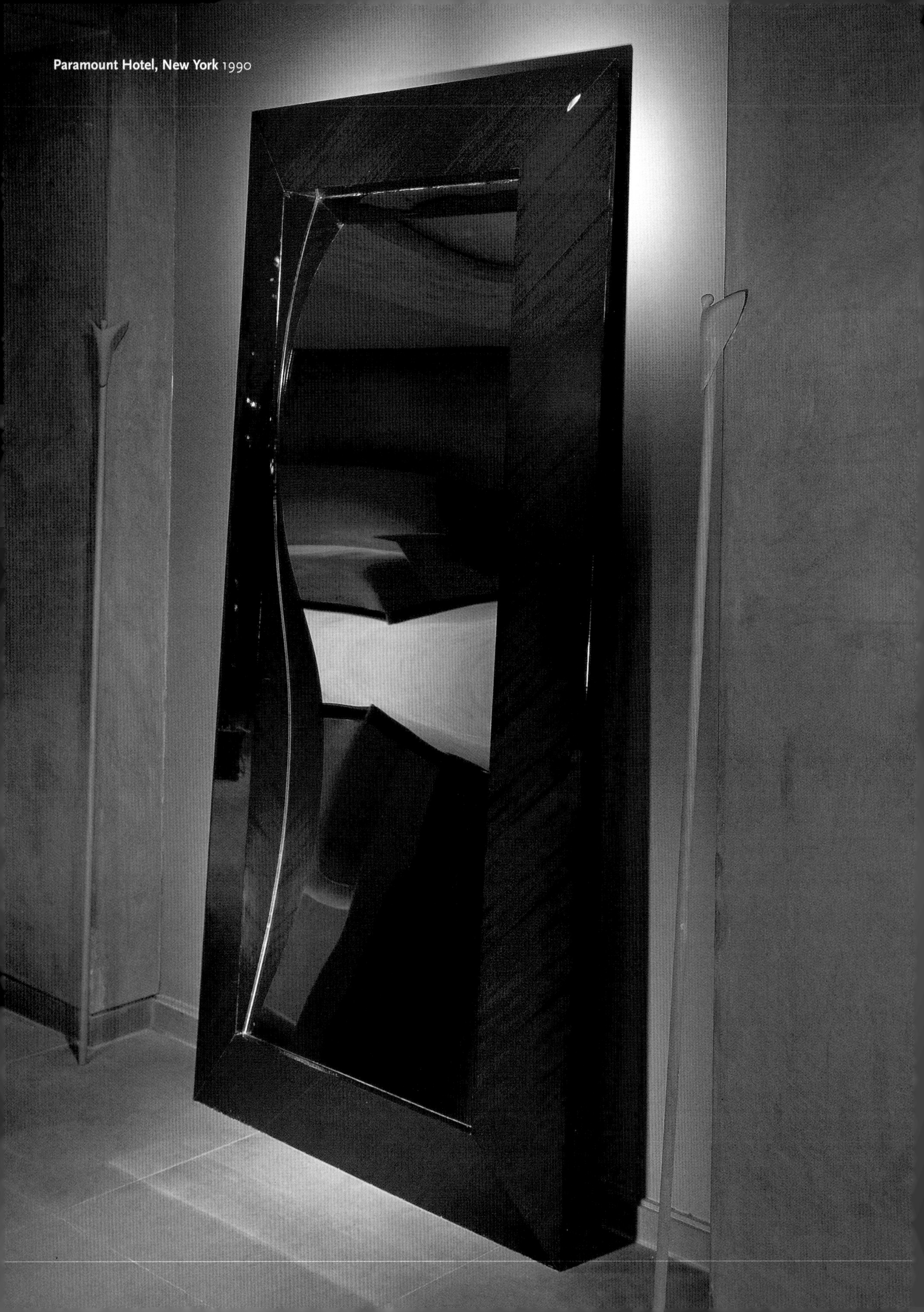

WARM AIR

SUN
RAIN
SNOW
CLOUDS
WARM
COLD

D.Sabàtti

MERCi POUR TOUT PAPA CHERi
JE T'AiME   ARA

Hotel Mondrian, West Hollywood 1996

He is back!!

Hotel Mondrian, West Hollywood 1996

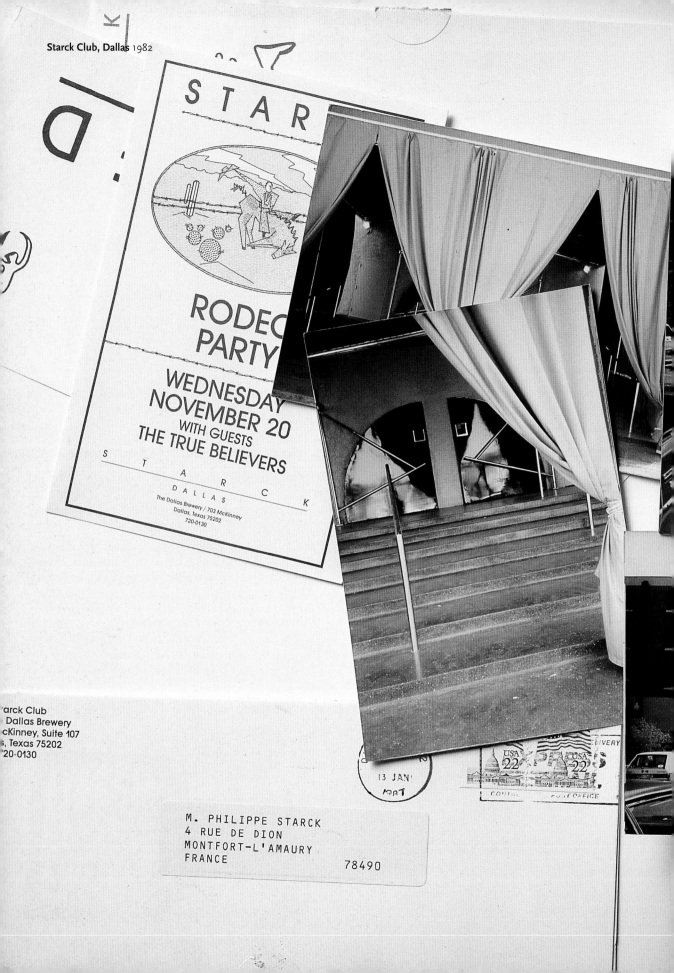

S T A R

RODEO
PARTY

WEDNESDAY
NOVEMBER 20
WITH GUESTS
THE TRUE BELIEVERS

S   T   A   R   C   K
D A L L A S
The Dallas Brewery / 703 McKinney
Dallas, Texas 75202
720-0130

arck Club
Dallas Brewery
cKinney, Suite 107
s, Texas 75202
20-0130

M. PHILIPPE STARCK
4 RUE DE DION
MONTFORT-L'AMAURY
FRANCE   78490

13 JAN
1987

USA 22   USA 22

STARCK CLUB 703 McKINNEY DALLAS TEXAS 75202
AMOUNT
DATE

L'amour est une espèce en voie de disparitio

Restaurant Manin, Tokyo 1987

Boutique Hugo Boss, Paris 1991

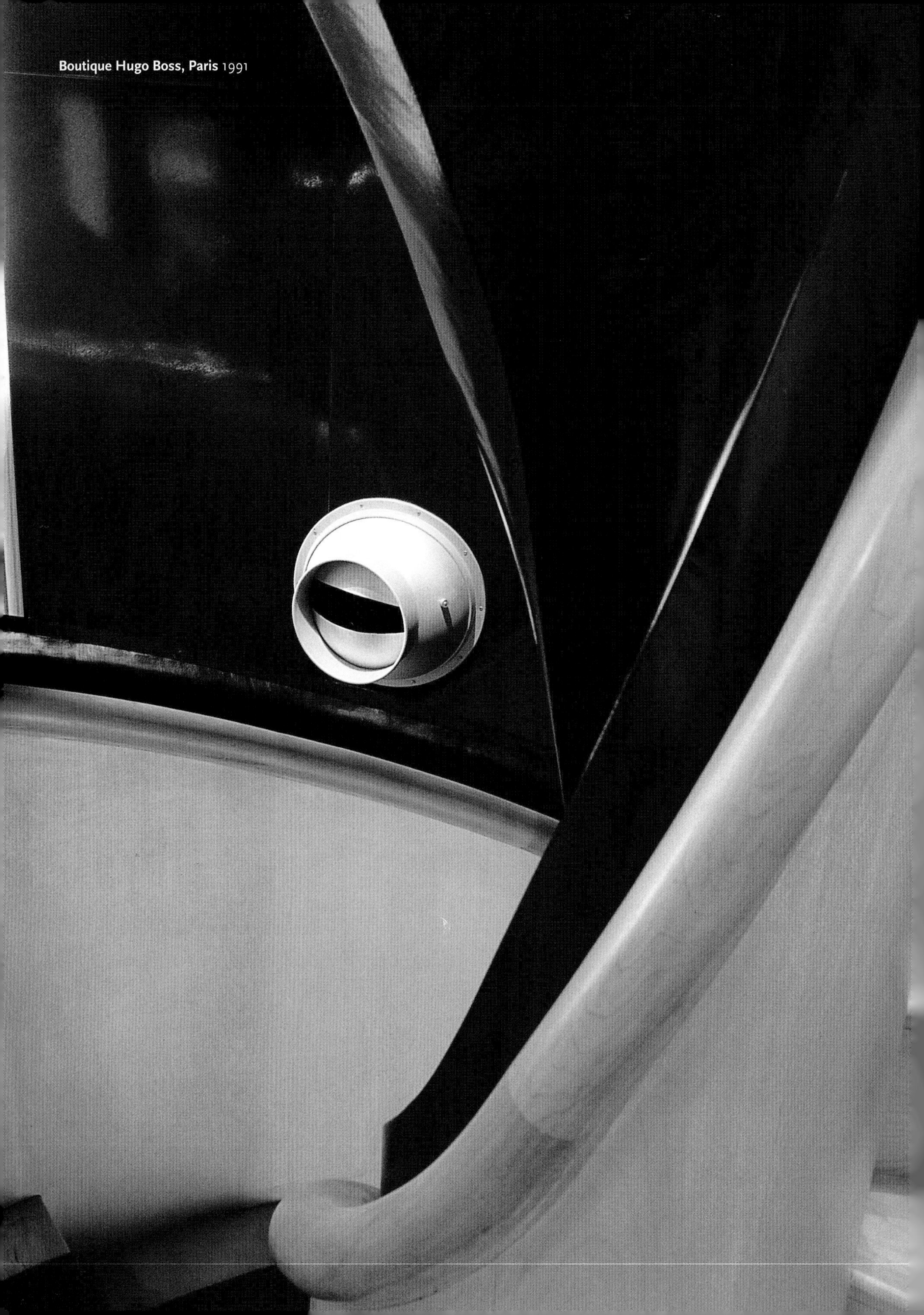

Salon Coppola, Milan 1992

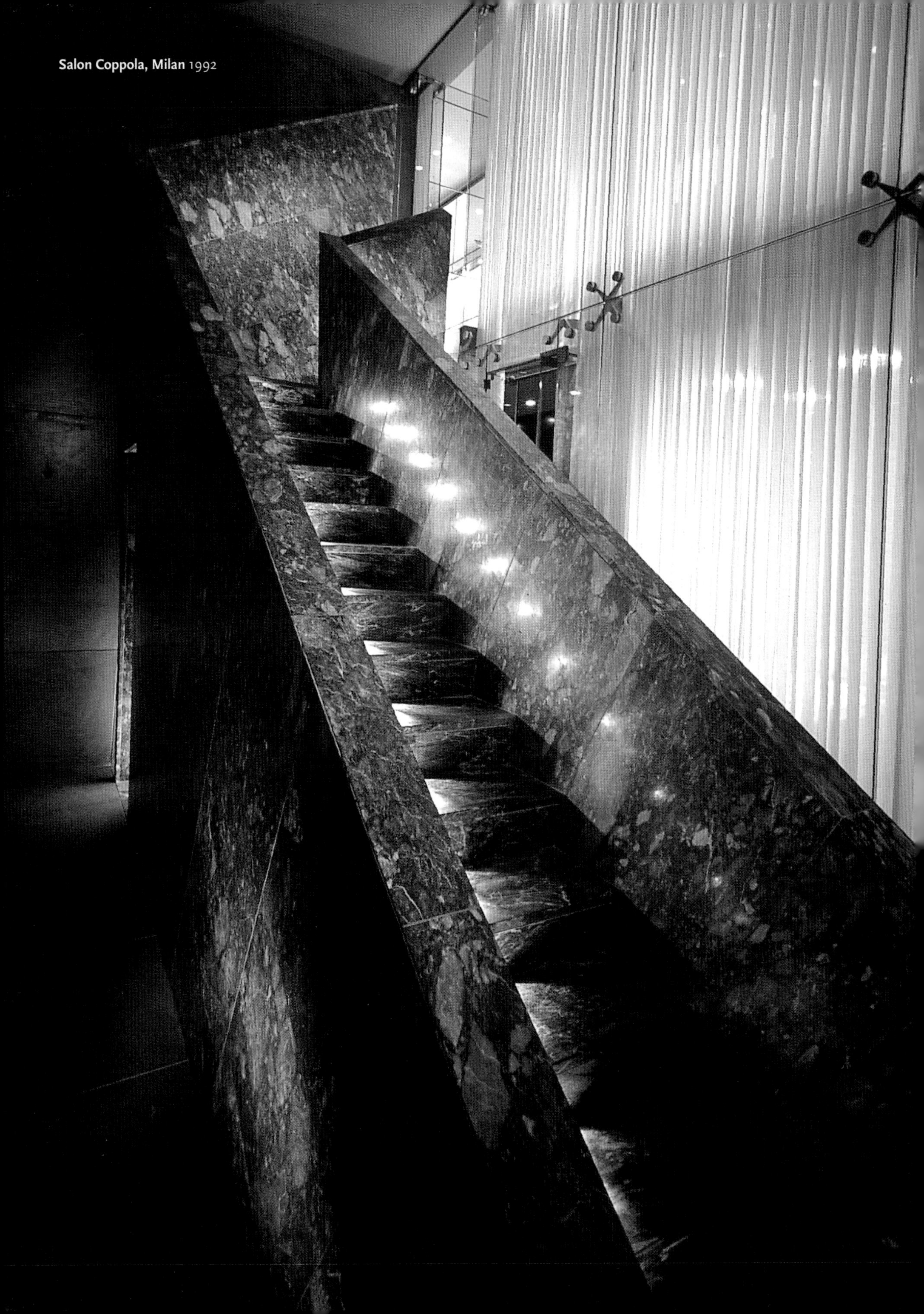

Nous sommes Dieu

Restaurant Teatriz, Madrid 1990

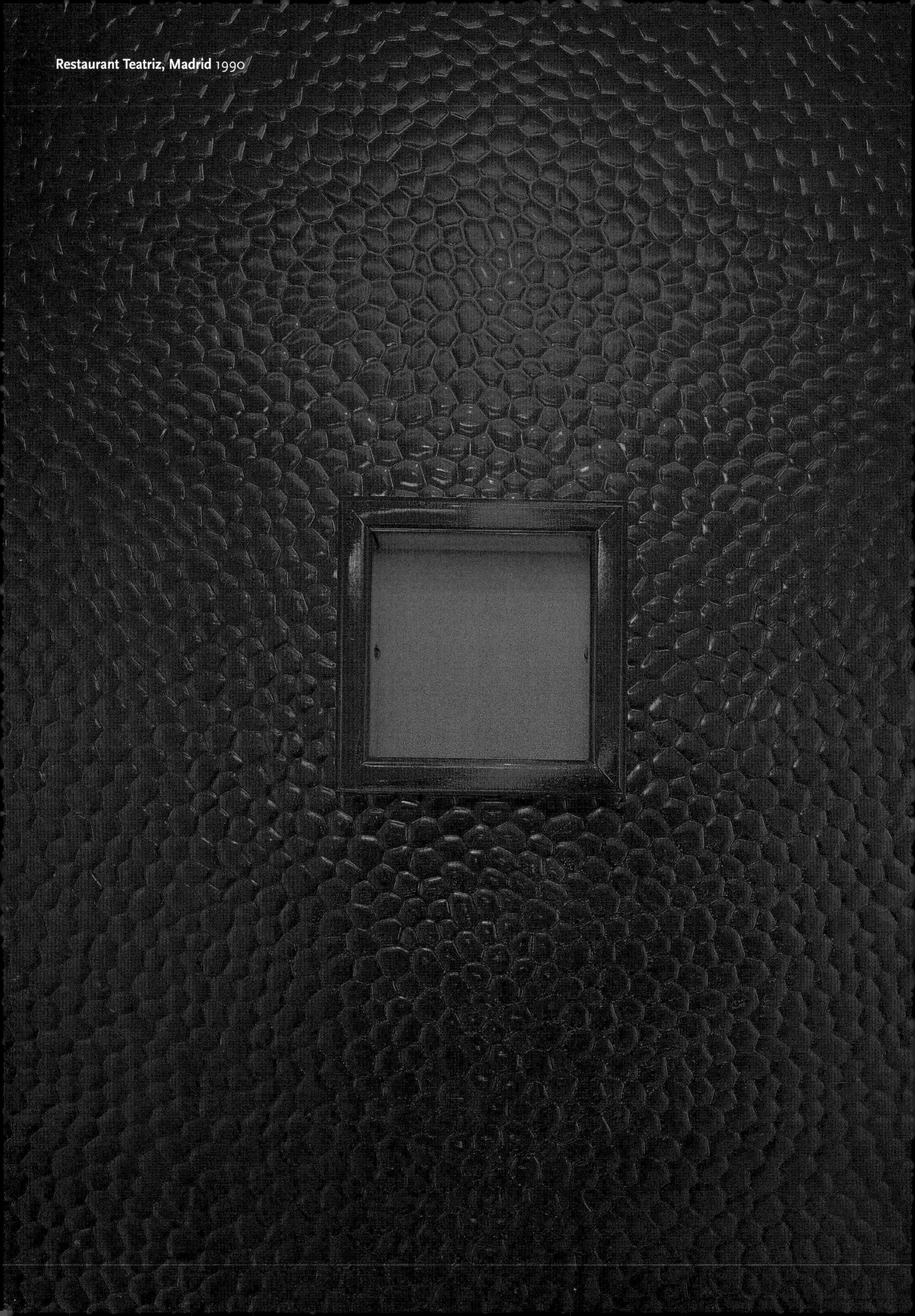

Restaurant Teatriz, Madrid, 1990

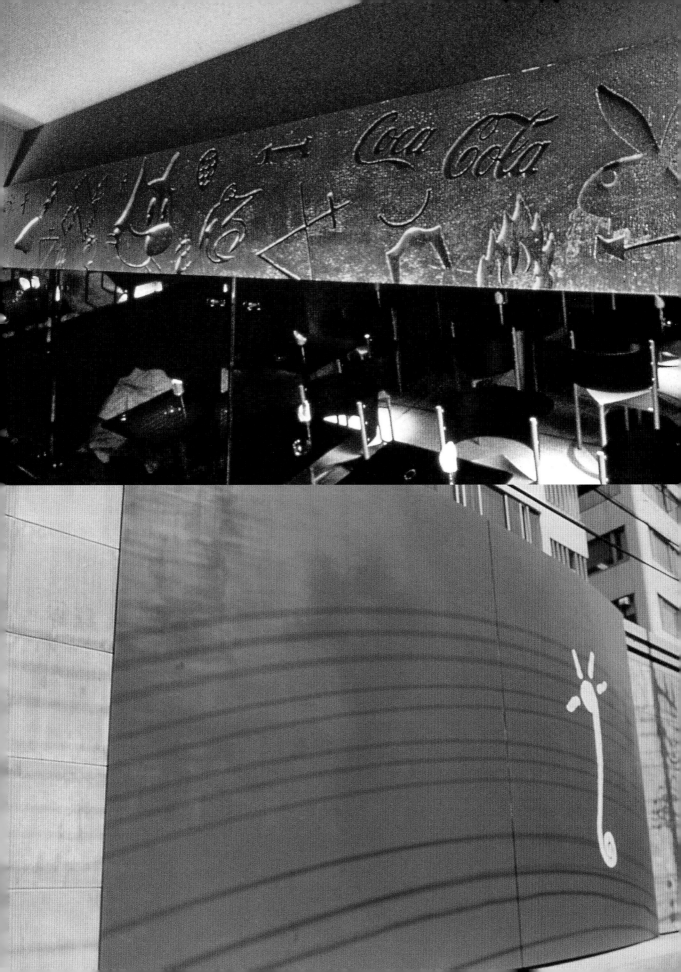

La Cigale, Paris 1988

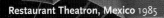

Restaurant Theatron, Mexico 1985

Delano Hotel, Miami 1995

7

Delano Hotel, Miami 1995

AN APPLE
A DAY
KEEPS
THE DOCTOR
AWAY

Restaurant Felix in the Peninsula Hotel, Hong Kong 1994

Restaurant Felix in the Peninsula Hotel, Hong Kong 1994

Oyster Bar in the Peninsula Hotel, Hong Kong 1994

Peninsula Hotel, Hong Kong 1994

Asia de Cuba Restaurant, New York 1997

STARCK
DECOUVRE
LE
SEX...

Everything has a Birth a Life a Death

12   Architecture

68   Interiors

152   Furniture

228   Industrial Design

392   Magma

400   Words

422   Overview

446   A–Z

Président M. 1984

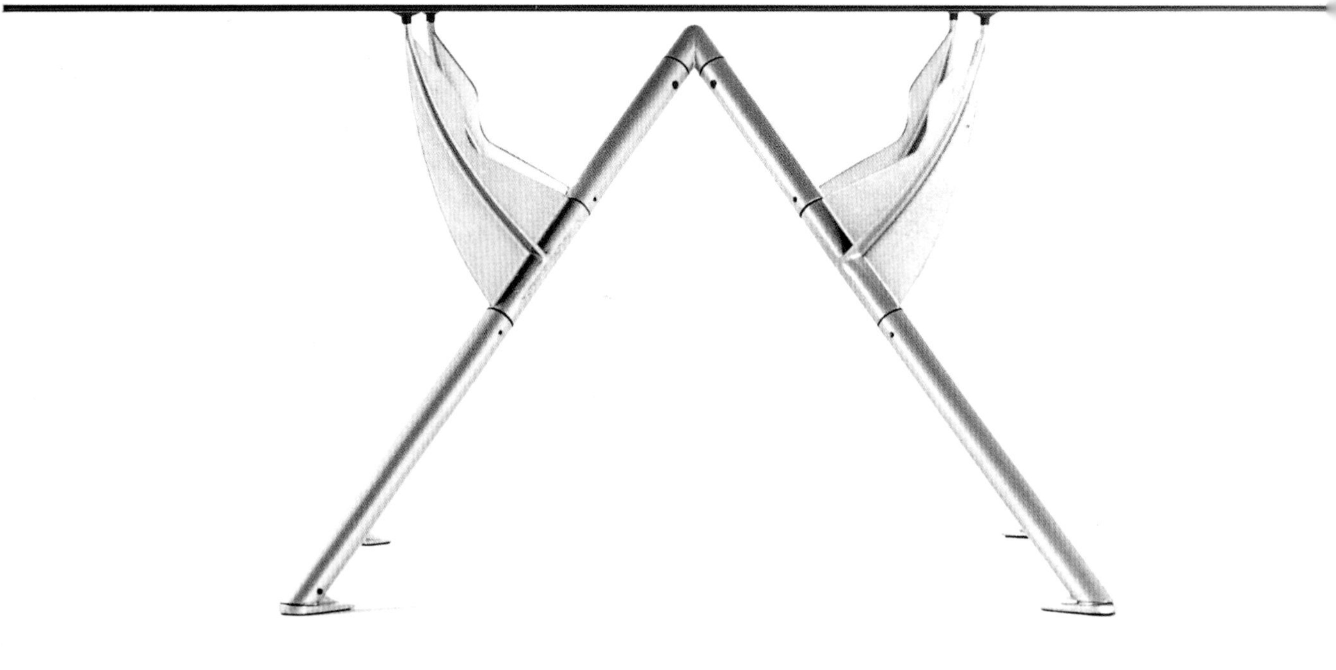

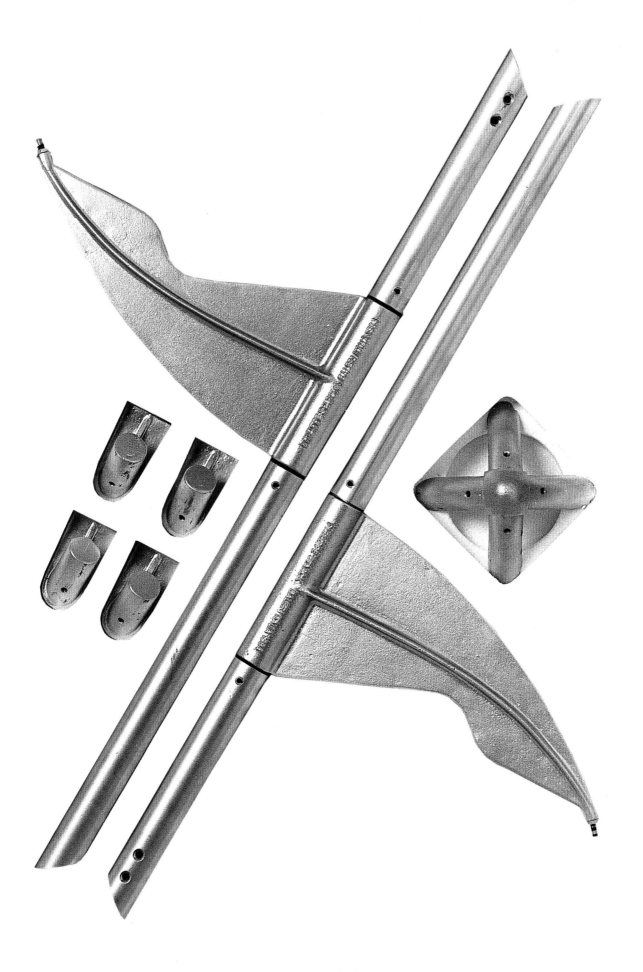

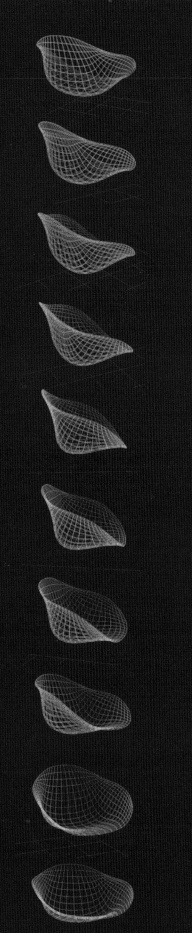

Partageons

Nous sommes des mutants

Saint Esprit and Napoléon 1999

Attila 1999

Gérons la décadence de l'Occident

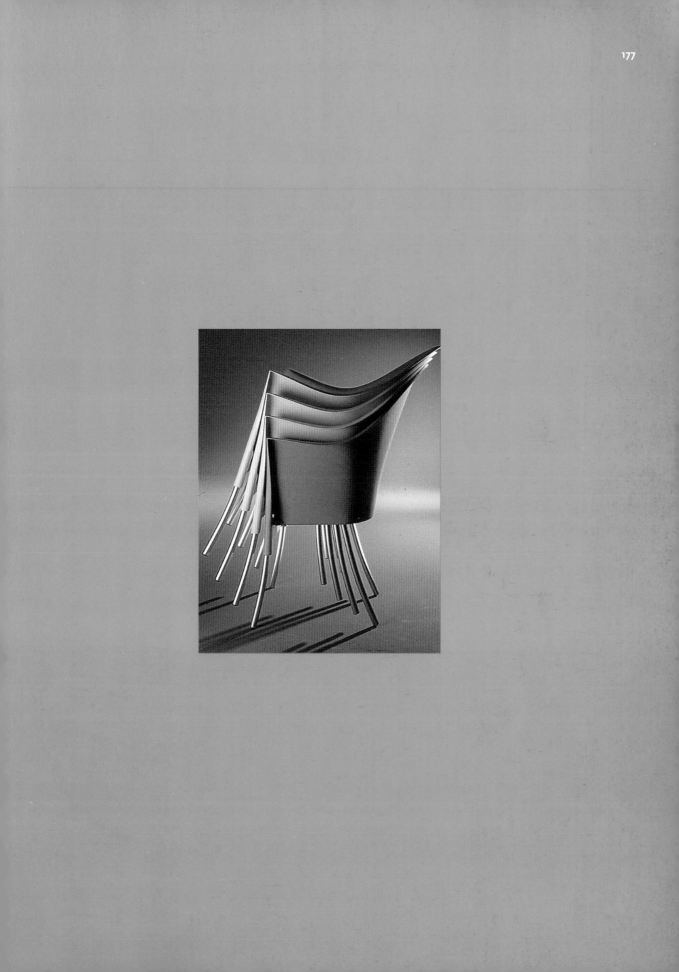

Asahy 1991 and **Paramount** 1991

Vicieuse 1992 and **Boom Rang** 1992

Boom Rang 1992 **Asahy** 1991

Royalton 1991

Lola Mundo 1988 and **Titos Apostos** 1985

J. (Série Lang) 1987

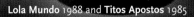

Costes 1984 and **Costes Alluminio** 1988

Pratfall 1985

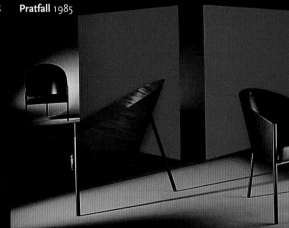

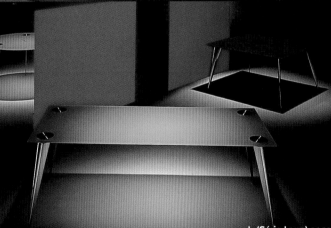

J. (Série Lang) 1991

1979

Colucci 1986 and **Tippy Jackson** 1985

Sarapis 1986 and **Von Vogelsang** 1985

Titos Apostos 1985

Romantica 1987   **Dick Deck** 1989

Costes Alluminio 1988

Bob Dubois 1987

Tessa Nature 1989

Cameleon 1992   **Placide of the Wood** 1989

Royalton Couch 1991

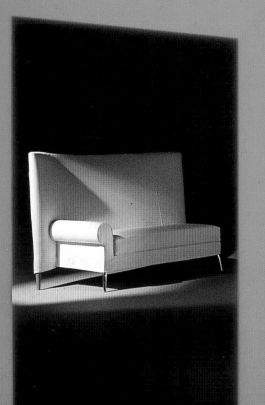

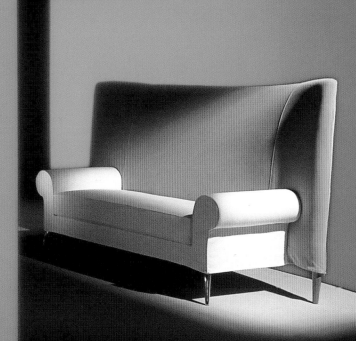

Royalton Long Chair and **Armchair** 1991

Asahy 1991 and **Paramount** 1991

Le paravent de l'autre 1992

Royalton Bed 1992

Royalton 1988

Big Nothing 1997

Cam El Eon 1999

Neoz 1997–1999

GLOIRE
Ô
GRAND
MOI
MOI

merci pour ce wonderfull NEW YEAR les MONDINO'S.

Hairdressing furniture 1989

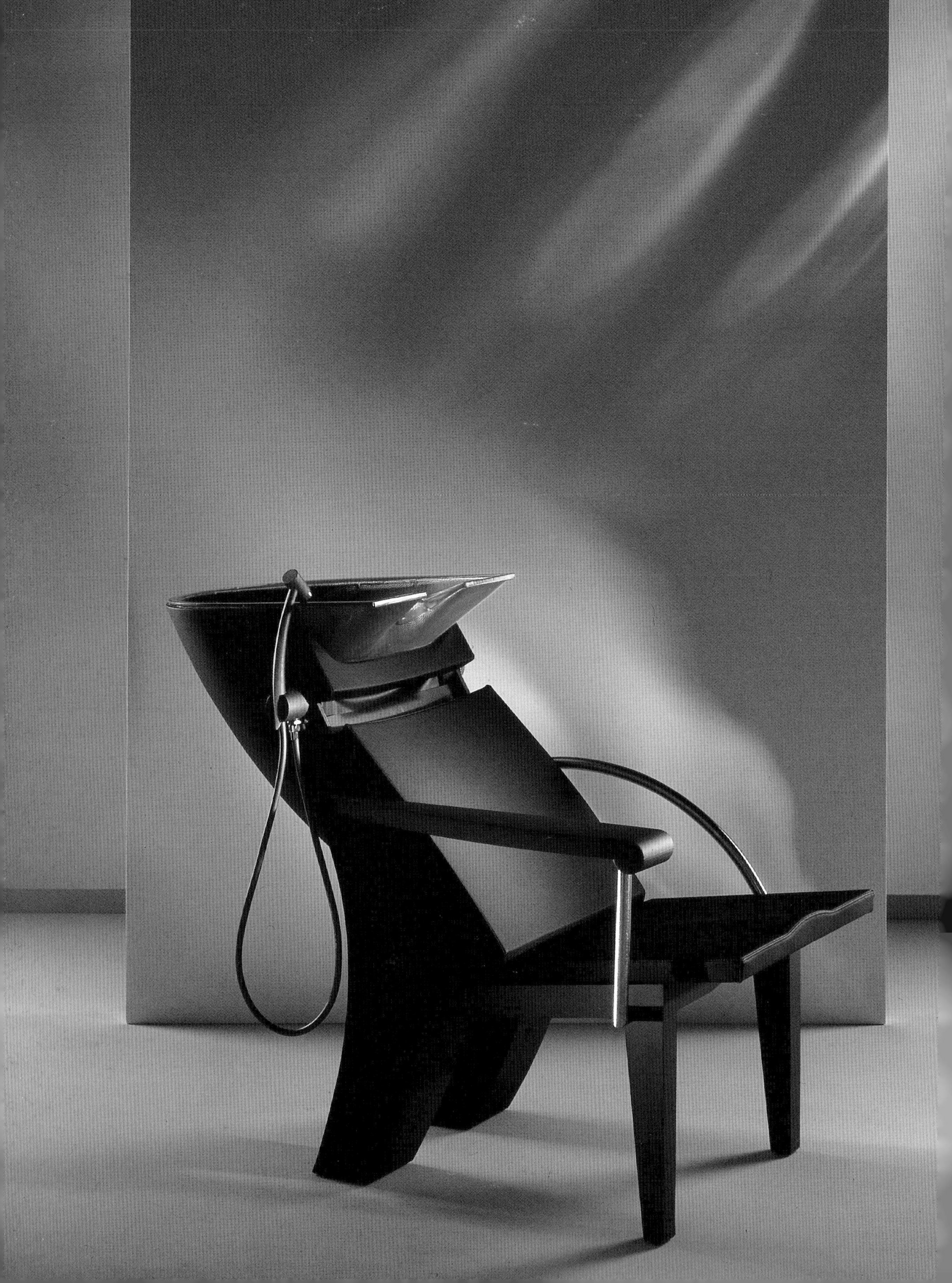

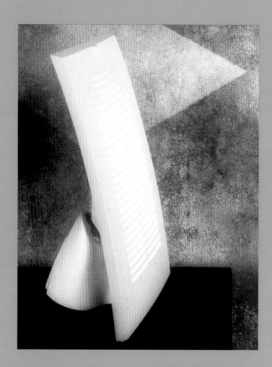

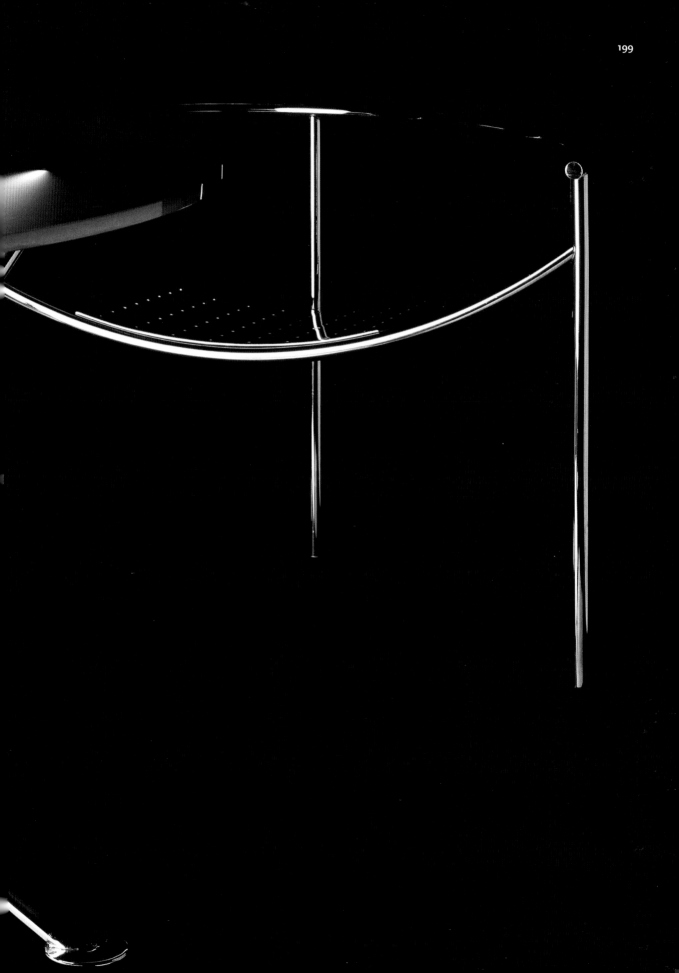

SUMO Table 199

M.T Minimum Table 1998

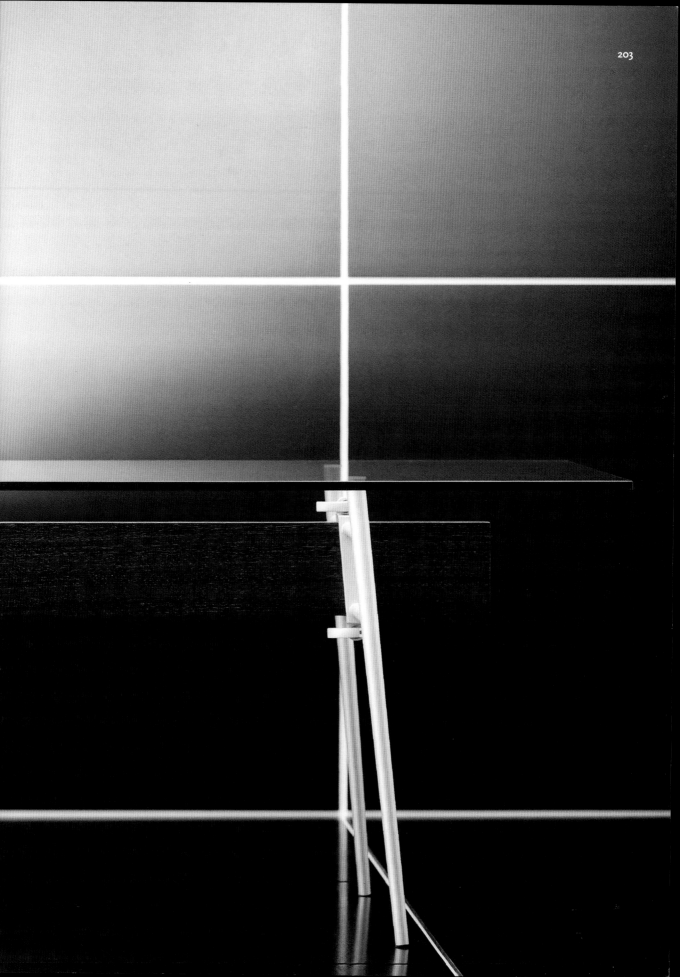

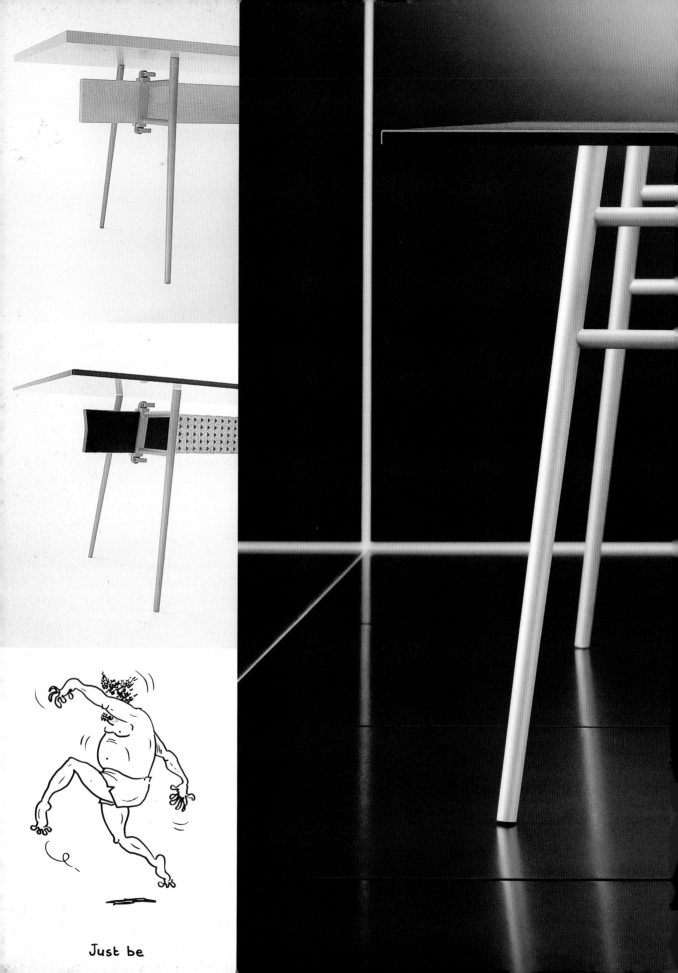

Just be

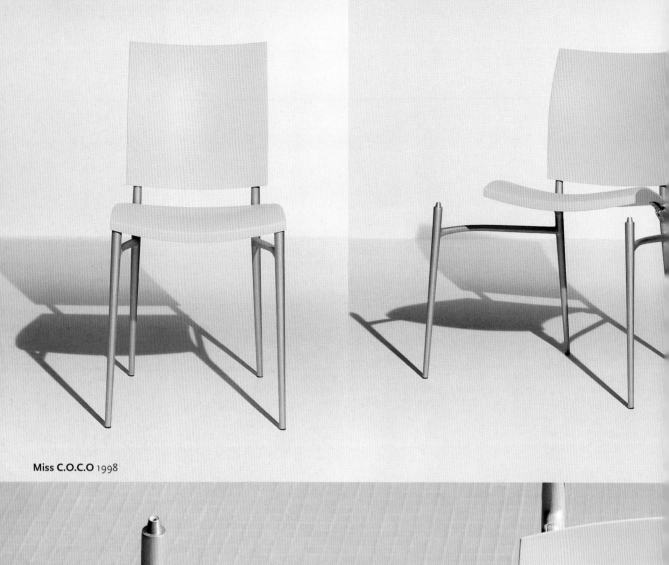

Miss C.O.C.O 1998

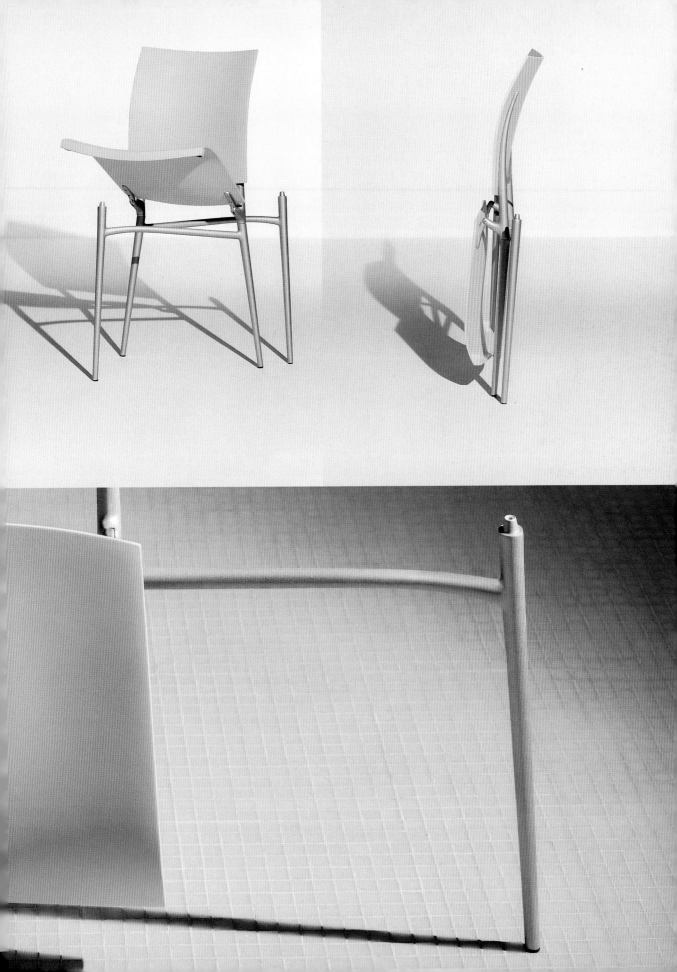

L.W.S Lazy Working Sofa 1998

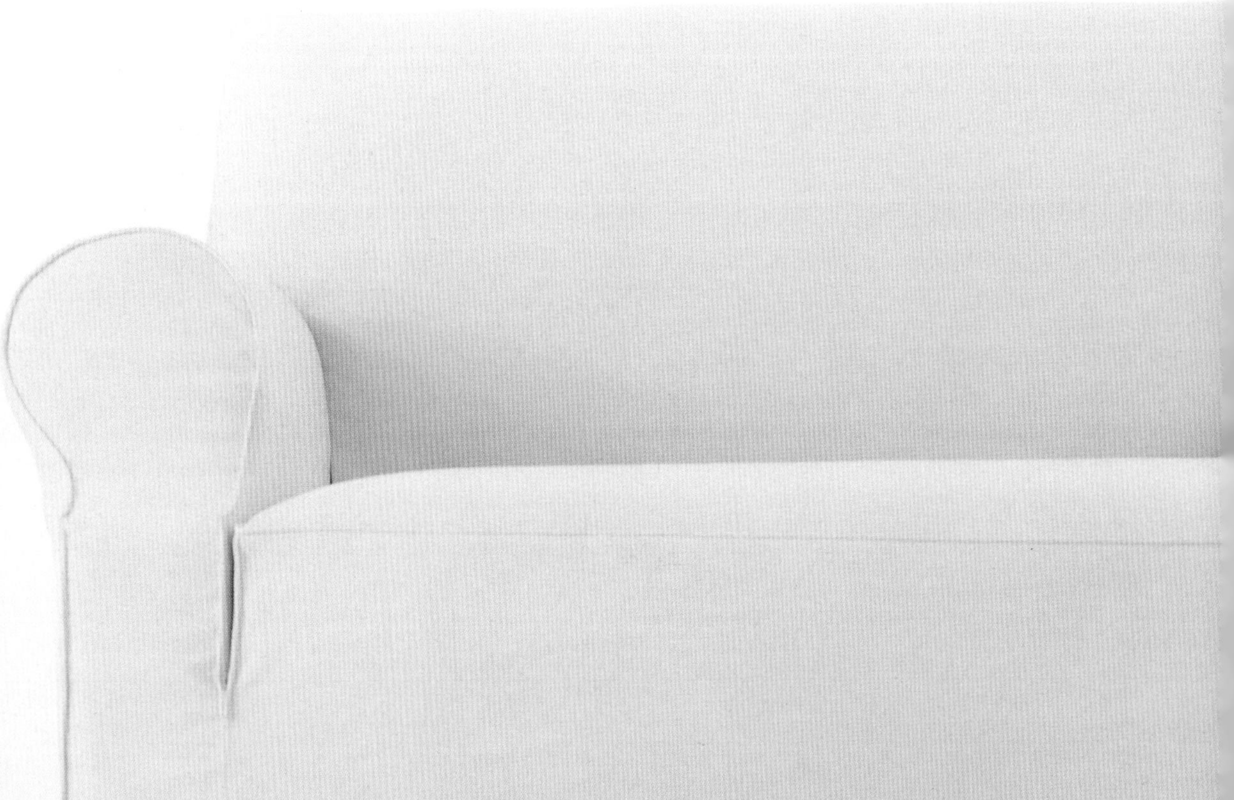

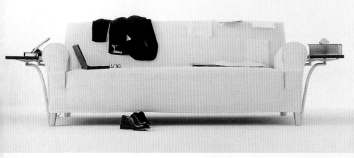

L'ESPRIT DE LA FORÊT
COLLECTION O.N.F.* 3 SUISSES BY STARCK

DEPUIS L'ORDONNANCE DE COLBERT (1669),
LES FORESTIERS SONT LES GARDIENS DE LA FORÊT
POUR LA CONSERVER, L'ENTRETENIR ET LA RENOUVELER.

LA FRANCE EST AUJOURD'HUI LE PAYS
LE PLUS FEUILLU D'EUROPE.

LA NOUVELLE COLLECTION DE PHILIPPE STARCK
VOUS DONNE L'ESPRIT DE LA FORÊT
AFIN QUE VOUS EN DEVENIEZ LES GARDIENS.

D ans le colis du meuble STARCK que vous commandez aux 3 SUISSES, vous trouverez une notice explicative vous permettant de contacter le Forestier de l'Office National des Forêts. Celui-ci vous remettra le rondin de bouleau brut qu'il choisira dans une forêt proche de chez vous (dans un rayon maximum de 150 km), ainsi que la plaque numérotée «Collection ONF/3 SUISSES by STARCK», qu'il scellera, en votre présence, sur la tranche du rondin. Pour contacter le Forestier, vous disposerez d'un numéro vert inscrit sur la notice ●

COLLECTION
ONF/3 SUISSES
by
STARCK
N° 00001

T A B L E S T A R C K en hêtre massif teinté et verni polyuréthane avec piétement (livré monté) possédant un système de serrage à l'intérieur de chaque pied pour le réglage du rondin. (le prix comprend le rondin de bouleau distribué par l'O.N.F. - Dimensions du rondin : 1,40 m x 13 à 14 cm de diamètre). RÉFÉRENCE : 791.0440. ● ● ● ● **F**

C O N S O L E S T A R C K en hêtre massif teinté et verni polyuréthane avec piétement (livré monté) possédant un système de serrage à l'intérieur de chaque pied pour le réglage du rondin. (le prix comprend le rondin de bouleau distribué par l'O.N.F. - Dimensions du rondin : 1,40 m x 13 à 14 cm de diamètre). RÉFÉRENCE : 791.5830. ● ● ● ● **F**

B A N C S T A R C K en hêtre massif teinté et verni polyuréthane avec piétement (livré monté) possédant un système de serrage à l'intérieur de chaque pied pour le réglage du rondin.(le prix comprend le rondin de bouleau distribué par l'O.N.F. - Dimensions du rondin : 1,40 m x 8 à 10 cm de diamètre) RÉFÉRENCE : 791.0740. ● ● ● **F**

Mister Bliss 1982   Dr. Sonderbar 1983   Pat Conley II 1986

Royalton Bar Stool 1988   Peninsula 1995   Théâtre du Monde 1984

Lundi Ravioli 1995   Lila Hunter 1988   Lio Comun 1991

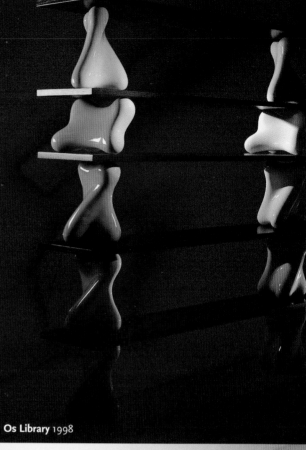

Monsieur X Rocking 1996

Os Library 1998

Popopo 1993

Monsieur X Chaise longue 1996

Cheap Chic 1997

Poaa 1999

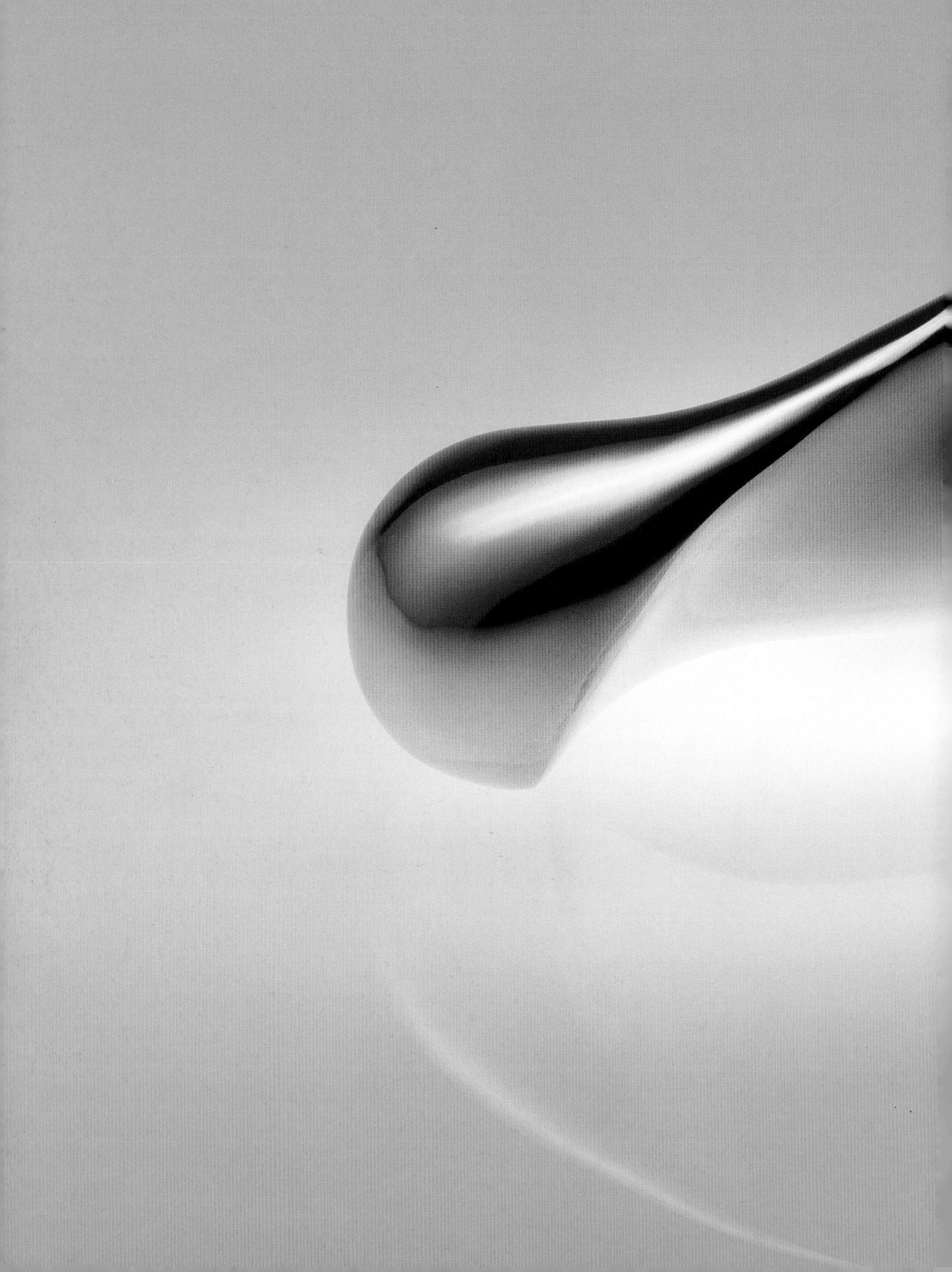

Dadada 1993

Pax Now

12   Architecture

68   Interiors

152 Furniture

228 **Industrial Design**

392 Magma

400 Words

422 Overview

446 A–Z

Plywood car (project) 1996

BAD BADS...

Doctor Life 1991 **Rosy Angelis** 1994

Miss Sissi 1990 **Romeo Moon** 1995

Light Lite 1992   Walla Walla 1994

Ara 1988

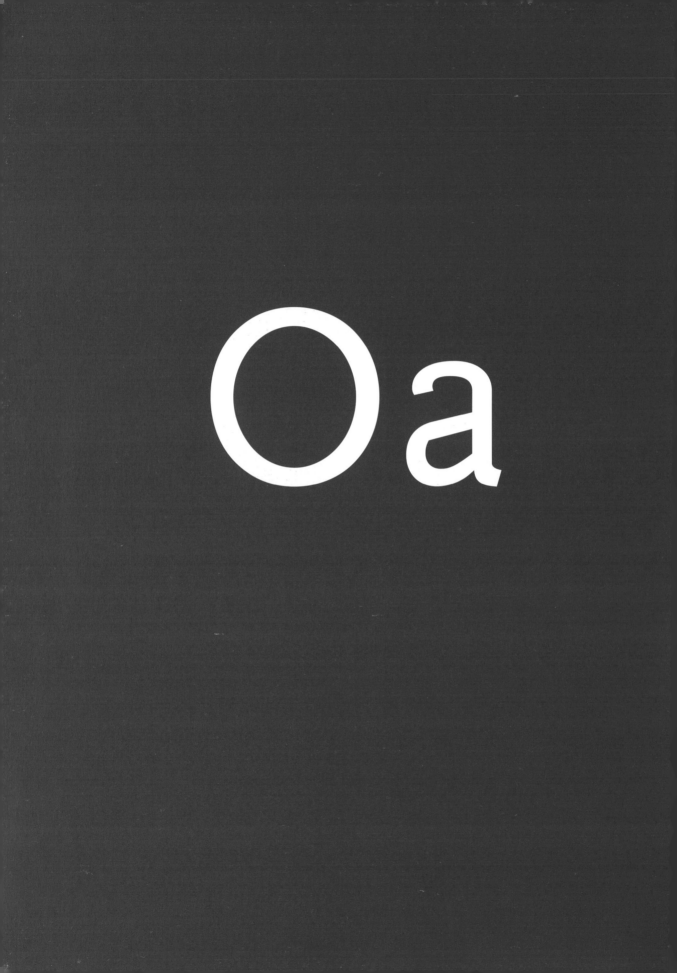

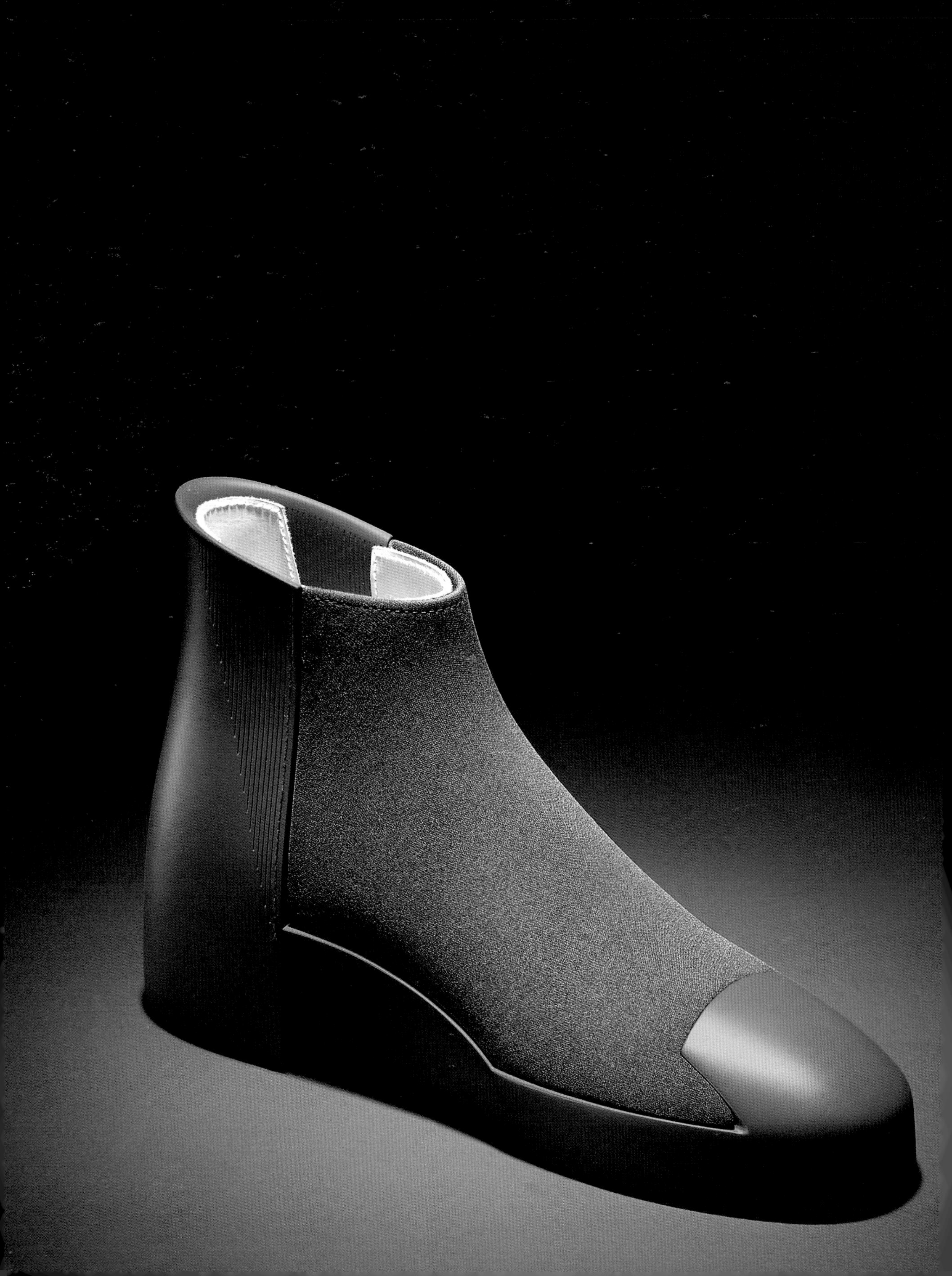

Shoe (prototype) 1996

We must share

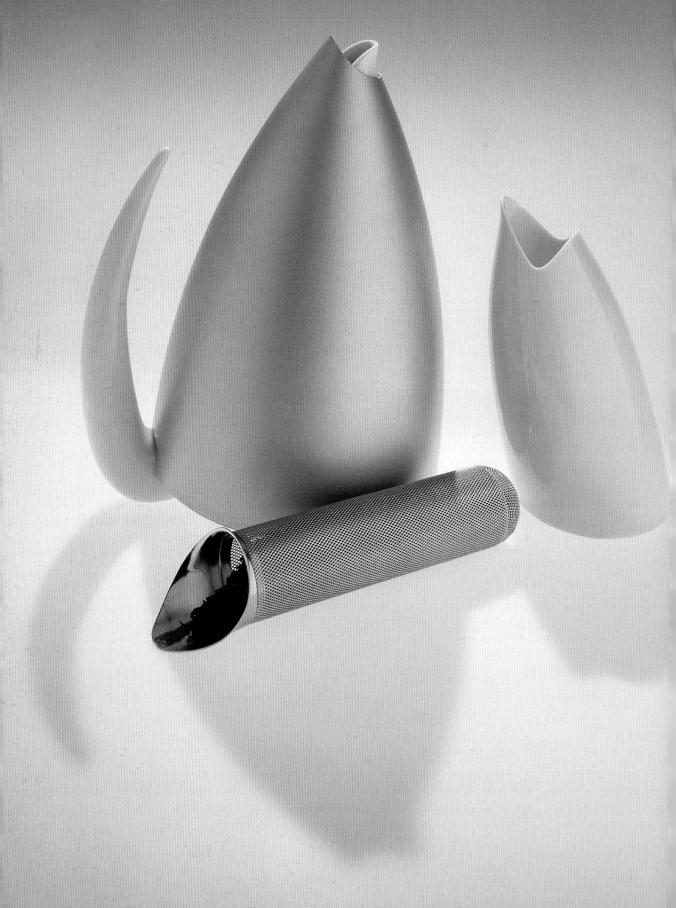

Mister Meumeu 1992

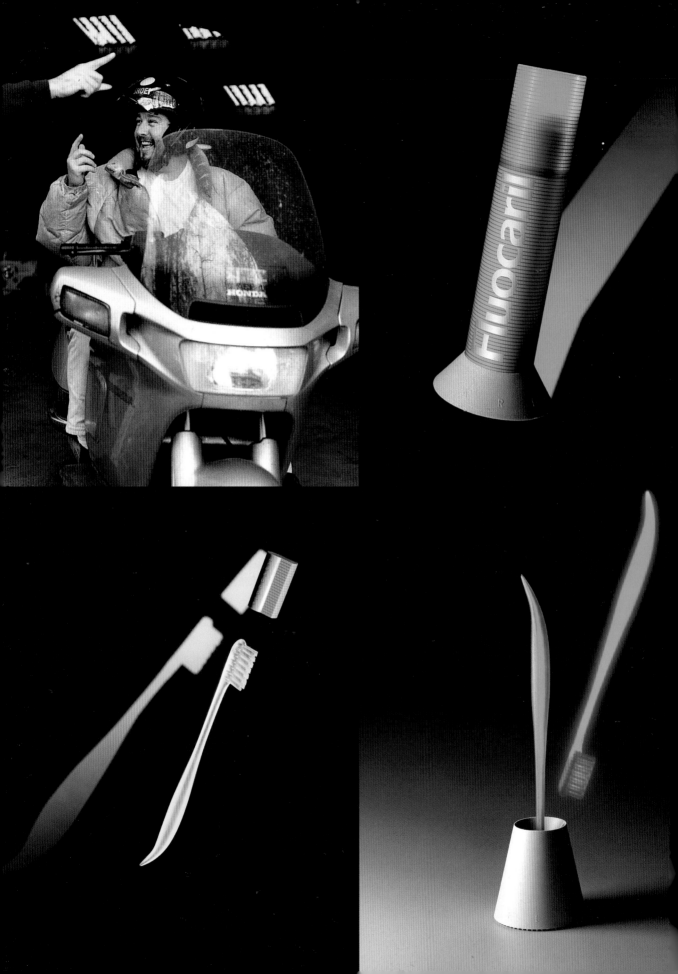

Washbasin 1994

Bathtub 1994

Toilet and bidet 1998

Bathtub 1998

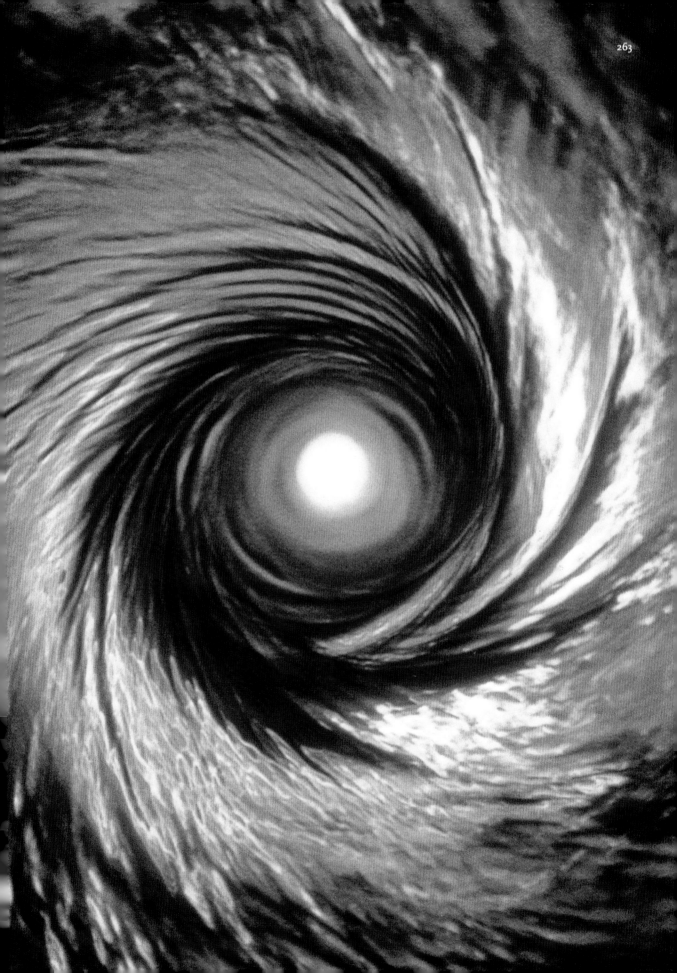

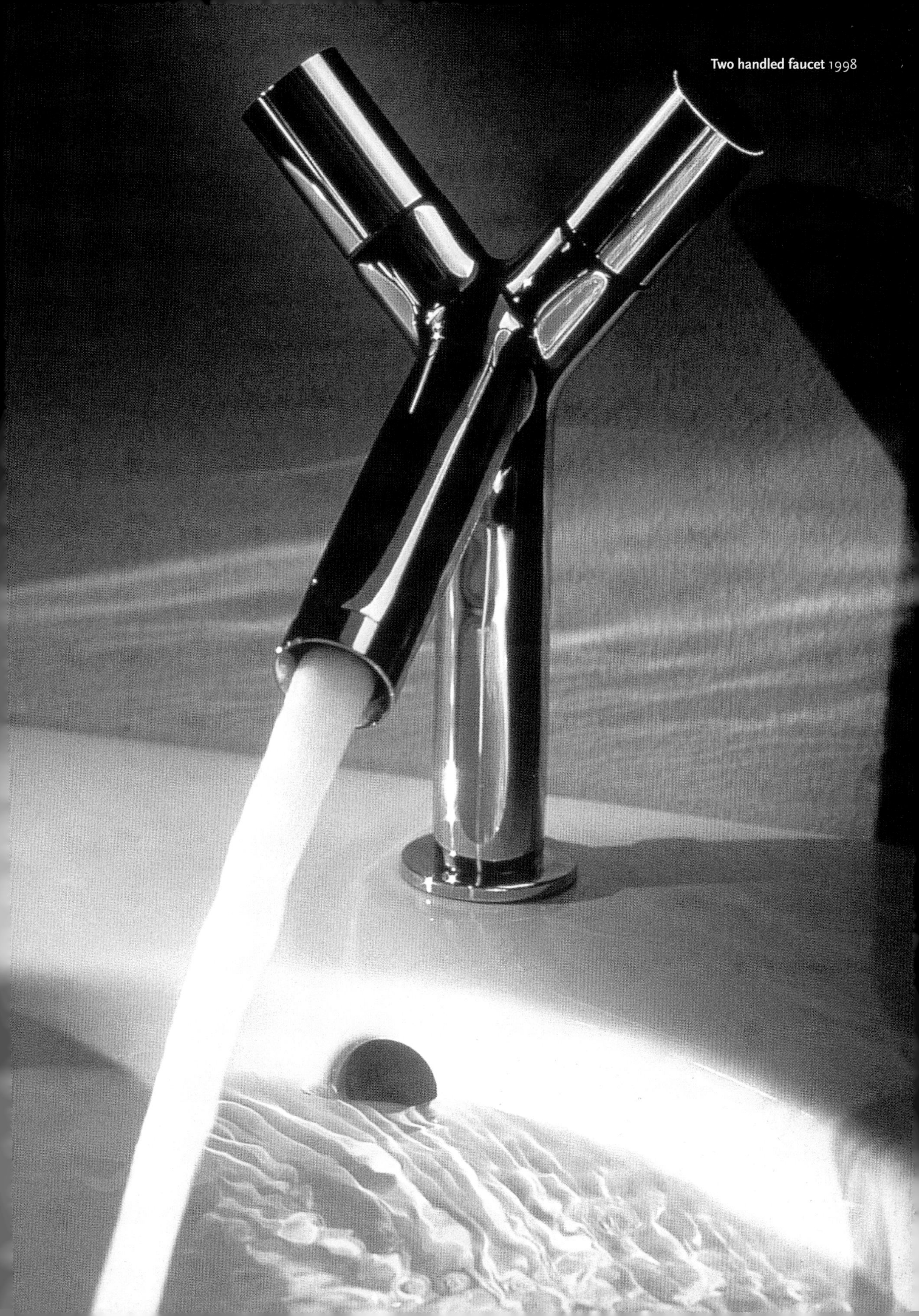

Two handled faucet 1998

SELF PORTRAIT
FORMENTERA 97.

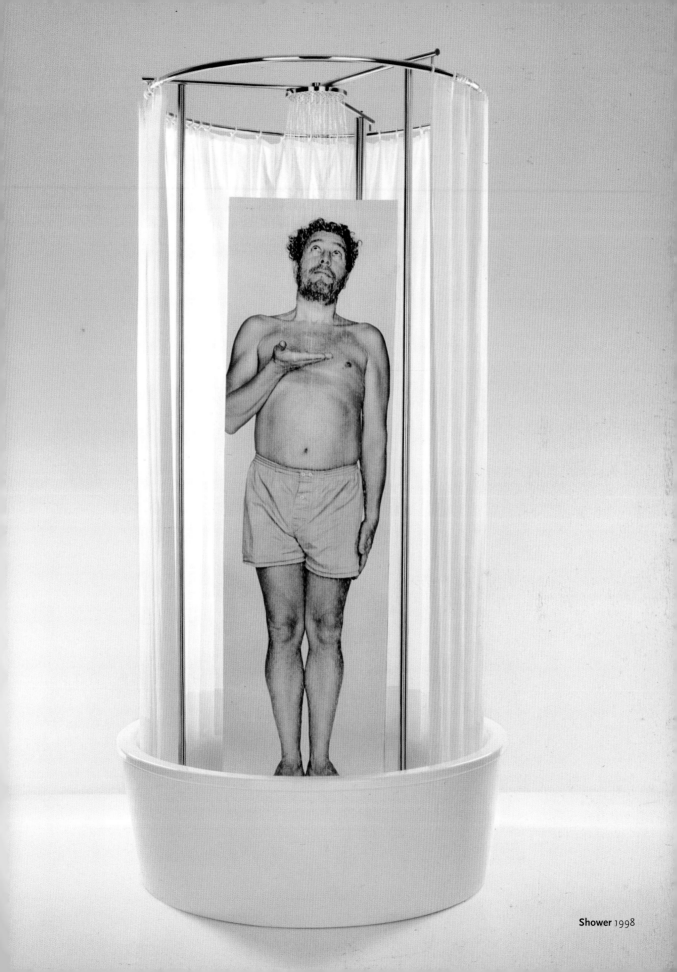

Shower 1998

First 41 S5 Voilier L Coque 1989

Beneteau Collection First 1988–1994
First 35.7, Voilier L Coque 1992

First 35 S5 Voilier L Coque 1988

Virtuelle 1997

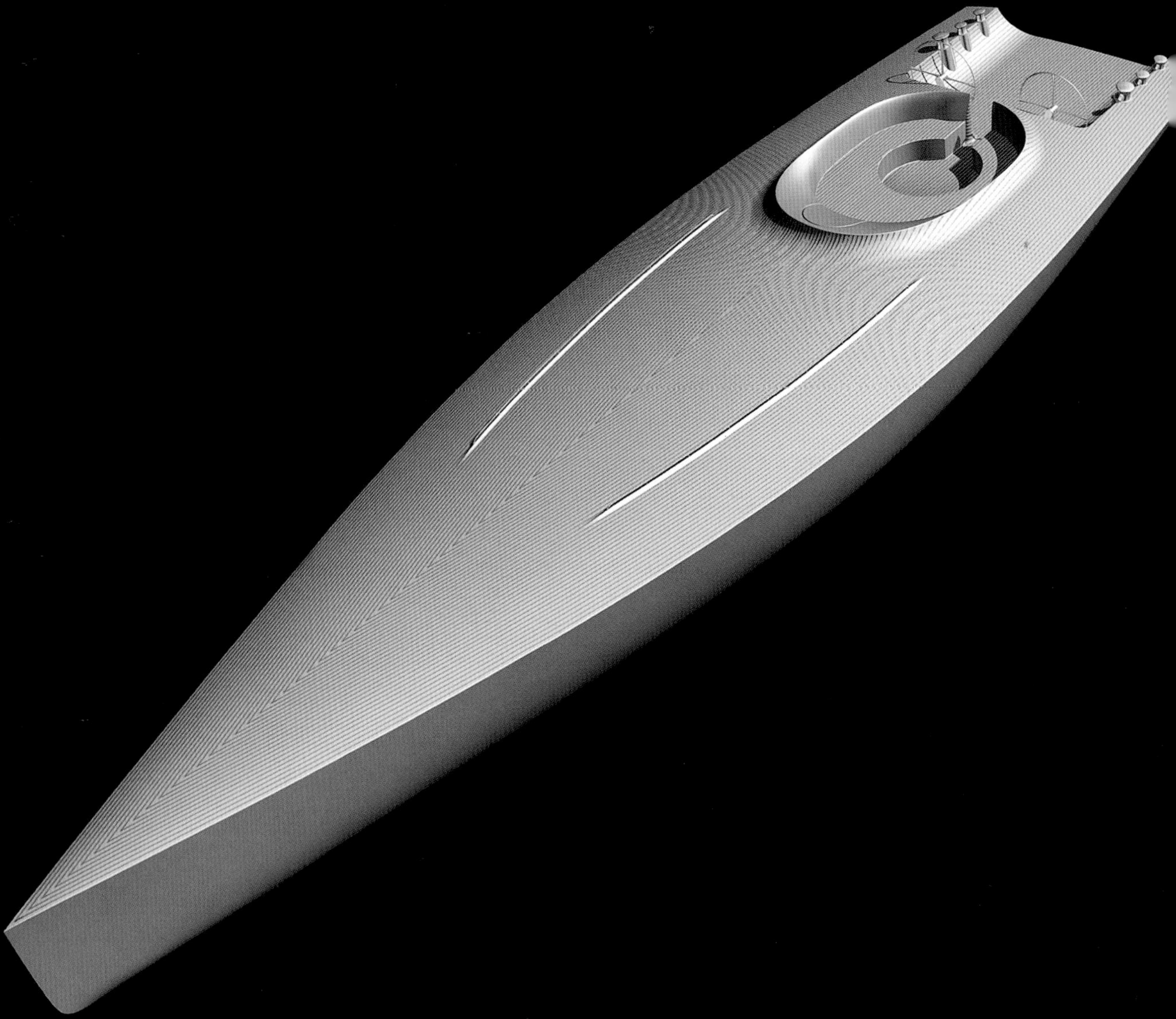

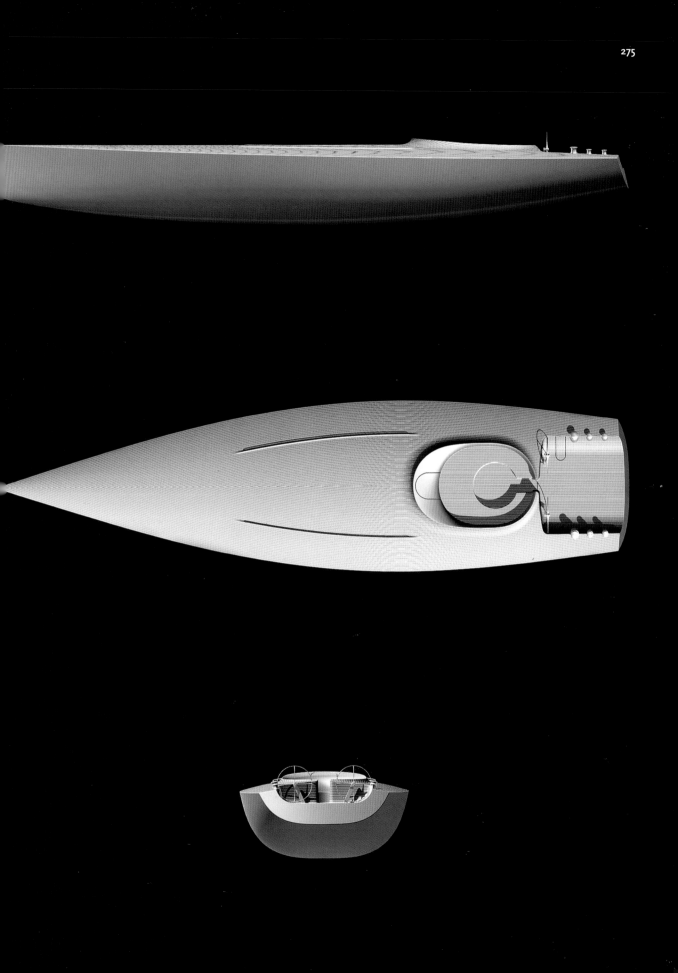

L'urgence est revenue

Plasmaa 1995

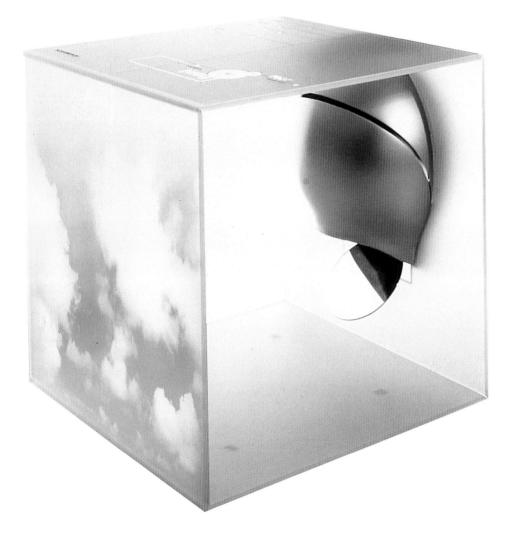

Cub 1996

Radio 1995

Video recorder 1995

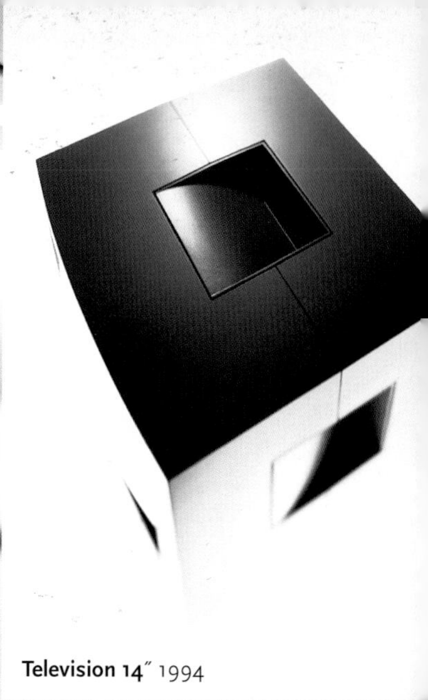

Television 14″ 1994

Speaker 16.9 1995

Don'O 1995

Television 14″ 1994

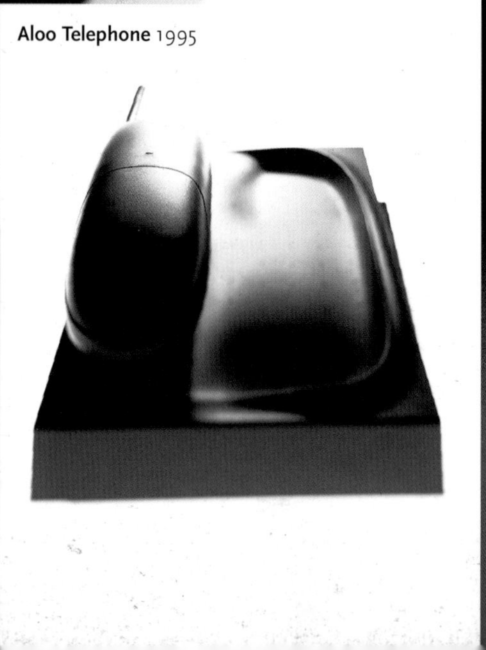

Aloo Telephone 1995

Speaker 199

Television 1994

Saba Television

Zéo TV 1994–1995

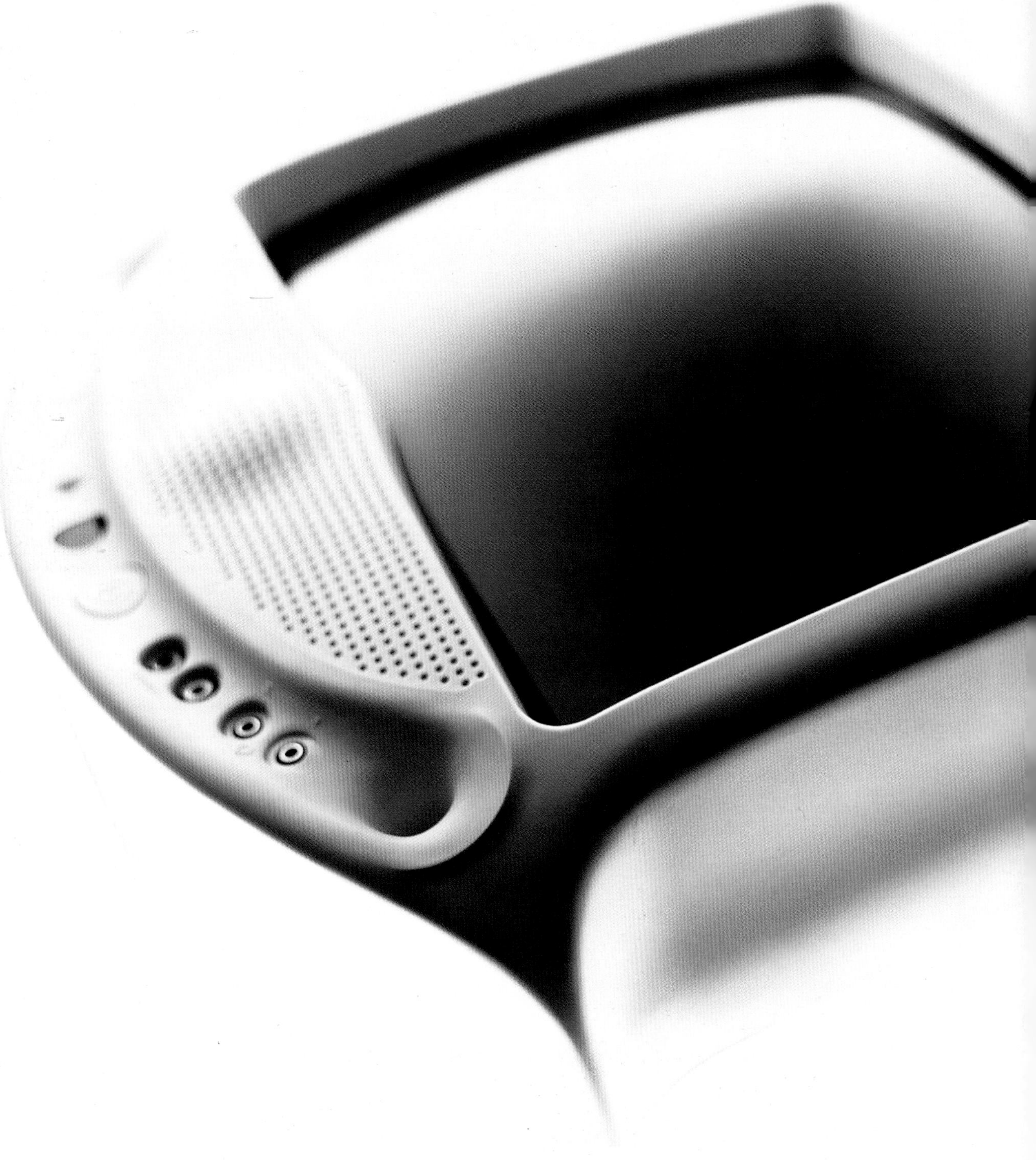

Oz TV 1994

Jim Nature TV 1994

Remote Control Unit (M 5107) 1994   Remote Control Unit 1994

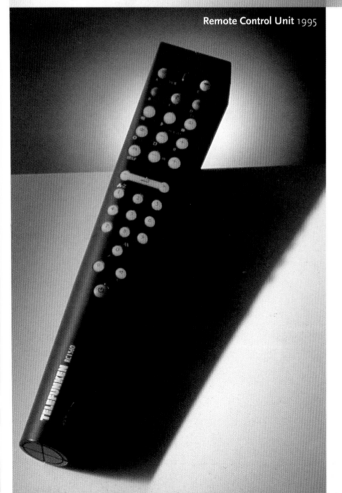

Remote Control Unit 1995

DES PARKINGS   DU SEX

1968   1998.

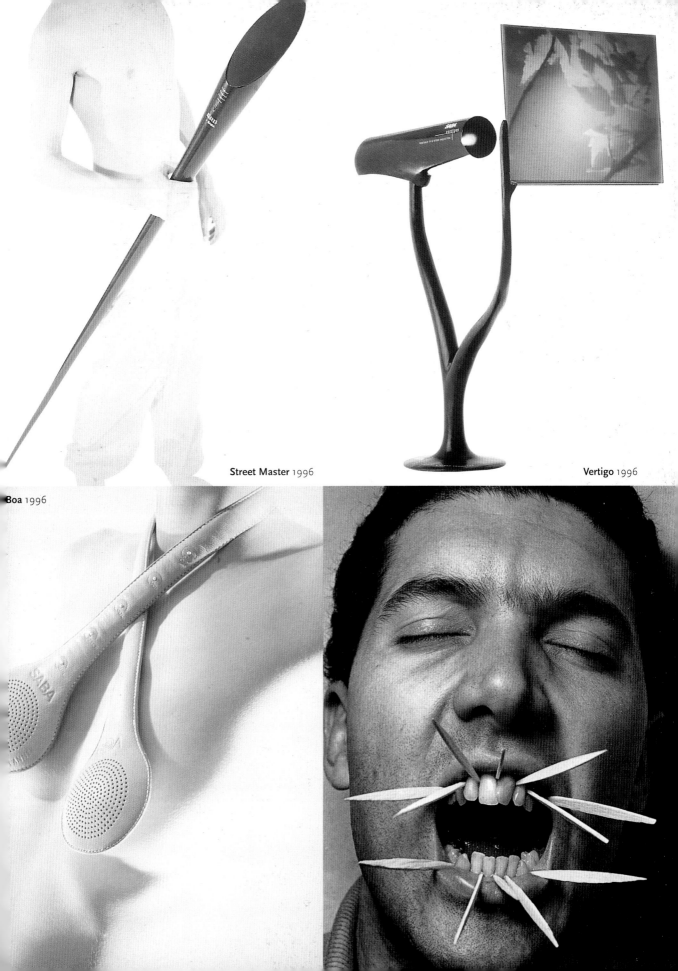

Street Master 1996

Vertigo 1996

Boa 1996

TV Partoo 1996

Icipari 1995

Lux Lux 1996

Comboo 1995

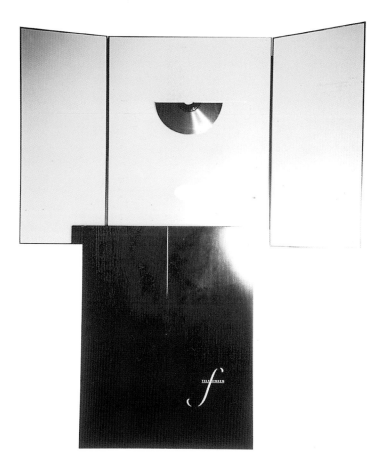

Toccata 1996

Les produits du groupe Thomson sont sous la direction artistique de
Philippe Starck. Certains sont créés par lui-même, d'autres sont
dessinés en collaboration ou par: Claude Bressan, Matali Crasset,
Mike Davidson, Elsa Frances, Bernard Guerrin, Patrick Jouin, Michael
Michalsky, Jérôme Olivet, Jean-Michel Policar, Andréa Quaglio,
Manuela Simonelli, Gérard Vergneau

Demain sera moins

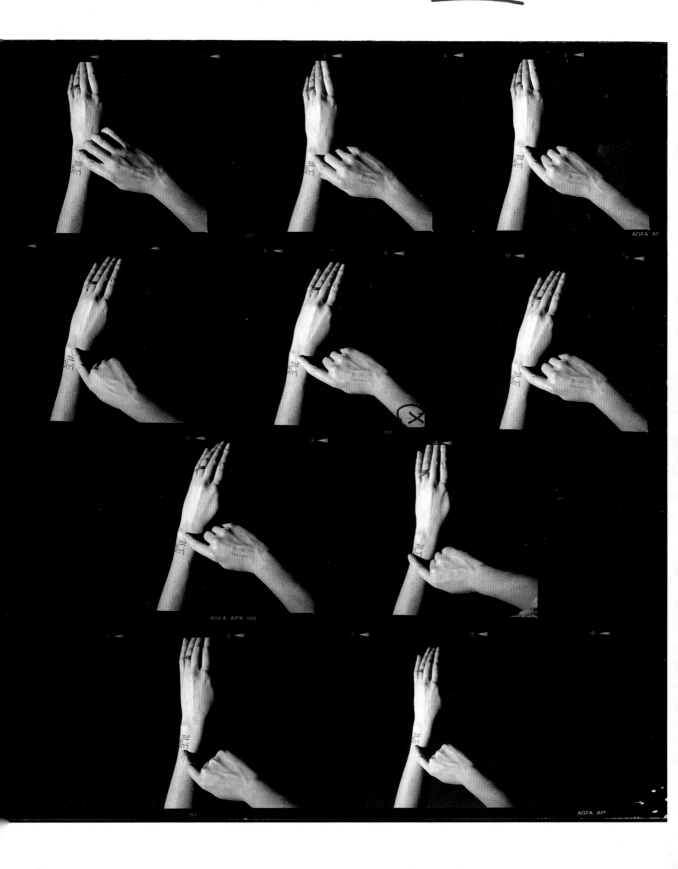

Montre digitale (project) 1996

Walter Wayle 1989

Moondog model 1987

Pour la vie 1990

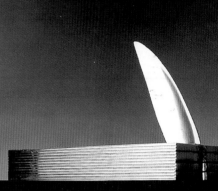

Laguiole model 1987

Jojo Long Legs 1991

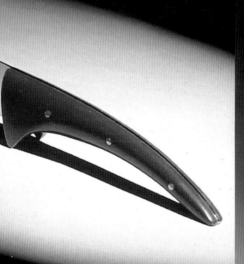

Jojo Long Leg 1991

Laguiole knife 1986

Pour la vie 1990

Joe Raspoutine 1987

Asahi model 1986

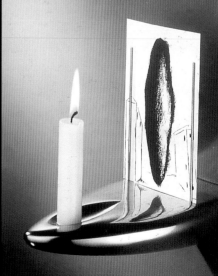

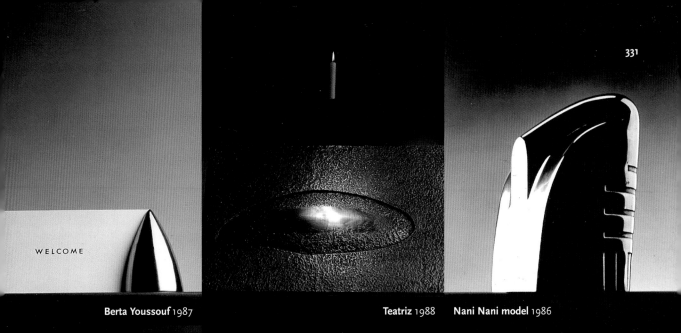

WELCOME

Berta Youssouf 1987

Teatriz 1988 **Nani Nani model** 1986

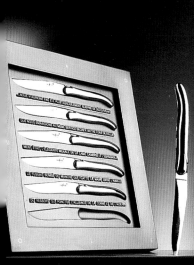

Laguiole Set 1986

O' Kelvin 1989 **Paramount IV** 1990

Miss Zenzen 1986

Paramount II 1990 **Pointus** 1986

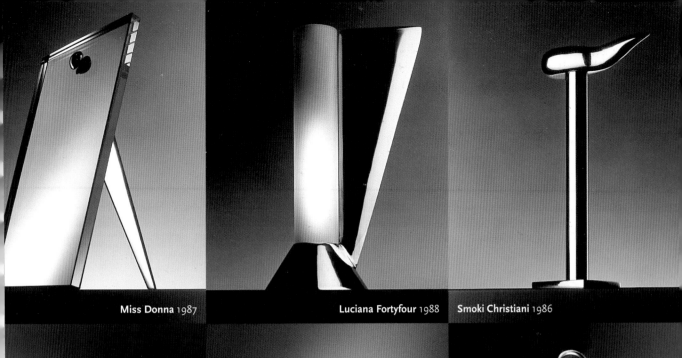

Miss Donna 1987

Luciana Fortyfour 1988

Smoki Christiani 1986

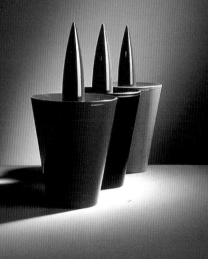

Tito Lucifer 1986

Joe Cactus 1990

Picfeu 1986

Mimi Bayou 1987

Chab Wellington 1987

Le Moult model 1987

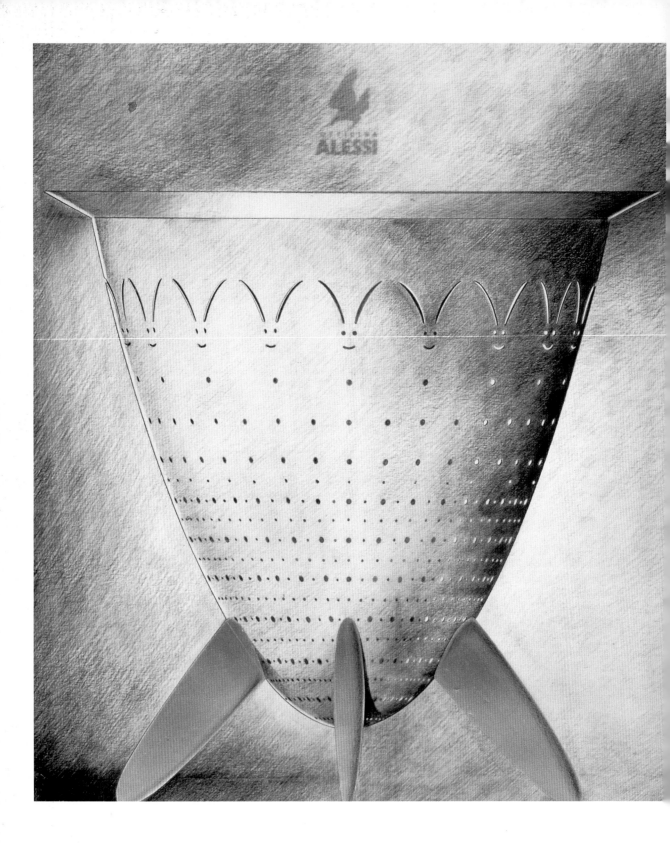

Max le Chinois 1990–1991

FRONT VIEW

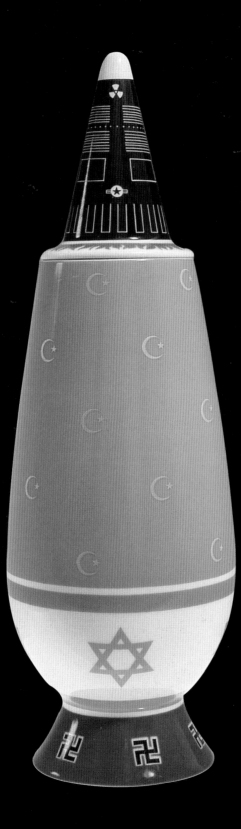

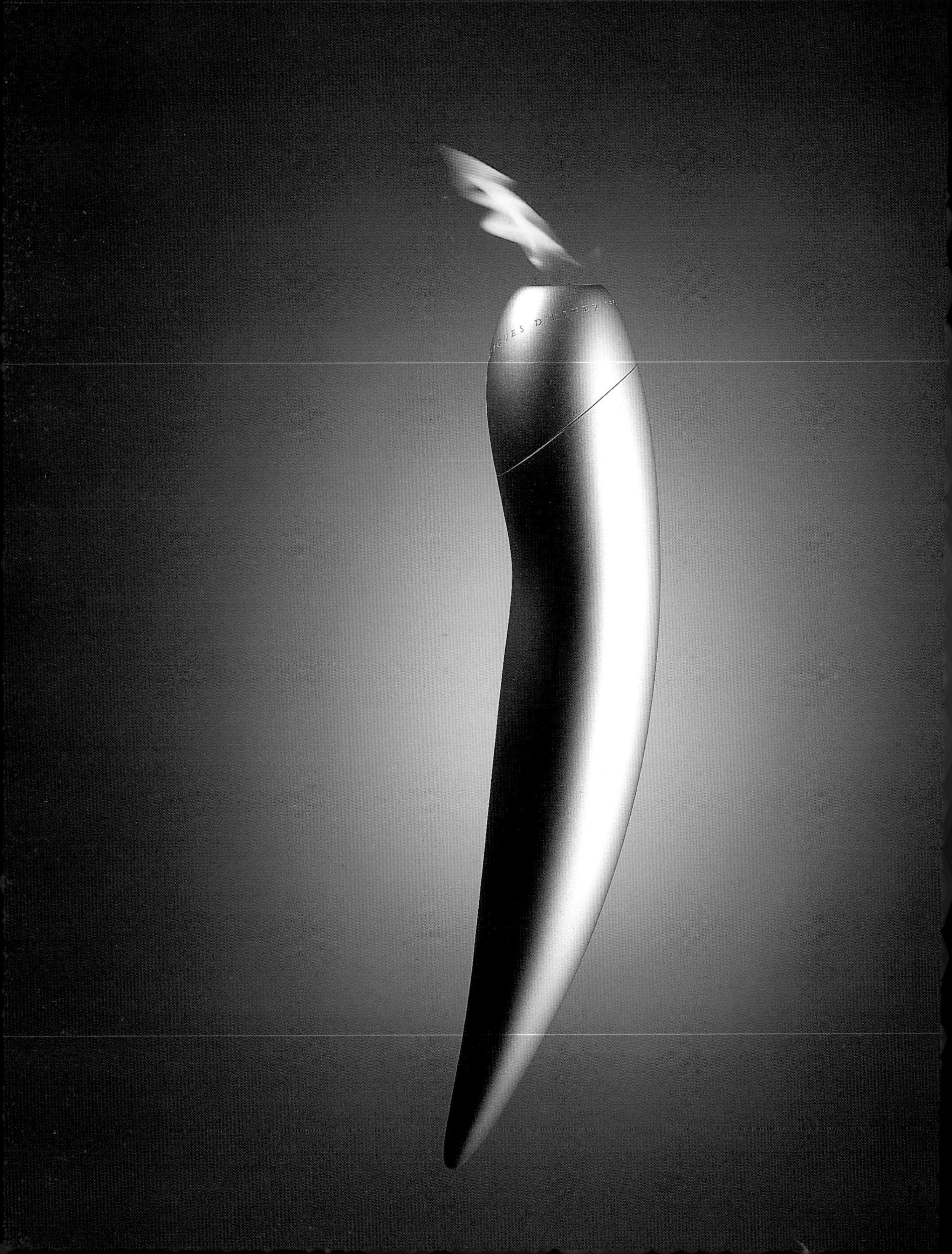

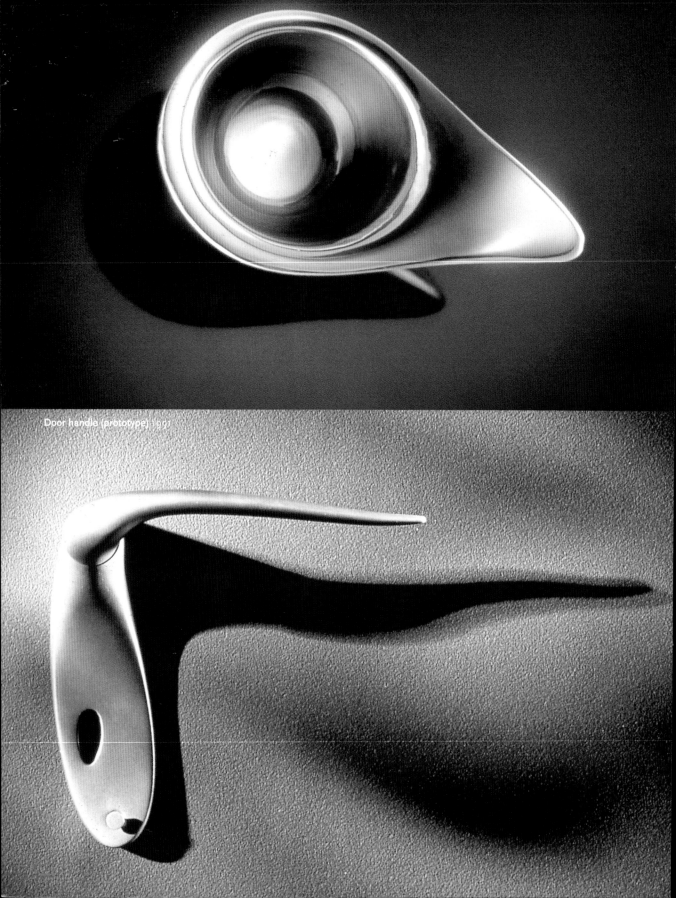

Door handle (prototype) 1991

Apriti 1991

S 1 Door handle 1991

Street lamp 1992

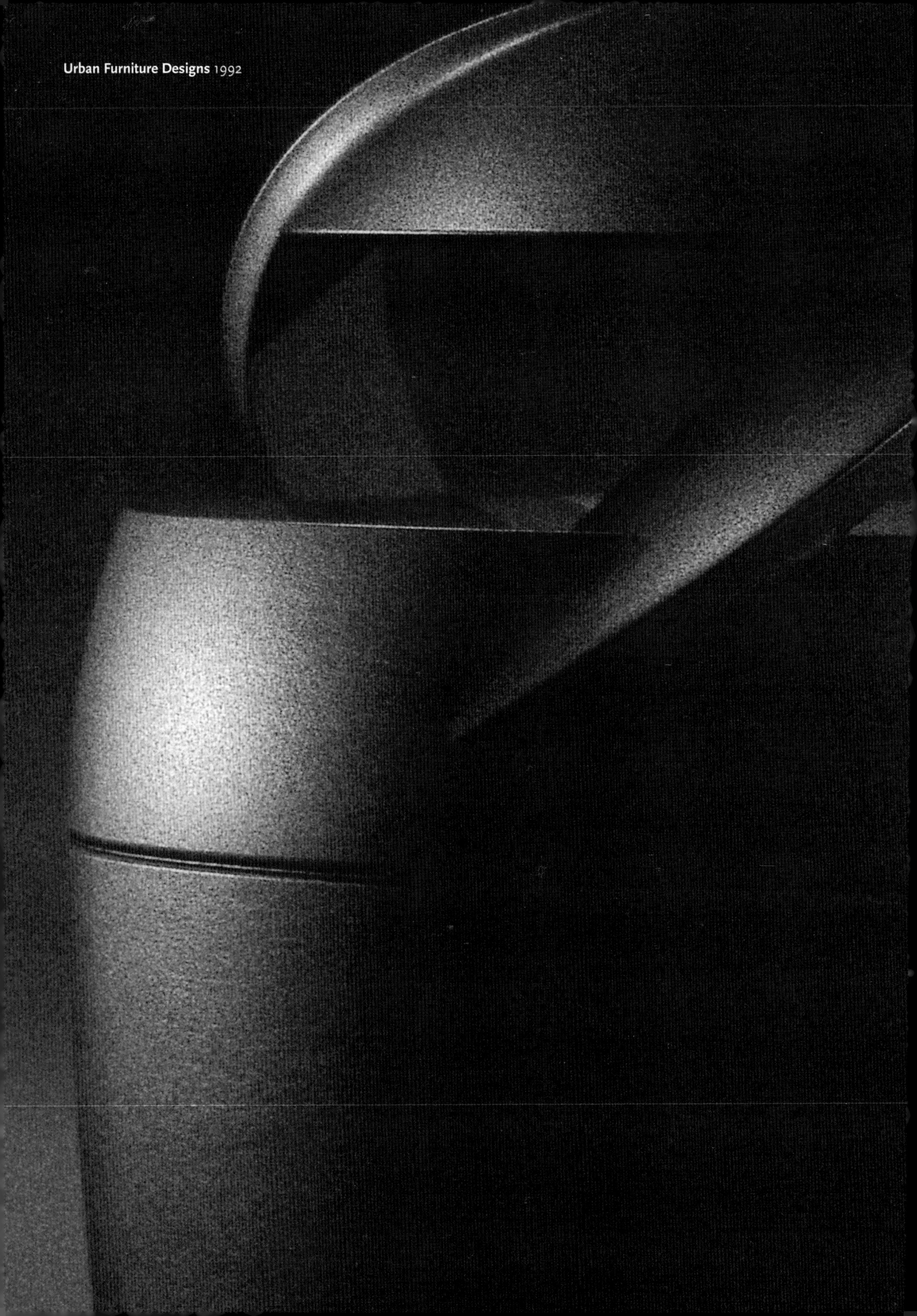
Urban Furniture Designs 1992

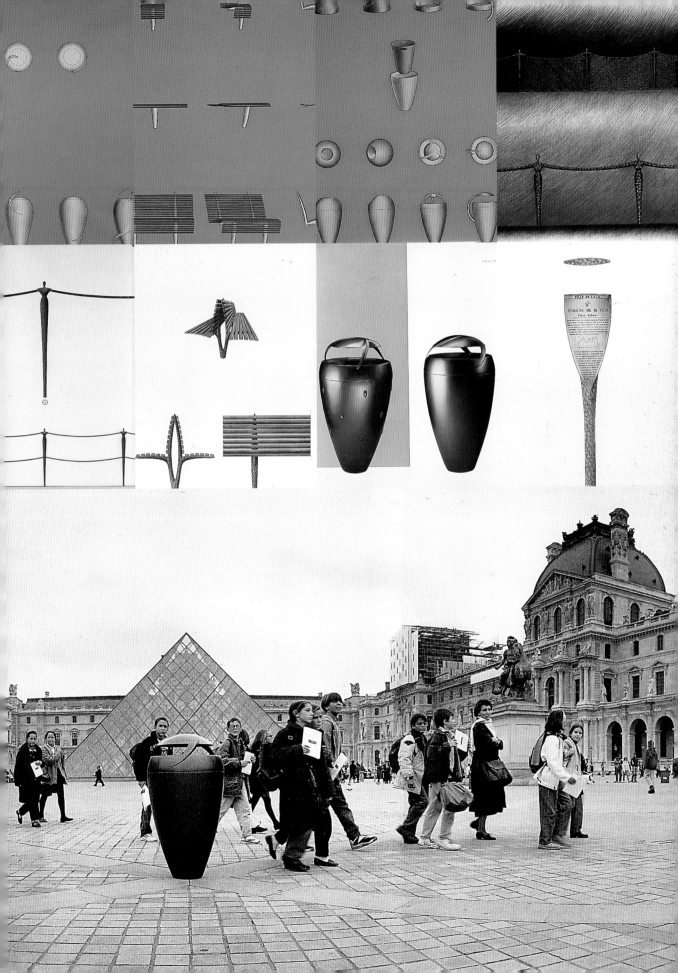

Mineral water bottle 1991

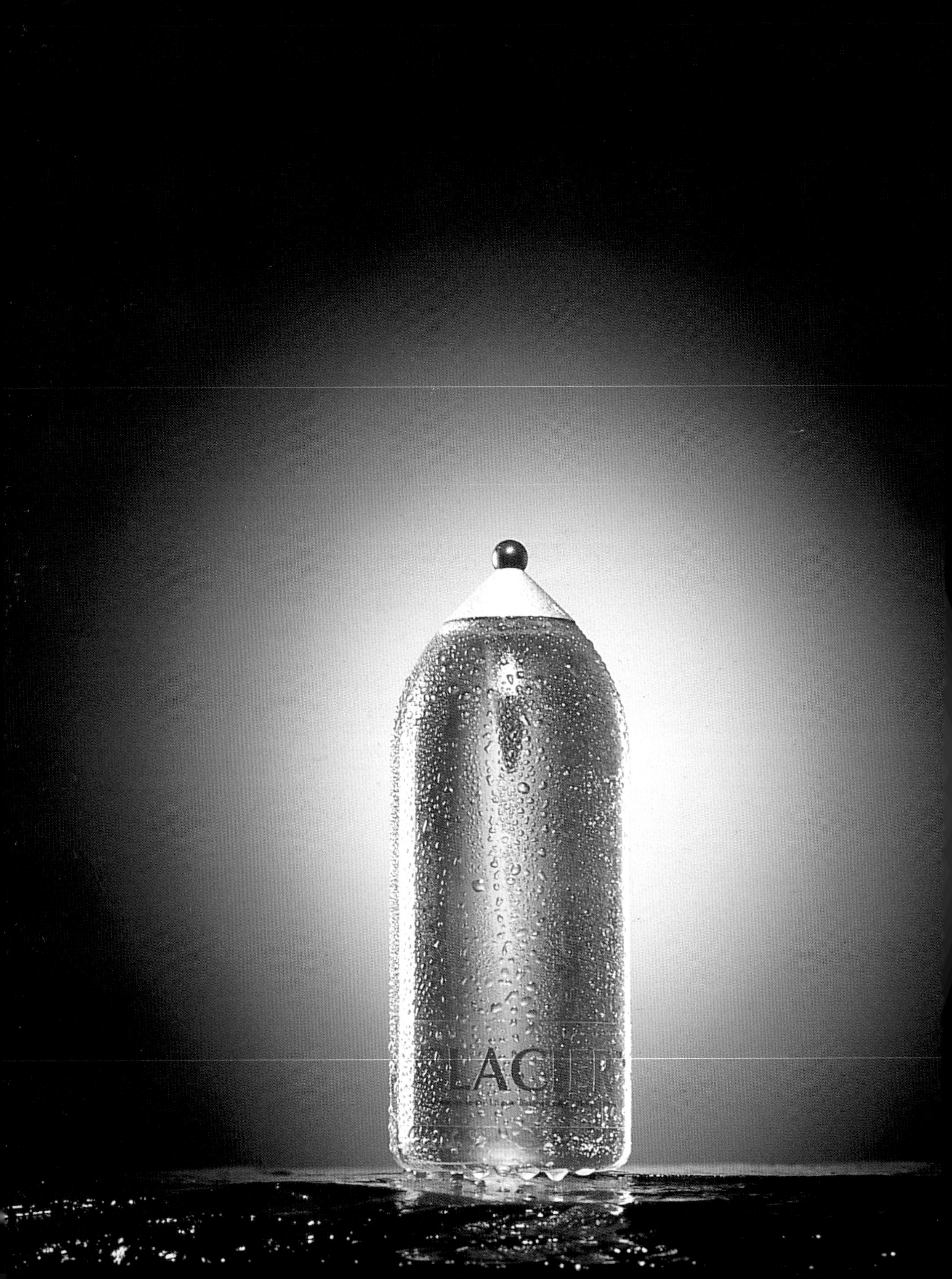

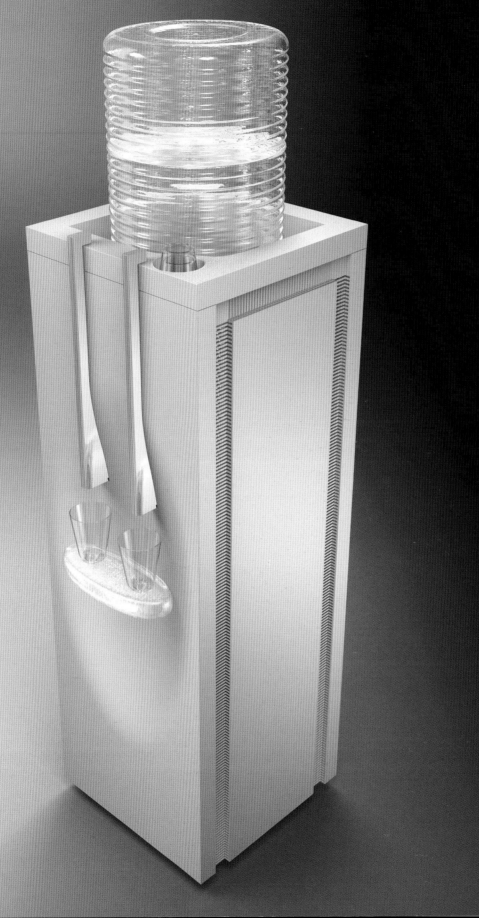

Ball Point Pen 1998

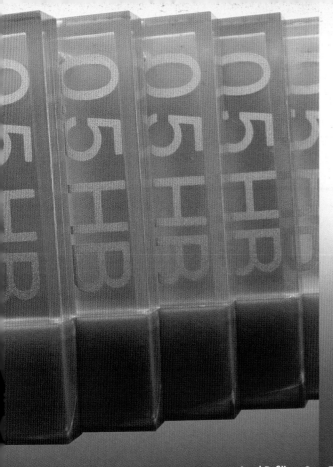

Lead Refill 1998 **Fluorescent Markers** 1998

Retractable pencil 1998 **Pencils** 1998

Toothbrush 1998

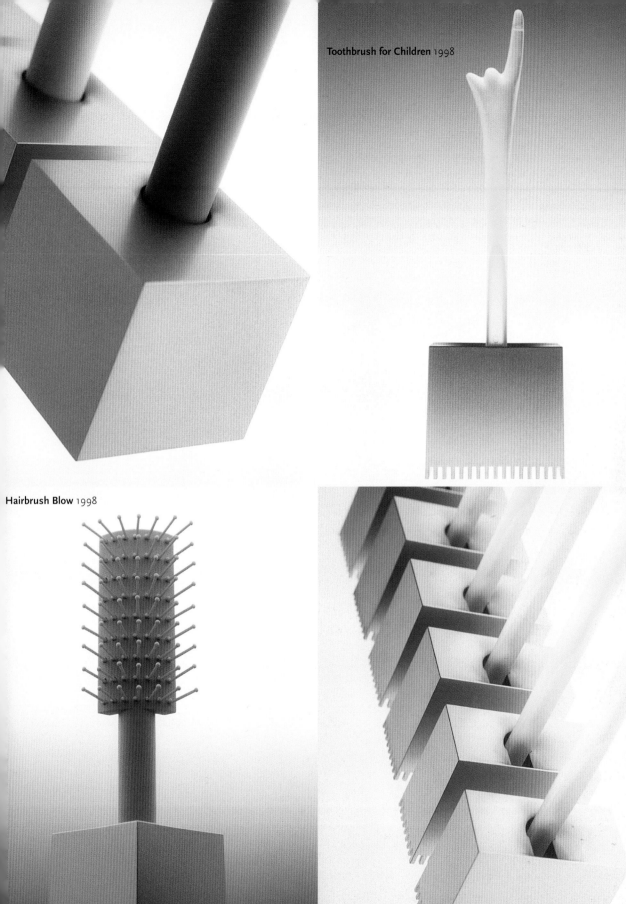

Toothbrush for Children 1998

Hairbrush Blow 1998

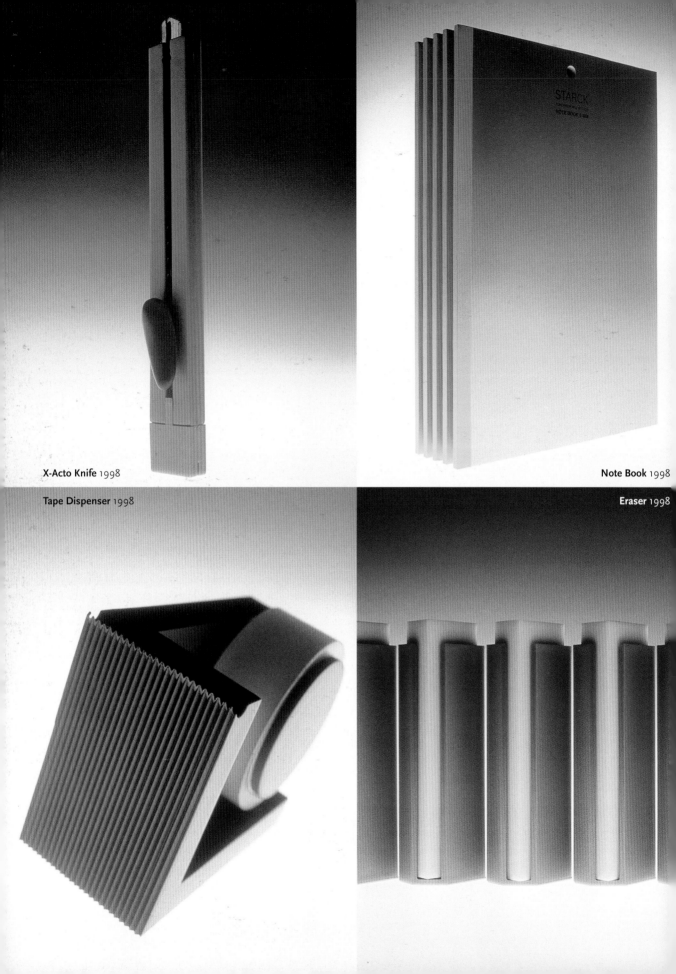

X-Acto Knife 1998

Note Book 1998

Tape Dispenser 1998

Eraser 1998

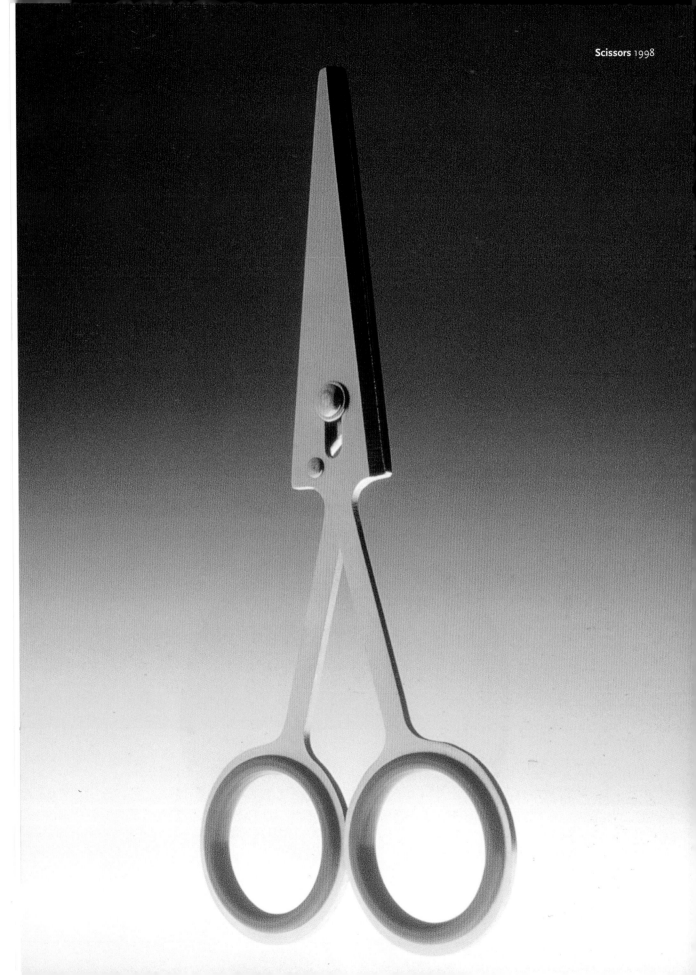

StarckNakedHOT 1999

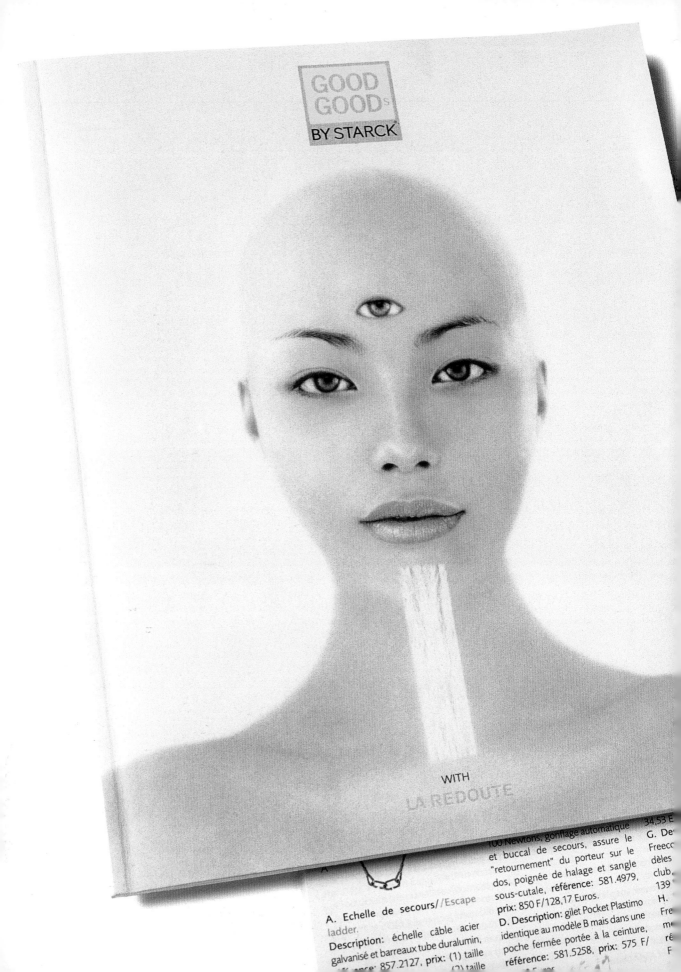

...équipements de protection provoquent souvent une réaction d'étonnement, ou d'inquiétude sur la santé mentale de celui qui s'en préoccupe. Je ...ceinture de sécurité lorsque je suis en voiture, le casque lorsque je roule en moto, et cela ne m'a jamais gêné. ...ologiques, chimiques, biologiques ou radiologiques, ne relève ni de la paranoïa, ni d'une prospective exagérément pessimiste: les exemples ...ents de ce type, en dehors de tout conflit militaire, seront malheureusement quotidiens et justifient certainement ces précautions. Banalement, on ...se limiter à répéter qu'il vaut mieux prévenir que guérir, surtout ce qui ne se guérit pas toujours.

...d equipment often provokes a surprised reaction, not to mention doubts about the mental health of anyone who gives some thought to the matter. I ...always fasten my seatbelt when I'm in a car, I wear a helmet on a motorcycle and that doesn't bother me at all. To be safely equipped for any possi... ...ological, chemical, or radioactive mishap is neither a symptom of paranoia nor the sign of an excessively pessimistic nature. ...es of this type of event, even in the absence of armed conflict, will unfortunately become routine occurrences, and certainly justify precautionary ...es. An ounce of prevention is worth a pound of cure, especially where there's a risk of incurability.

ncendie,
oxyde de
radioacti-
or,   gaz
monoxide
detector.
sseur mono-
m, fonctionne
fixe au mur à
ond, détecte la
de de carbone,
rence 895.2523,
0 Euros.
étecteur Legrand
stique (butane,
ville), signal visuel
e puissance (85dB à
secteur 9VDC/220v
ns 120x 60x28mm,
5730 prix: 590 F/88,96

Description: avertisseur d'incen-
Legrand, détecteur de fumée
mestique avec sirène de forte
ssance (85dB à 1m) et vo-
t lumineux, livré avec pile (9v)
accessoires de fixation, diamètre
5cm, hauteur 3,8cm, référence:
596.5640, prix: 295 F/44,48 Euros.

micro
el mo-
touch
prix:

L. Description: Radiatest Pekly, dê-
tecteur de radio-activité de poche,
alarme sonore et visuelle, très haute
sensibilité, poids 150g, dimensions
102x60x26mm, référence:581.5444
prix: 1290 F/194,52 Euros.

et micro
Ericsson
58, 788,
rix: 329

Tous les équipements de protection
dans ces deux pages en 24h chez
vous: +80 F/12,06 Euros.

Masque protection voies respiratoires (filtres vendus séparément)//Respirator mask (filters sold separately).
scription: masque Giat dérivé du masque de protection de l'armée française, assure la protection des voies respiratoires en filtrant l'air en fonction des ...es utilisés, couvre-face à large visière panoramique souple qui s'adapte parfaitement aux formes du visage (2 tailles), 2 soupapes d'expiration, ...et inspiratoire, demi-masque interne et système de ventilation de la visière évitant la buée, brides réglables, sangle de portage, poids 500g, livré sans ...ouche (vendues ci-dessous), références: taille homme 666.7430, prix: 1500 F/226,18 Euros. taille femme 581.7099,

...filtre protection accidents chimiques large spectre, grande autonomie//Broad-spectrum large-capacity filter for chemichal impurities.
...scription: cartouche filtrante Giat A2B2E2K2P3 combinée vapeurs organiques, gaz et vapeurs inorganiques, vapeurs acides, dioxyde de soufre, ammo-
...uche (poussières radiologiques comprises), ne produit pas d'oxygène, poids 370g, modèle plus performant que modèle O, référence:

...filtre poussières total, poussières radiologiques comprises//Normal capacity filter for chemical impurities.
...7226, prix: 365 F/55,04 Euros.

...filtre protection accidents chimiques large spectre, capacité normale//Normal capacity filter for chemical impurities.
...scription: cartouche filtrante Giat A1B1E1K1P3 à large spectre spécifique, pour aérosols, gaz et vapeurs organiques, gaz et vapeurs inorganiques,
...oxyde de soufre, ammoniac, filtre poussières total, ne produit pas d'oxygène, poids 240g, référence: 581.7200, prix: 325 F/49,01 Euros.

...filtre poussières total (poussières radiologiques comprises)//Dust and particle filter (including radiological dust).
...scription: cartouche filtrante Giat P3 pour toutes les poussières, notamment poussières radiologiques, ne produit pas d'oxygène, référence: 581.7102,
...: 155 F/23,37 Euros.

Non-products for non-consumers

One fine day, several million years ago, Ms Cromignonne and Mr Abominet fell in love with their offspring. A new era dawned. Madame strove to protect her infant, Monsieur to improve posterity. Together, the two of them – the pragmatic mother and the idealistic, visionary father – invented the naïve concept of Progress, which was to be expressed chiefly through the creation and manufacture of tools supposed to make our lives easier and even to contribute to our happiness. Much, much later – that is to say, in our times – it became evident that the most generous ideals tend to be the first to degenerate.

Man found himself many a time a slave to the tools he created to serve him. Although there are a few rare objects whose integrity, practicality, and sense of purpose has remained intact, a plethora of others exist only for themselves, without humour, love or fancy. Farewell, dreams of happiness... As I matured, I realized I could try to correct an injustice to which I was myself probably an accomplice.

Being neither a philosopher, nor a sociologist, nor a statesman, and lacking the intelligence to grapple with the problem on theoretical grounds, I decided to be pragmatic.

Grasping the wills and won'ts, the needs and desires of the citizen I would like to have as a friend and neighbour, I attempted to describe the equipment he or she is likely to carry, and maybe, through him or her catch a glimpse of the society in which I would like to see my children and those of my friends growing up. What a vast, pretentious and naive scheme.

I set about trying to find, collect, correct, or create (where necessary) objects which were honest, responsible, and respectful of people. Not necessarily beautiful objects, but good objects.

I soon realized I was facing an impossible task. After research and selection, very few products came up to my stringent standards. Yet, although the ones I approved were still far from my ideal of perfection, they did convey a certain spirit: an alternative direction, a new way of being.

Today, I am able to offer you a catalogue of these objects, a compendium I like to call a catalogue of "non-products for non-consumers." The non-consumer is an individual who is alert and wary, but also open, creative, enthusiastic, and finally extremely upstream and modern.

I hope that as you peruse these objects and the commentaries which accompany them, you will be able to recognize yourself as a member of the free and unincorporated tribe of non-consumers.

Further, I hope that you will be the ones to track down and create objects which, tomorrow morning, will constitute the future of the second compendium, so that, little by little, we can raise this collection to the level of our vision, and that the success of its "moral market", by setting an example, will mark out a new relationship between mankind, tools and their manufacture.

Cromignonne and Abominet could then see their dreams come true, and our children could at last go on new adventures.

To our future mistakes

Non-products are confronted with a grid of requirements based on criteria such as justification for existence, integrity of purpose, longevity, moral elaboration, didacticism, political significance, symbolic social significance, sexual significance, human responsibility, fair cost, fair price, creativity and, sometimes, humour, poetry and respect.

Naturally, none of the objects in this collection is fully satisfactory in each of the above respects. But each one is an endeavour, a mutation, an effort... This annual compendium, by definition immune to the whims of fashion, will therefore grow thicker as the years advance. Since it is impossible to be completely lucid, we shall make further mistakes – our mistakes will be the items which will be taken away from the catalogue. This page will give an account of these mistakes and make them into a constructive experience.

To our futures

This first catalogue is just a means of priming the pump. I am not a professional in mail-order merchandising, and, as a result, this first try is probably too personal. But the catalogue is a means to an end, a tool. You now possess it, put it to work. Take notes, make drawings, snap photos. Describe your needs and your dreams as catalyzed by what appears here. Send us your suggestions and ideas. You can also upload information to the Good Goods catalogue website at www.goodgoods.tm.fr. My mission here is about to end. Now it's up to you to destroy and reconstruct your future. Thank you.

Philippe Starck

Nicht-Produkte für Nicht-Konsumenten

Eines schönen Tages, vor einigen Millionen Jahren, verliebten sich Frau Cromignonne und Herr Abominet in ihren Nachwuchs. Ein neues Zeitalter brach an. Madame wollte unbedingt ihr Kind beschützen; Monsieur die Nachwelt verbessern. Zusammen erfanden die beiden – die pragmatische Mutter und der idealistische, visionäre Vater – das naive Konzept des Fortschritts, das hauptsächlich durch die Erschaffung und Herstellung von Geräten zum Ausdruck gebracht wurde, die uns das Leben erleichtern und sogar zu unserem Glück beitragen sollten. Erst viel, viel später – in unserem Zeitalter – zeigte sich, daß die edelsten Ideale oft die ersten sind, die zur Degeneration neigen.

Oft mußte der Mensch entdecken, daß er zum Sklaven der Geräte geworden war, die er erfunden hatte, damit sie ihm dienen. Zwar gibt es einige wenige Objekte, deren gute Qualität, Bedienbarkeit und Nützlichkeit erhalten geblieben sind, doch allzu viele andere sind reiner Selbstzweck, ohne Humor, Liebe oder Phantasie. Lebt wohl, Träume vom Glück ... Als ich heranreifte, erkannte ich, daß ich vielleicht ein Unrecht wiedergutmachen könnte, das ich wahrscheinlich selbst mitverschuldet hatte.

Weil ich weder ein Philosoph bin, noch ein Soziologe, noch ein Staatsmann, weil ich nicht intelligent genug bin, das Problem theoretisch anzugehen, beschloß ich, pragmatisch zu handeln. Ich versuchte, die Wünsche und Bedürfnisse meines Mitbürgers, den ich gerne als Freund und Nachbarn hätte, zu erfassen – das, was er will und was er nicht will – und die Gegenstände zu beschreiben, mit denen er sich umgeben möchte, um vielleicht durch ihn hindurch einen Blick auf eine künftige Gesellschaft werfen zu können, in der ich meine Kinder und die meiner Freunde aufwachsen sehen möchte. Was für ein gewaltiges, prätentiöses und naives Programm.

Ich bemühte mich also darum, Objekte zu finden, zu sammeln, zu verbessern oder (wenn nötig) zu gestalten, die den Menschen gegenüber ehrlich, verantwortlich und respektvoll sind. Nicht unbedingt schöne Objekte, aber gute Objekte. Doch schon bald wurde mir bewußt, daß ich mir ein unerreichbares Ziel gesetzt hatte. Nach einem intensiven Such- und Auswahlprozeß konnten nur sehr wenige Produkte meinen strengen Maßstäben genügen. Und selbst die Produkte, die meine Billigung fanden, waren meilenweit von meinem Ideal der Perfektion entfernt. Dennoch sprach aus ihnen eine gewisse Geisteshaltung, eine alternative Richtung, eine neue Lebensauffassung. Heute kann ich Ihnen einen Katalog dieser Objekte anbieten, ein Kompendium, das ich als einen Katalog von »Nicht-Produkten für Nicht-Konsumenten« bezeichnen möchte. Der Nicht-

Konsument ist ein Mensch, der wachsam und argwöhnisch ist, aber auch offen, kreativ, enthusiastisch und schließlich äußerst fortschrittlich und modern. Ich hoffe, daß Sie sich als Mitglied der freien und ungebundenen Gruppe der Nicht-Konsumenten erkennen, wenn Sie sich diese Objekte ansehen und die Begleitkommentare lesen. Außerdem hoffe ich, daß Sie zu denen gehören werden, die weitere Objekte aufspüren und gestalten, so daß wir schon bald ein zweites Kompendium zusammenstellen und diese Sammlung Schritt für Schritt auf das Niveau unserer Vision anheben können. Der beispielgebende Erfolg dieses *moral market* würde ein neues Verhältnis zwischen Menschen, Geräten und ihrer Herstellung deutlich machen.

Cromignonne und Abominet könnten dann ihre Träume verwirklicht sehen, und unsere Kinder könnten endlich neue Abenteuer erleben.

Zu unseren künftigen Fehlern

An Nicht-Produkte werden Anforderungen gestellt, die auf Kriterien wie den folgenden beruhen: Existenzberechtigung, Zweckdienlichkeit, Langlebigkeit, moralischer und didaktischer Anspruch, politische Bedeutung, symbolische gesellschaftliche Bedeutung, sexuelle Bedeutung, menschliches Verantwortungsbewußtsein, faire Kosten, faire Preise, Kreativität und manchmal Humor, Poesie und Respekt. Natürlich kann keines der Objekte in dieser Sammlung diesen Kriterien in jeder Hinsicht voll genügen. Aber jedes einzelne stellt eine Bemühung, einen Versuch dar. ... Dieses jährlich erscheinende Kompendium – gegen die Launen der Mode per definitionem immun – wird deshalb Jahr für Jahr umfangreicher werden. Weil immer die Gefahr besteht, daß man sich irrt und täuschen läßt, werden wir auch künftig Fehler machen – unsere Fehler werden die Objekte sein, die aus dem Katalog herausgenommen werden. Auf dieser Seite werden wir über unsere Fehler Rechenschaft ablegen und unsere Lehren daraus ziehen.

Zu unserer Zukunft

Dieser erste Katalog kann nur der Anfang sein. Ich bin kein professioneller Versandhändler, und deshalb ist dieser erste Versuch wahrscheinlich zu persönlich ausgefallen. Doch dieser Katalog ist ein Mittel zum Zweck, ein Werkzeug. Nutzen Sie ihn. Machen Sie Notizen, Zeichnungen, Fotos. Lassen Sie sich von den hier vorgestellten Objekten anregen, und beschreiben Sie Ihre Bedürfnisse und Träume. Schicken Sie uns Ihre Vorschläge und Ideen. Der Good-Goods-Katalog hat auch eine Internet-Adresse: www.goodgoods.tm.fr. Damit ist meine Mission fürs erste beendet. Jetzt liegt es an Ihnen, Ihre Zukunft zu zerstören und wiederaufzubauen. Vielen Dank.

Philippe Starck

Des non-objets pour des non-consommateurs

Un jour, il y a quelques millions d'années, Madame Cromignonne et Monsieur Abominet tombèrent amoureux de leur progéniture. C'était assez nouveau. Madame voulait protéger sa descendance, Monsieur voulait l'améliorer. A eux deux – elle pragmatique, lui théorique et visité – ils inventèrent l'idée naïve du progrès dont l'un des principaux moyens d'expression passa par la création et la production d'outils censés nous apporter une vie meilleure et même du bonheur. Bien plus tard – c'est-à-dire aujourd'hui – on peut s'apercevoir que les jolies idées sont généralement les premières à dégénérer.

L'Homme se retrouva bien souvent esclave d'outils créés pour le servir. Si certains rares objets auront l'honnêteté, la rigueur et le respect de leur mission, une pléthore d'autres ne rouleront que pour eux, sans humour ni amour, ni fantaisie. Adieu, rêves de bonheur. L'âge venant, je me suis dit que j'essaierais bien de corriger une histoire dont j'ai sûrement été moi-même complice.

N'étant pas philosophe, sociologue, politique... ni même assez intelligent pour attaquer le problème sur le plan théorique, j'ai décidé d'être pragmatique.

Par ses acceptations, ses refus, ses souhaits et ses nécessités nécessaires, j'ai tenté de décrire l'équipement du citoyen que j'aimerais avoir comme voisin et ami. Et, peut-être, entrevoir à travers celui-ci la société où j'aimerais voir grandir mes enfants, et les enfants de mes amis.

Vaste, prétentieux et naïf programme.

J'ai donc essayé de trouver, collecter, corriger, ou créer quand il le fallait, des objets honnêtes, responsables, respectueux de la personne. Des objets pas forcément beaux, mais des objets bons.

Je me suis vite aperçu que je m'attaquais à une mission impossible : après recherches et sélections, assez peu d'objets passèrent à travers ma grille d'exigence. De plus, les objets retenus étaient loin d'être aussi parfaits que je l'aurais voulu, mais on pouvait déjà y reconnaître un esprit, une nouvelle direction, une autre façon d'être.

Ces objets, je vous les propose aujourd'hui dans ce catalogue que j'aimerais appeler catalogue des « non-produits pour des non-consommateurs ». Des non-consommateurs conscients et suspicieux, mais aussi ouverts, créatifs, enthousiastes et finalement profondément à contre-courant, modernes.

J'espère qu'à travers ces objets et les commen-

taires qui les accompagnent, vous pourrez vous reconnaître comme membre de la tribu libre et infédérée des non-consommateurs. J'espère aussi que c'est vous qui débusquerez et créerez les objets qui, demain matin, constitueront le futur du deuxième recueil. Afin que, petit à petit, il soit à la hauteur de notre ambition et que, le succès de son *moral market* créant l'exemple, puisse apparaître une nouvelle relation entre l'Homme, la production et les objets.

Cromignonne et Abominet pourraient alors voir leurs rêves se réaliser, et nos enfants repartir – enfin – vers de nouvelles aventures.

A nos futures erreurs

Les non-produits doivent passer à travers une grille d'exigence dont les critères sont, entre autres, légitimité à exister, honnêteté du service, longévité, élaboration morale, didactisme, sens politique, sens de la représentation sociale, sens sexuel, responsabilité humaine, coût juste, prix juste, créativité et quelquefois, poésie, humour et respect.

Evidemment, aucun des objets de ce recueil ne satisfait en totalité aux exigences posées. Mais ils tentent, essaient, commencent. Ce recueil annuel, par définition à l'abri des modes et des démodés, ne fera ainsi que se compléter au fil des ans.

Parce qu'il est difficile de ne pas se laisser séduire, tromper, et de s'abuser soi-même, nous ferons encore des erreurs : nos erreurs seront les produits que nous ferons disparaître de ce recueil. Nous ne jouerons pas de l'oubli et cette page en rendra compte, afin que ces échecs nous soient utiles.

A nos futurs

Ce premier recueil n'est qu'une façon d'« amorcer la pompe ». Je n'ai pas vocation à faire du commerce par correspondance, et, pour cette raison, sa première version est sans doute trop personnelle. Mais ce catalogue n'est qu'un outil. Il est entre vos mains : servez-vous en. Notez, dessinez, photographiez, décrivez et signalez dans ces pages vos rêves, vos préoccupations. Envoyez-nous toutes vos suggestions, vos idées. Vous pouvez également expédier vos informations sur le site Internet du recueil Good Goods, www.goodgoods.tm.fr. Ma mission est ici sur le point de se terminer : c'est à vous qu'il appartient maintenant de détruire et reconstruire votre futur.

Merci.

Philippe Starck

N.C
NO CREATION
NO CHEMICAL
The N.C brand clothing and household linen I am bringing out satisfies two specifications. No Creation is a conscious effort to reject the creative approach. I want to summon up a prototype of a garment or piece of household linen with time-honoured qualities, a prototype already familiar to the collective memory, immune to the vagaries of fashion. No Chemical means that I am producing these goods using natural materials which have not undergone any chemical treatments or processing. The respect we owe the environment is above all respect we owe ourselves as human beings. Our line of N.C cotton garments made in Peru labeled Stop Cocaine Go Organic responds to moral need as well. The growth of organic cotton is been and encouraged by the Peruvian government as an incentive to farmers to quit growing coca (from which cocaine is made) as a cash crop. Currently, the inorganic cotton crop is responsible for 20% of the total pesticides used in agriculture. These chemicals are harmful to human health both in the field and later, when the inorganically grown cotton is in contact with the skin. The Skal (Eko label) attests to the exclusively organic quality of the cotton we use, which is grown and processed without the addition of chemicals. Skal is an international inspection agency recognized by the European Union, and its standards for ecological purity are the most demanding. The same is true for a pure alpaca wool or alpaca-wool blend garments: the quality of the yarns and natural hues (pure alpaca wool in a natural state is available in a wide variety of tints) enables us to offer clothing that is just as good as, if not better than, similar products which have been processed with chemical pollutants. For technical reasons certain N.C garments have not yet been awarded the Eko label from Skal. Nevertheless, they have been made respecting strict ecological standards.

A. **Produit:** Big Baby, **label:** N.C, **description:** grenouillère hiver et demi-saison 70% laine 30% alpaga, jauge 12, certificat Eko (Skal), **références:** noir 520.5298, camel 520.5212, anthracite 520.5220, **tailles:** 1 (S), 2 (M), 4 (XL), 5 (XXL), **prix:** 1290 F/194,52 Euros.

Tous les vêtements N.C des pages 10, 11, 12, 13, **en 24 heures chez vous:** +80F/ 12,06 Euros.

A

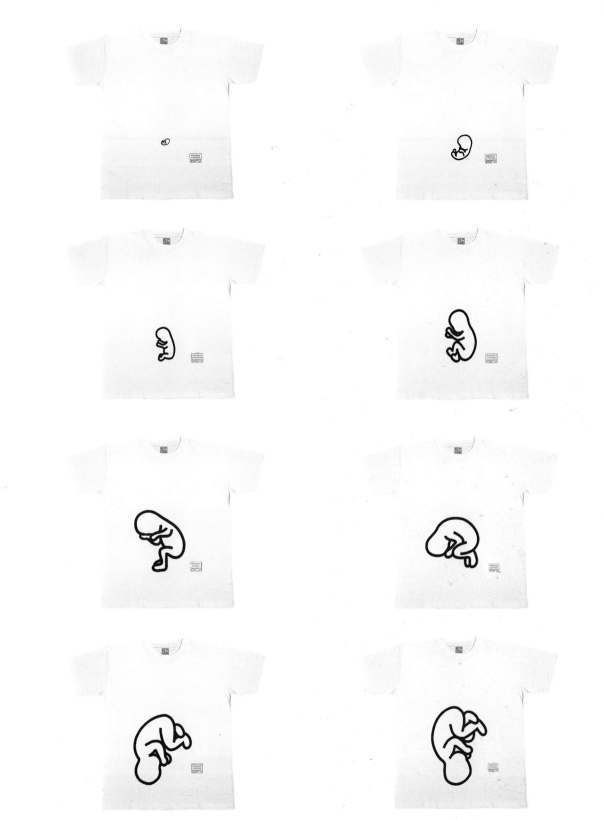

Design: Patricia Bailer, produit: 9 months T-Shirts, label: N.C, fabricant: Bo Weevil, date de conception: 1997, date de production: 1998, description: série de 8 T-Shirts pur coton couleur blanc naturel où est imprimé un fœtus aux différentes étapes de son développement, taille: le T-Shirt est de plus en plus grand pour s'adapter à la morphologie de la femme enceinte, référence: 857.4421, prix: 900 F/135,71 Euros les 8 T-Shirts, en 24h chez vous: +80 F/12,06 Euros.

N.C. Political T-Shirts. L'expérience et la réflexion m'ont conduit à synthétiser quelques conclusions élémentaires.Elles sont devenues de courtes phrase: qui appartiennent, à mon sens, au registre de l'évidence. J'ai choisi d'imprimer 8 de ces phrases sur un T-Shirt, un support simple et efficace, pour rappeler à ceux qui les porteront, ou les liront, que nous ne pouvons pas toujours faire l'économie de la responsabilité et de l'action. Le coton de ces T-Shirts est nat cultivé et traité sans produits chimiques ni pesticides, qualité garantie par le label Eko (Skal).

N.C. Political T-Shirts. Experience and contemplation have led me to draw certain basic conclusions. Expressed in the form of short maxims, they belon what I see as the realm of universal wisdom. I have decided to print eight of these statements on a T-Shirt, a simple and direct form of communication, to re all those who will wear or read them that we cannot always afford the luxury of irresponsibility and inertia. The natural unbleached cotton in these T-Shi grown and processed without chemical additives or pesticides, according to Eko (Skal) standards.

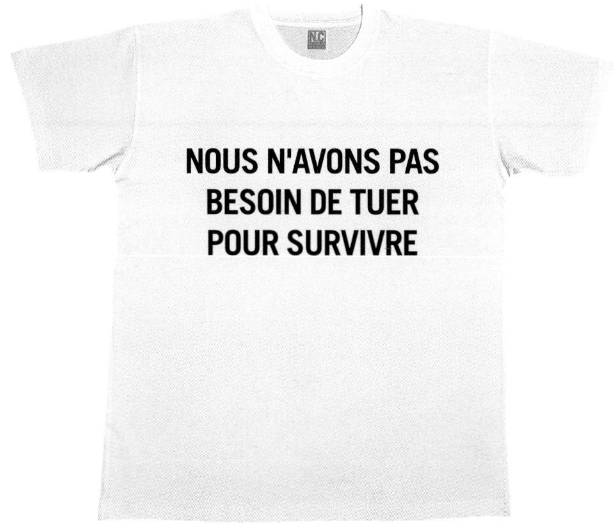

**NOUS N'AVONS PAS
BESOIN DE TUER
POUR SURVIVRE**

**TOMORROW
WILL BE
LESS**

**NOUS SOMMES
DES MUTANTS**

WE ARE GOD

esign: Philippe Starck, **produit:** Political T-Shirts, **label:** N.C, **fabricant:** Bo Weevil, **date de conception:** 1997, **date de production:** 1998, **description:** T-Shirt
r coton blanc naturel, message imprimé en noir, **références:** God is…858.0006, Le civisme…853.7950, Nous n'avons…854.5685, Tomorrow…851.8300,
oral…852.6745, L'amour…851.8866, Nous sommes…851.9609, We are…853.3016, **tailles:** 1 (S), 3 (L), 5 (XXL), **prix:** 150 F/22,62 Euros, **en 24h chez vous:**
0 F/12,06 Euros.

A   B

OAO: nous sommes ce que nous mangeons. L'homme est un écosystème où l'esprit est indissociable du corps et de sa nourriture, dans une relation d'intim interdépendance. S'il est largement admis que l'alimentation a une influence sur la santé du corps, il est tout de même curieux que l'on ne reconnaisse pas aus communément son rôle vis-à-vis de la qualité de la pensée. La gamme de produits OAO est un accès créatif à une nourriture organique moderne. Son intégri biologique est garantie par le laboratoire Lima Expert, précurseur de l'alimentation organique, qui assure depuis plus de 40 ans une sélection rigoureuse de s aliments biologiques. L'alimentation biologique sera – hélas – une mode, mais elle laissera un acquis important: une nouvelle norme de qualité alimentai Lorsque l'on peut manger de la nourriture ayant poussé dans un sol non traité aux engrais industriels et n'ayant subi aucun adjuvant chimique, il ne faut p hésiter. Meilleurs pour la santé, les produits bio nous permettent aussi de retrouver des goûts que l'on avait tendance à oublier. OAO, mangeons intelligent.

OAO: We are what we eat. Man is an ecosystem in which mental synergy is an integral part of the body and its food; a web of intimately interdepende and intertwined processes. Oddly enough, although it seems to be commonly accepted that diet has an influence on physical health, people are relucta to acknowledge its impact upon mental energy. The OAO product line is a creative approach to modern organic self-care. Its biological integrity has be tested by Lima Expert laboratories, foundation-layers for quality health foods. For over 40 years, Lima has been setting standards for organically grow naturally processed foods. Unfortunately the "health-food craze" will turn out to be a mere passing fad. But it will have left an imprint on the way we eva uate what we eat. When it is possible to obtain products free of any chemical additives, which have been grown in soil uncontaminated by industrial fe tilizers, we should not hesitate. You will find that organic foods are not only healthier, they are tastier as well. OAO, eat smart.

A. Produit: huile d'olive Sei Colli OAO, **partenaire:** Lima Expert, **description:** huile à base d'olives issues de l'agriculture biologique récoltées à la ma première pression à froid, **contenance:** 1 x 75cl, **référence:** 968.3577, **prix:** 99 F/14,93 Euros (prix au litre 132 F/l - 19,91 Euros/l).

B. Produit: huile d'olive San Vito OAO, **partenaire:** Lima Expert, **description:** huile à base d'olives issues de l'agriculture biologique récoltées à la ma première pression à froid, plus rare et délicate que la Sei Colli, **contenance:** 1 x 75cl, **référence:** 968.3585, **prix:** 119 F/17,94 Euros (prix au lit 159 F/l - 23,98 Euros/l).

C. Produit: riz thaï mi-complet OAO, **partenaire:** Lima Expert, **description:** riz thaï mi-complet issu de l'agriculture biologique, **poids:** 6 boîtes x 500g, **référence:** 956.3954, **prix:** 89 F/13,42 Euros (prix au kilo 29,67 F/kg - 4,47 Euros/kg).

C

D. Produit: riz basmati complet OAO, **partenaire:** Lima Expert, **description:** riz basmati complet issu de l'agriculture biologique, **poids:** 6 boîtes x 500g, **référence:** 956.3717, **prix:** 89 F/13,42 Euros (prix au kilo 29,67 F/kg - 4,47 Euros/kg).

D

E. Produit: spaghetti mi-complets OAO, **partenaire:** Lima Expert, **description:** spaghetti mi-complets issu de l'agriculture biologique, **poids:** 12 boîtes x 500g, **référence:** 956.4187, **prix:** 119 F/17,94 Euros (prix au kilo 19,83 F/kg - 2,99 Euros/kg).

E

Produit: pâtes semini mi-completes OAO, **partenaire:** Lima Expert, **description:** pâtes semini, à base de blé dur semi-complet issu de l'agriculture biologique, **poids:** 12 boîtes x 500g, **référence:** 956.7747, **prix:** 119 F/17,94 Euros (prix au kilo 19,83 F/kg - 2,99 Euros/kg).

F

Produit: sel de sésame OAO, **partenaire:** Lima Expert, **description:** condiment à base de graines de sésame grillées issues de l'agriculture biologique et de sel marin, **poids:** 6 pots x 100g, **référence:** 956.6746, **prix:** 75 F/11,31 Euros (prix au kilo 125 F/kg - 18,85 Euros/kg).

G

Produit: sel marin OAO, **partenaire:** Lima Expert, **description:** sel marin récolté à Noirmoutier, **poids:** 6 x 200g, **référence:** 968.5529, **prix:** 59 F/8,90 Euros (prix au kilo 49,17 F/kg - 7,42 Euros/kg).
Produit: poivre noir en grains OAO, **description:** poivre noir de Madagascar issu de l'agriculture biologique, **poids:** 6 pots x 80g, **référence:** 969.3335, **prix:** 75 F/11,31 Euros (prix au kilo 156,25 F/kg - 15,56 Euros/kg).

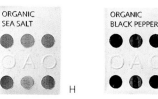

H

I

E. Gel nettoyant moussant Starck with Bioderma™. Très doux (sans savon), émollient et filmogène, il permet le nettoyage efficace du visage et du corps tout en évitant le dessèchement et la fragilisation. Il est adapté à tous les types de peaux (homme, femme, enfant), ne pique pas les yeux et peut même être utilisé comme shampooing pour les très jeunes enfants ou les nourrissons. Sans parfum.
Starck with Bioderma™ foaming cleansing gel. This extremely mild, detergent-free gel cleans the face and body without dehydrating and leaves the skin with a silky glow. It is safe for people of all ages, even children, does not sting the eyes, and can be used even as a shampoo for infants or very young children. Fragrance free.
Produit: gel nettoyant moussant Starck with Bioderma™, **description:** flacon-pompe 250ml, **référence:** 689.1934, **prix:** 85 F/12,82 Euros (34 F/dl – 5,13 Euros/dl).

Tous les Starck with Bioderma **en 24h chez vous:** +80 F/12,06 Euros.

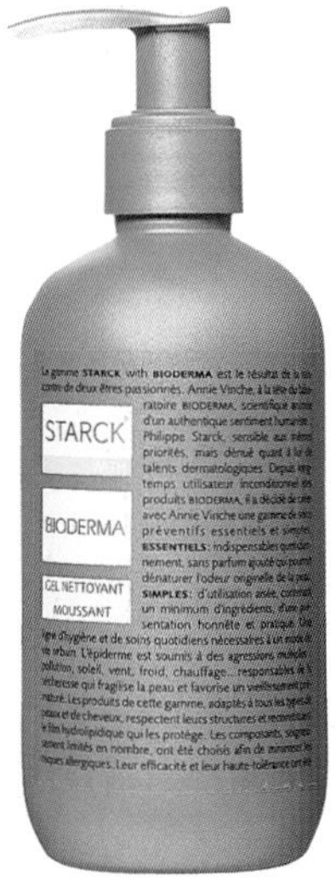

E

Starck with Bioderma™. La gamme Starck with Bioderma™ est le résultat de ma rencontre avec Annie Vinche, à la tête du laboratoire Bioderma™. Une scientifique rare, animée d'un authentique sentiment humaniste. Je suis sensible aux mêmes priorités, mais malheureusement tout à fait dénué de talents dermatologiques. Depuis longtemps utilisateur de ses produits, j'ai décidé de créer avec elle une gamme de soins préventifs essentiels et simples. Essentiels: indispensables quotidiennement, sans parfum ajouté qui pourrait dénaturer l'odeur originelle de la peau. Simples: d'utilisation aisée, contenant un minimum d'ingrédients, d'une présentation honnête et pratique. L'épiderme est soumis à des agressions multiples (pollution, soleil, vent, froid, chauffage...) responsables de la sécheresse qui fragilise la peau et entraîne un vieillissement prématuré. Adaptés à tous les types de peaux et de cheveux, les produits de la gamme Starck with Bioderma™ respectent leur structure et reconstituent le film hydrolipidique qui les protège. Les composants, soigneusement limités en nombre, ont été choisis afin de minimaliser les risques allergiques. Leur efficacité et leur haute tolérance ont été testées en milieu hospitalier dermatologique.
Starck with Bioderma™. This range is the result of my encounter with Annie Vinche, head of Bioderma™ Laboratories. She is an exceptional scientist, inspired by genuinely humanistic motivations. Although I am driven by the same prerogatives, I am forced to admit that I lack the dermatological talents. As a longtime user of Bioderma™ products, I decided to create, with her, a line of essential, preventive skin care products, an indispensable daily routine without artificial perfumes liable to mask the skins natural fragrance. Simple products, easy to use, containing few ingredients and packaged in an honest, practical manner. Skin is subjected to a variety of attacks from pollution, sun, wind, cold, central heating and so on, leading to dehydration and premature ageing of the skin. Adapted to all skin and hair types, Starck with Bioderma™ products respect the epidermal structure and restore the hydrolipidic film which protects it. The ingredients, carefully screened down to a bare minimum, have been chosen for their hypoallergenic properties. Their effectiveness and safety have been clinically tested.

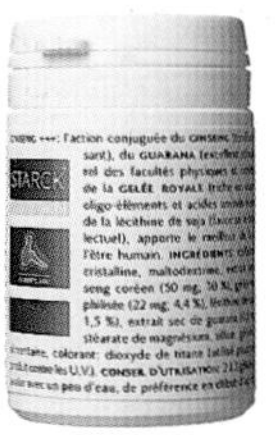

E

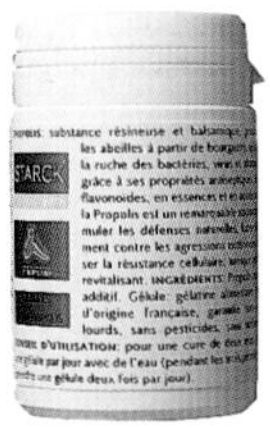

F

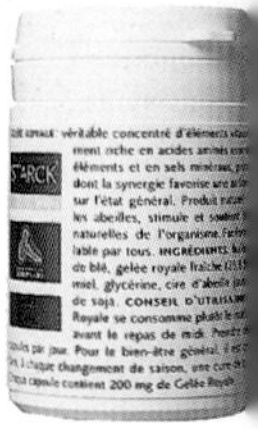

E. Ginseng+++ Starck with Europ-Labo. Complexe fortifiant, dynamisant et stimulant général de l'organisme, tant sur un plan physique que psychique. Un concentré de substances naturellement prodigieuses: ginseng, guarana, gelée royale et lécithine de soja.
Starck with Europ-Labo ginseng+++. A complex which fortifies, energizes, and stimulates the organism, on both a psychic and physical level. It is a concentration of naturally powerful substances: ginseng, guarana, royal jelly, lecithin.
Produit: Ginseng+++ Starck with Europ-Labo, **contenance:** 55 gélules, **référence:** 701.6140, **prix:** 95 F/14,32 Euros, **en 24h chez vous:** +80F/12,06 Euros.

F. Gélules de propolis Starck with Europ-Labo. Tonique général et revitalisant. Riche en flavonoïdes, en essences et en acides naturels, elle est un remarquable soutien pour stimuler les défenses naturelles, lutter efficacement contre les agressions extérieures et favoriser la résistance cellulaire et la vitalité de l'organisme.
Starck with Europ-Labo propolis capsules. Propolis, a general revitalizing tonic, rich in bioflavinoids, essences, and natural acids. Propolis boosts the body's resistance to disease, arms it against outside agression, and promotes the organism's vitality and cellular resilience.
Produit: Gélules de propolis Starck with Europ-Labo, **contenance:** 75 gélules, **référence:** 705.4980, **prix:** 65 F/9,80 Euros, **en 24h chez vous:** +80F/12,06 Euros.

G. Gelée royale fraîche Starck w[...] Labo. Reconstituant et stimulant, r[...] défenses naturelles de l'organisme. E[...] tre des éléments vitaux et convient [...] Particulièrement recommandée aux [...] périodes de croissance, aux convale[...] personnes âgées, aux personnes [...] stressées, déprimées.
Starck with Europ-Labo fresh ro[...] tonic and stimulant, it reinforces the b[...] ral defenses. This concentrate of vital[...] beneficial to people of all ages, bu[...] cially recommended for young pe[...] growth spurts, convalescents, elde[...] and anyone who feels tired, depress[...] ject to stress.
Produit: Gelée royale fraîche Starck [...] Labo, **contenance:** 65 capsules, [...] 704.4496, **prix:** 95 F/14,32 Euros, e[...] vous: +80F/12,06 Euros.

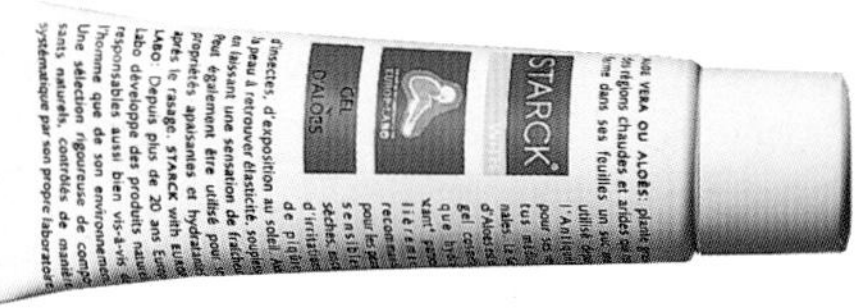

H

H. Gel d'aloes Starck with Europ-Labo. Gel hydratant*. L'aloe vera, ou aloès, est une plante grasse des régions chaudes et arides qui renfer[...] feuilles un suc amer utilisé depuis l'Antiquité pour ses vertus médicinales. Gel cosmétique qui convient à toutes les peaux, particulièrement r[...] en cas de fragilité cutanée, en cas d'irritations, de piqûres d'insectes, d'exposition au soleil. Il aide la peau à retrouver élasticité et souplesse en[...] sensation de fraîcheur. Propriétés apaisantes et cicatrisantes. Bénéfique après le rasage. *Hydratation des couches supérieures de l'épiderme.
Starck with Europ-Labo aloe vera gel. A moisturizing gel*. Aloe Vera is a succulent plant which grows in hot, arid regions. Its leaves contain [...] which has been used for medicinal purposes since Antiquity. This gel treatment is suitable for all skin types, and is especially recommended fo[...] skin irritation due to chapping, insect bites, sunburn, or windburn. It restores the skin's elasticity and softness leaving a refreshing feeling. Heal[...] properties. A good after-shave treatment. *Moisturization of the skin's outer layer.
Produit: Gel d'aloes Starck with Europ-Labo, **contenance:** 50ml, **référence:** 739.5205, **prix:** 45 F/6,79 Euros (prix au décilitre: 90F/dl), **en 24h** [...] +80F/12,06 Euros.

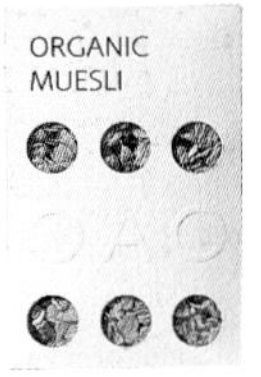

A

A. Produit: muesli aux fruits OAO, **partenaire:** Lima Expert, **description:** mélange équilibré à base de fruits et de noix (raisins secs, noisettes, pommes séchées), épeautre (céréale à valeur nutritive élevée), pétales de maïs et Sarrasin, issus de l'agriculture biologique, **poids:** 6 boîtes x 375g, **référence:** 958.9708, **prix:** 129 F/19,45 Euros (prix au kilo 57,33 F/kg - 8,64 Euros/kg).

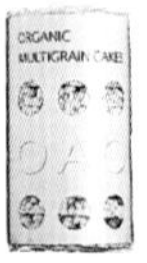

B

B. Produit: galettes multicéréales OAO, **partenaire:** Lima Expert, **description:** galettes à base de riz et de céréales mélangées issus de l'agriculture biologique, **poids:** 12 paquets x 100g, **référence:** 968.0578, **prix:** 75 F/11,31 Euros (prix au kilo 62,50 F/kg - 9,42 Euros/kg).

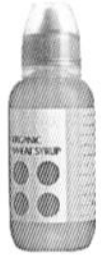
C

C. Produit: sirop de blé OAO, **partenaire:** Lima Expert, **description:** sirop de blé (sucres lents) issu de l'agriculture biologique, pour sucrer les aliments, les boissons, ou à tartiner, **contenance:** 6 flacons x 420g, **référence:** 969.6083, **prix:** 119 F/17,94 Euros (prix au kilo 42,22 F/kg - 7,12 Euros/kg).

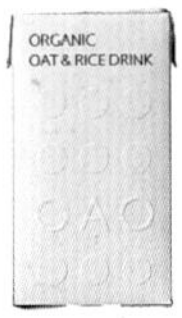

D

D. Produit: lait d'avoine et de riz OAO, **partenaire:** Lima Expert, **description:** boisson rafraîchissante végétale à base d'avoine et de riz complet issus de l'agriculture biologique, aromatisée à la vanille, substitut idéal, froid ou chaud, du lait ou du filtrat de soja, **contenance:** 12 briques x 1l, **référence:** 967.8670, **prix:** 169 F/25,48 Euros (prix au litre 14,08 F/l - 8,12 Euros/l).

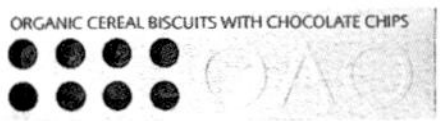

E

E. Produit: biscuits aux céréales et éclats de chocolat OAO, **partenaire:** Lima Expert, **description:** biscuits préparés à base de céréales (flocons d'avoine, de maïs) et de cacao issus de l'agriculture biologique, **poids:** 14 paquets x 150g, **référence:** 968.0934, **prix:** 189 F/ 28,50 Euros (prix au kilo 90 F/kg - 13,57 Euros/kg).

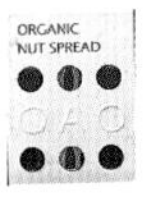

F

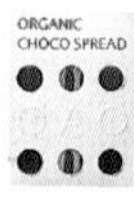

G

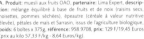

F. Produit: pâte à tartiner aux noisettes OAO, **partenaire:** Lima Expert, **description:** à base de noisettes sélectionnées issues de l'agriculture biologique, **poids:** 6 pots x 250g, **référence:** 970.0552, **prix:** 169 F/ 25,48 Euros (prix au kilo 112,67 F/kg - 16,99 Euros/kg).
G. Produit: pâte à tartiner au chocolat OAO, **description:** goût exceptionnel, à base de noisettes et de cacao issus de l'agriculture biologique, **poids:** 6 pots x 250g, **référence:** 970.0560, **prix:** 219 F/ 33,02 Euros (prix au kilo 146 F/kg - 22,01 Euros/kg).

L'abus d'alcool est dangereux pour la santé, consommez avec modération

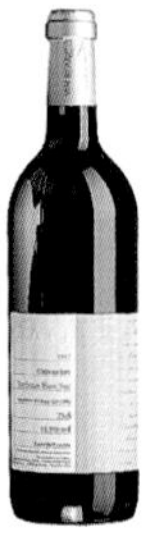
H

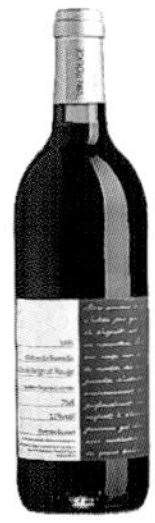
I

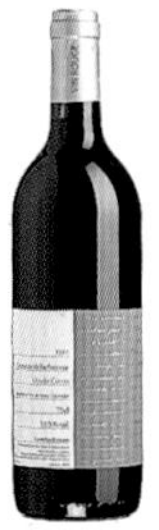
J

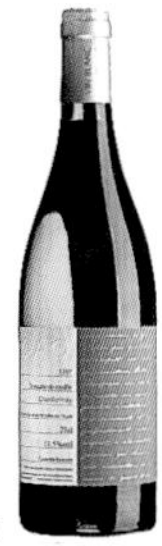
K

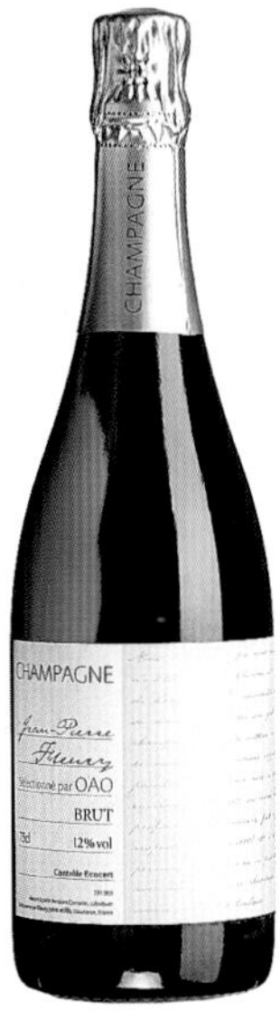

L

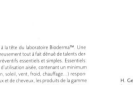

Champagne. Depuis 1992, Jean-Pierre Fleury cultive l'ensemble de son vignoble en bio-dynamie: un choix de culture qui respecte l'écosystèm[...] totalement les engrais industriels, remplacés par des traitements à base végétale et minérale. Initiée par Jean-Pierre Fleury et son ami Poirrier, c[...] profondément moderne fait appel au respect, à l'honnêteté et à l'amour de la personne qui consommera ce produit. Outre son goût plus authenti[...] pagne est le prototype des nouveaux rapports qu'il est possible d'entretenir avec la production, son environnement, et soi-même. Consommé ave[...] c'est une grande source de bonheur. Produit sur une petite surface, ce champagne biologique n'est malheureusement proposé qu'en série limitée [...]
Champagne. In 1992, Jean-Pierre Fleury converted his entire vineyard to biodynamic farming techniques. This venture respects the ecosystem [...] usual industrial fertilizers and pesticides, and using plant- and mineral-based treatments instead. Initiated by Jean-Pierre Fleury and his friend Poi[...] foundly modern approach based on an appeal to the integrity, honesty, and discernment of the people who will later consume the product. This c[...] only tastes more genuine, it is also a model for the new synergy developing between production techniques, nature, and the soil. Imbibed in mo[...] great source of pleasure. However, because this organic champagne is grown in small quantities, it is available only as a limited edition of number[...]
H. Produit: Champagne Jean-Pierre Fleury, sélectionné par OAO, **partenaire:** Lima Expert, **description:** Champagne brut issu de raisins c[...] biologique, mis en bouteille au domaine, **contenance:** 75cl, **référence:** 970.8057, **prix:** 200 F/30,16 Euros (prix au litre 266,67 F/l - 40,21 E[...]

I. Produit: Château Jarr 1997 OAO, **partenaire:** Lima Expert, **description:** Bordeaux blanc sec, issu de raisins de l'agriculture biologique, ap[...] trôlée, produit et mis en bouteille au domaine, **contenance:** 75cl, **référence:** 970.7603, **prix:** 59 F/8,90 Euros (prix au litre 78,67 F/l - 11,87[...]
J. Produit: Château le Barradis 1995 OAO, **partenaire:** Lima Expert, **description:** Côtes de Bergerac rouge, appellation contrôlée, vin iss[...] l'agriculture biologique, mis en bouteille au château, **contenance:** 75cl, **référence:** 970.3713, **prix:** 89 F/13,42 Euros (prix au litre 118,67 F/l - [...]
K. Produit: Domaine de Barbarossa 1997 OAO, **partenaire:** Lima Expert, **description:** vin de Corse rouge issu de raisins de l'agriculture biol[...] lation contrôlée, mis en bouteille au domaine, **contenance:** 75cl, **référence:** 970.0692, **prix:** 59 F/8,90 Euros (prix au litre 78,67 F/l - 11,87 [...]
L. Produit: Domaine de Coulée 1997 OAO, **partenaire:** Lima Expert, **description:** Chardonnay, vin blanc de pays de la Hte vallée de l'Aude, iss[...] l'agriculture biologique, mis en bouteille au domaine, **contenance:** 75cl, **référence:** 970.7891, **prix:** 69 F/10,40 Euros (prix au litre 92 F/l - 13,[...]

Tous les produits alimentaires des pages 6 à 9 **en 24h chez vous:** +99 [...]

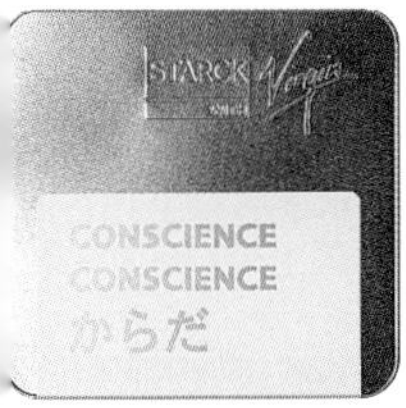

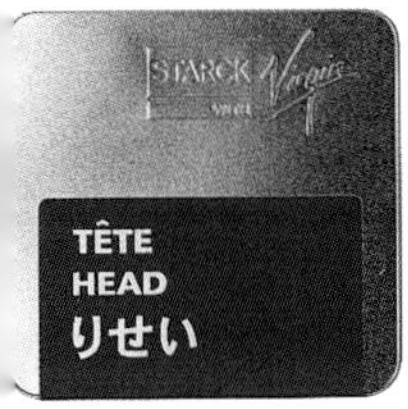

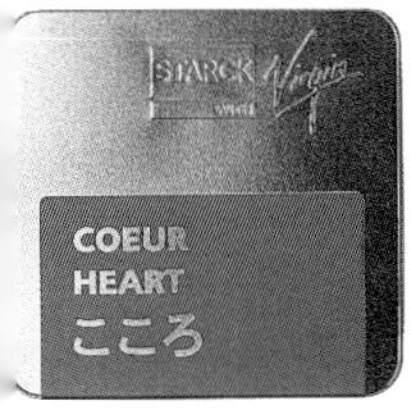

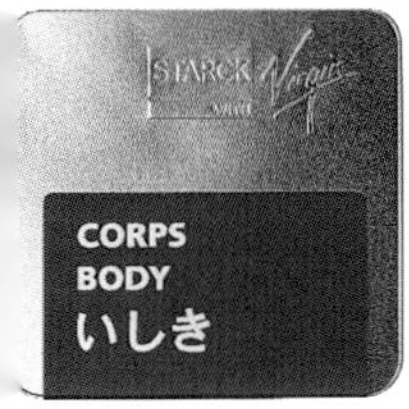

CD Thème Starck with Virgin. J'ai eu le bonheur de naître dans la musique, et de pouvoir continuer à y vivre. Elle est certainement l'un des éléments qui influe le plus sur mon travail créatif: j'ai toujours une mélodie dans la tête. J'aime avant tout le son, quelle que soit sa nature, sa culture ou son époque, pour la diversité des émotions fondamentales auxquelles il donne accès. En recueillant dans quatre disques les compositions musicales pour lesquelles j'ai le plus de gratitude, j'ai voulu transmettre différents sentiments, correspondants à des moments et des envies distincts de l'existence de chacun. Ces quatre disques marquent le début d'une collection qui se prolongera dans notre catalogue suivant, avec de nouveaux enthousiasmes. Je veux aussi remercier ici tous les artistes et les maisons de disques qui ont accepté de nous céder leurs titres pour ces quatre compilations. Sans eux et leur musique, je ne serais rien.
Starck with Virgin theme CD. It was my good fortune to be born musically, and to have been able to continue my life that way. There's always a tune dancing through my mind, and I'm sure this is one of the most significant elements influencing my creative work. Above all, I love sound, regardless of its cultural or epochal source, for the simple reason that it opens the listener to such a broad spectrum of emotions. My purpose in assembling these four records of musical compositions to which I owe the most gratitude, is to convey the various feelings which resonate within all of us at distinct moments in our individual experience. These four discs are the starting point of a collection which will expand as new enthusiasms are added in the catalogue to follow. I would like to thank all the artists and recording companies who were willing to participate in putting together these four anthologies. Without them and their music, I would be nothing.

A. Conscience – nous rappeler que tout est politique, que des artistes se préoccupent toujours de militantisme et d'engagement//Conscience – reminding us that every act is political, that artists draw their inspiration from a commitment to an ideal.
Conscience*. Patti Smith (People Have the Power), Curtis Mayfield (New World Order), Pato Banton (Pato Banton 's Opinion PT2), Carlos Puebla (Hasta Siempre - Che Guevara), Lou Reed (Swords of Damocles), John Lennon (Instant Karma), David Bowie (Heroes), Leslie Winner (John Says), Latcho Drom (Balada Conducatoruili), Ben Harper (Oppression), P.I.L (Acid Drop), Pascal Comelade (La Bella Ciao)...
Produit: CD Thème Conscience Starck with Virgin, **référence**: 592.3875, **prix**: 149 F/ 22,47 Euros.

B. Tête – une aide à la concentration et au rêve//Mind – the seat of concentration and reverie.
Tête*. Hiroshi Fujiwara (Hard Boiled Dub), Alpha (My Things), Robert Wyatt (Maryan), Michael Nyman (The Promise), Marianne Faithfull (Sleep), Philip Glass (Secret Agent), David Byrne/Brian Eno (Regiment), Nusrat Fateh Ali Khan/Michael Brook (Lament, extrait de Night Song), Moon Dog (Bird's Lament), Lou Reed/John Cale (A Dream), Laurie Anderson (The Night Flight From Houston), Pascal Comelade (Oh Caroline)...
Produit: CD Thème Tête Starck with Virgin, **référence**: 592.3867, **prix**: 149 F/ 22,47 Euros.

C. Cœur – l'intention de vous faire pleurer comme une midinette, à chaque note et sans scrupules//Heart – urging us to sob like overwrought teenyboppers at each note, unashamedly.
Cœur*. Robert Wyatt (Sea Song), The Velvet Underground with Nico (Femme Fatale), Lou Reed & John Cale (Hello It's Me), Nilsson (Everybody's Talkin' – B.O. Midnight Cowboy), PJ Harvey/Pascal Comelade (Love Too Soon), Lou Reed (Street Hassle), Nusrat Fateh Ali Khan (Yeh Jo Halka Saroor Sae), Marianne Faithful (Times Square), Manna (Who Changed The Order), Nico Faquito (Al Veiven De Mi Carreta), Bonga (Mona ki n'Gixica), Pascal Comelade (Ti Amo)...
Produit: CD Thème Coeur Starck with Virgin, **référence**: 592.2950, **prix**: 149 F/ 22,47 Euros.

D. Corps – sans préjugés culturels, son seul but est de faire bouger. Un caillou n'y résisterait pas//Body – free of cultural bias, its single goal is to bring about motion. A pebble would not, could not, remain inert.
Corps*. Liquid Liquid (Cavern), L'orchestre National de Barbès (Alaoui), Dillinger (Funky Punk), Billy Idol (Dancin'with Myself), Urban Dance Squad (Deeper Shade Of Soul), Lou Reed (Sweet Jane), U-Roy (Jah Son Of Africa), P.I.L (Warrior), Iggy Pop (NightClubbing), The Fun Lovin' Criminals (Fun Lovin' Criminals), Paul Simon (The Obvious Child), Waldeck (Wake Up), Manna (Hoggin 'A' Dub), Pascal Comelade (Rock Del Veneno)...
Produit: CD Thème Corps Starck with Virgin, **référence**: 592.3859, **prix**: 149 F/ 22,47 Euros.

*Liste des titres provisoire, sous réserve de l'accord des ayants-droit.

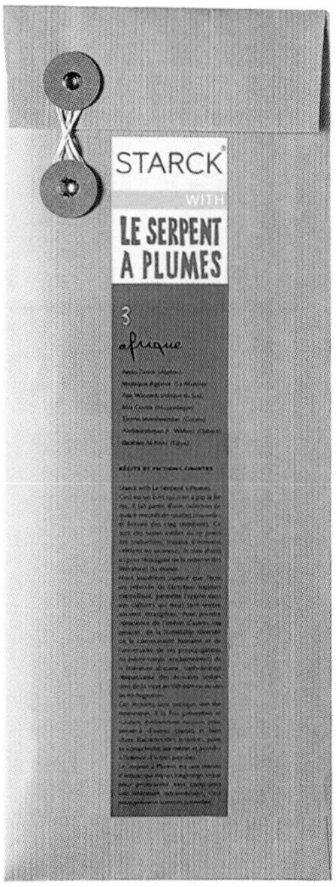

A

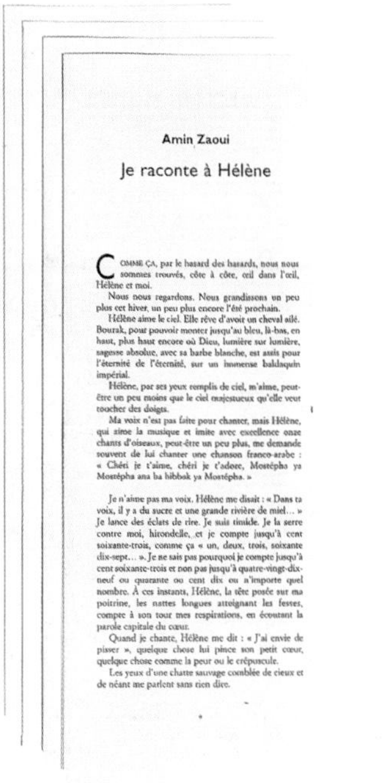
Amin Zaoui

Je raconte à Hélène

Comme ça, par le hasard des hasards, nous nous sommes trouvés, côte à côte, œil dans l'œil, Hélène et moi.
Nous nous regardons. Nous grandissons un peu plus cet hiver, un peu plus encore l'été prochain.
Hélène aime le ciel. Elle rêve d'avoir un cheval ailé. Bourak, pour pouvoir monter jusqu'au bleu, là-bas, en haut, plus haut encore où Dieu, lumière sur lumière, sagesse absolue, avec sa barbe blanche, est assis pour l'éternité de l'éternité, sur un immense baldaquin impérial.
Hélène, par ses yeux remplis de ciel, m'aime, peut-être un peu moins que le ciel majestueux qu'elle veut toucher des doigts.
Ma voix n'est pas faite pour chanter, mais Hélène, qui aime la musique et imite avec excellence onze chants d'oiseaux, peut-être un peu plus, me demande souvent de lui chanter une chanson franco-arabe : « Chéri je t'aime, chéri je t'adore, Mostépha ya Mostépha ana ba hibbak ya Mostépha. »

Je n'aime pas ma voix. Hélène me disait : « Dans ta voix, il y a du sucre et une grande rivière de miel... » Je lance des éclats de rire. Je suis timide. Je la serre contre moi, hirondelle, et je compte jusqu'à cent soixante-trois, comme ça « un, deux, trois, soixante dix-sept... ». Je ne sais pas pourquoi je compte jusqu'à cent soixante-trois et non pas jusqu'à quatre-vingt-dix-neuf ou quarante ou cent dix ou n'importe quel nombre. À ces instants, Hélène, la tête posée sur ma poitrine, les nattes longues atteignant les fesses, compte à son tour mes respirations, en écoutant la parole capitale du cœur.
Quand je chante, Hélène me dit : « J'ai envie de pisser », quelque chose lui pince son petit cœur, quelque chose comme la peur ou le crépuscule.
Les yeux d'une chatte sauvage comblée de cieux et de néant me parlent sans rien dire.

aisselle concentré Starck with Ecover. Il serait inconséquent de croire que la nature puisse tirer profit d'un liquide vaisselle, comme elle le fait ı des fourmis. Mais puisque nous ne pouvons pas encore nous passer de détergents, la politesse minimale est de chercher sérieusement à li- âts. Les détergents entraînent notamment une modification de la tension superficielle de l'eau, ce qui leur permet de nettoyer facilement, mais suite l'asphyxie des insectes, de la faune et de la flore aquatiques. Comme si, pour l'homme, l'air était brusquement remplacé par de l'eau. Le elle Starck with Ecover est efficace, mais il s'emploie à rétablir aussi vite que possible la tension superficielle de l'eau par l'utilisation de com- rels et de combinaisons chimiques plus élémentaires. Notre responsabilité ne doit pas s'arrêter au bouchon de l'évier.
Ecover concentrated dishwashing liquid. It would be naive to believe that the ecosystem could benefit from a dishwashing liquid the way it ees or ants. But since we human parts still require clean utensils, the least we can do is limit the damage we wreak in pursuit of hygiene. The ents alter the surface tension of the water to promote cleaning, which, in passing, asphyxiates insects, the aquatic fauna and flora, as if, with- the air we breathe became water. Concentrated dishwashing liquid Starck with Ecover is efficient; but it also restores natural water surface ten- ly as possible, by using natural components and elementary chemical compounds. Our responsibilities go well beyond the sink drain.
de vaisselle concentré Starck with Ecover, **description**: flacon-pompe 250ml, **référence**: 540.5718, **prix**: 45 F/6,79 Euros (180 F/l - 27,16 Euros/l)

ant en poudre Starck with Ecover. Ce blanchissant en poudre s'utilise pour les textiles blancs en complément de la lessive Starck with Ecover. i azurants optiques, il respecte la peau. La compatibilité dermatologique de tous les produits Starck with Ecover est maximale.
Ecover whitening additive. This powdered whitener can be added to white loads in conjunction with Starck detergent with Ecover. Free of ners and bleach, it respects the skin. All Starck products with Ecover display maximal dermatological compatibility.
chissant en poudre Starck with Ecover, **description**: 250g x 2, **référence**: 540.6706, **prix**: 30 F/4,52 Euros le lot de 2 boîtes (60 F/kg g).

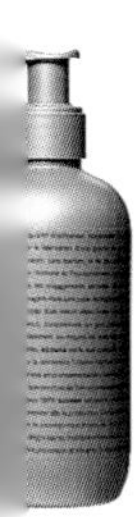

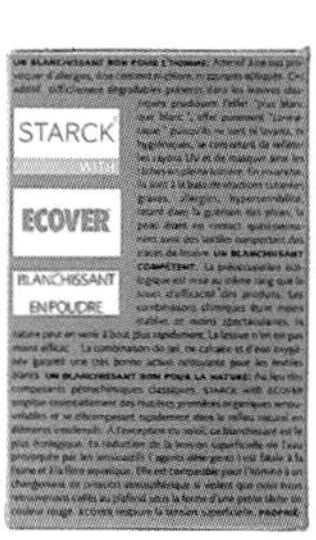

B

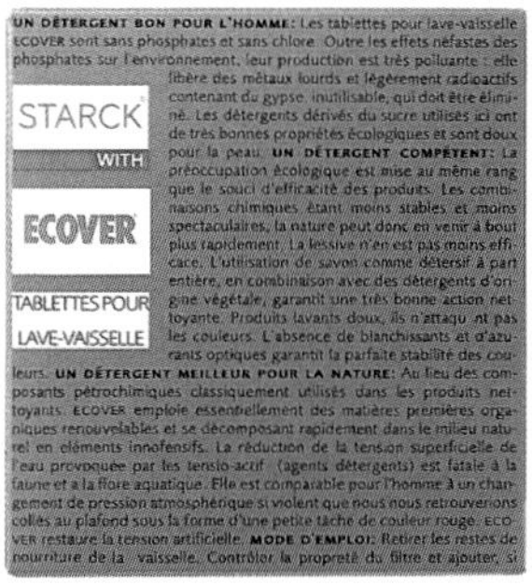

C

pour lave-vaisselle Starck with Ecover. Les tablettes pour lave-vaisselle Starck with Ecover sont sans phosphates et sans chlore. Au lieu des pétrochimiques classiquement employés, Ecover choisit des matières premières organiques, végétales ou minérales, renouvelables (ici, des érivés du sucre). Ecover recherche la meilleure dégradabilité finale, et non la biodégradabilité primaire telle que définie par la loi, qui est insuf- sts sont le plus souvent effectués par les fabricants de détergents classiques dans une eau à 20 degrés, sur des bactéries "professionnelles", détergents, donc dans des conditions très éloignées d'une situation authentique. La dégradation secondaire, préférée ici, s'attache à ce que se faire disparaître plus facilement tous les éléments nuisibles encore présents après la perte du pouvoir lavant des produits détergents.
Ecover tablets for automatic dishwashers. These dishwashing tablets are free of phosphates and bleach. Instead of the petrochemical com- ly found in such products. Ecover opts for organic raw materials from renewable plant or mineral sources (in this case, detergents derived from r is formulated to achieve the best final biodegradability, instead of the primary biodegradability as defined by law, which is insufficient. In usually conducted by manufacturers of conventional detergents at water temperatures of 70 degrees Fahrenheit, on "professional" bacteria etergent. These simulated conditions thus bear little resemblance to real-life situations. The purpose of measuring secondary degradation, as ıake it easier for nature to eliminate all the harmful elements which linger after the detergent has exhausted its washing power.
tes pour lave-vaisselle Starck with Ecover, **description**: 25 pastilles x 20g, **référence**: 746.7087, **prix**: 75 F/11,31 Euros (150 F/kg - 22,62 Euros/kg).

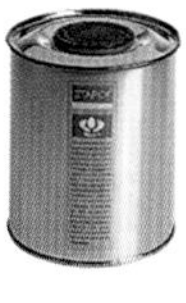
A

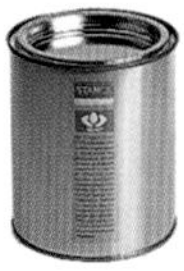
B

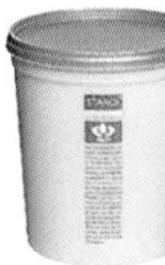
C

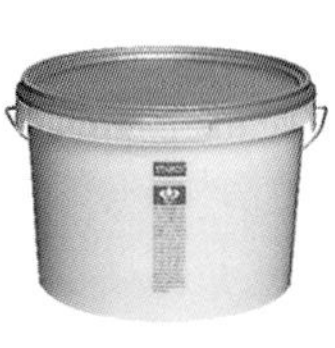

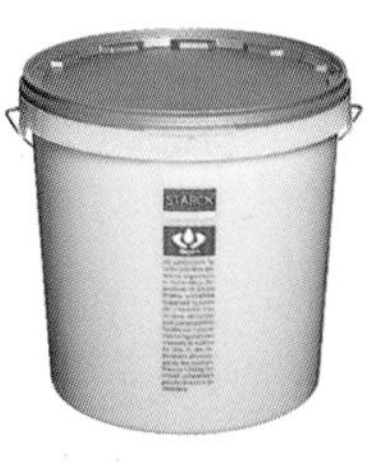

A. Diluant Starck with Biofa. Produit diluant à base d'essences naturelles (écorces d'agrumes et minérales). Il permet de diluer la laque et de nettoyer les instruments et pinceaux ayant été en contact avec laques et vernis, sans entrainer de dommages pour la santé et l'environnement. Les matières premières organiques et minérales des produits Starck with Biofa se décomposent rapidement dans le milieu naturel en éléments inoffensifs. Ce diluant accomplit même la prouesse de sentir naturellement bon.
Starck with Biofa thinner. A paint thinner made of natural essences (minerals and citrus peels). It is designed to thin varnish and clean brushes and rollers which have been used to apply varnish and gloss, with no adverse effects on health or the environment. The organic and mineral raw materials used in the Starck Biofa product line break down rapidly as products harmless to the natural environment. Moreover, this thinner even passes the odor test with flying colors.
Produit: diluant Starck with Biofa, **contenance**: 0,75l, **référence**: 532.2626, **prix**: 45 F/6,79 Euros (prix au litre : 60 F/l / 9,05 Euros), **en 24h chez vous**: +149 F/22,47 Euros.

B. Laque Starck with Biofa. Laque satinée pour la protection et la décoration du bois, du plâtre et des métaux. Les peintures de cette gamme offrent un niveau d'efficacité comparable, sinon supérieur, aux peintures à composants pétrochimiques: rendement élevé, odeur agréable, qualité de couleurs et sont sans danger pour la santé. Elles ont en revanche un temps de séchage partiellement plus long. Les peintures naturelles Starck with Biofa, en remplissant parfaitement leurs fonctions, sans polluer ni l'homme ni la nature, démontrent qu'un produit efficace n'est pas nécessairement nocif. Le nécessaire respect de l'environnement est d'abord respect de l'homme.
Starck with Biofa varnish. Satin-finish varnish for the protection and decoration of wood, plaster, and metal surfaces. The varnishes in this range display performances equal to or even greater than those available with petrochemical-based paints: high yield, pleasant odour, and colour quality, while presenting absolutely no health hazard. They merely require slightly longer drying times. Starck natural paints with Biofa fulfill their purpose admirably without damaging either the environment or human beings. A product does not have to be harmful to be effective.
Produit: laque Starck with Biofa, **contenance**: 0,75l, **références**: voir en page 45, références 31 à 35 **prix**: 95 F/14,32 Euros (prix au litre : 126,67 F/l / 19,09 Euros), **en 24h chez vous**: +149F/22,47 Euros.

C. Peinture Starck with Biofa. Peinture murale naturelle, satinée, diluable à l'eau, sans solvant. A la différence des peinture classiques elle ne contient pas de substances chimiques (solvants notamment) susceptibles d'avoir des incidences sur la santé. Le Toluol (benzène méthylique), classiquement utilisé dans les peintures, peut entraîner une pollution des habitats 5 fois plus élevée que dans la rue. Les composants naturels (matières premières organiques et minérales) des peintures Starck with Biofa respectent la santé de l'homme. Cette gamme de couleur exclusive est une proposition fondée sur l'une de mes compétences majeures: la maîtrise du sens et des implications physiologiques des couleurs. Mais ce n'est qu'un conseil, certainement pas une directive de décorateur.
Starck with Biofa paint. Natural, water-soluble, satin-finish emulsion wall paint. Unlike conventional paints, it contains none of the chemical solvents or substances which are liable to manifest their toxicity to the human organism. Toluene, the methyl benzene ordinarily used in paint, can raise the pollution level in the private dwelling to nearly fivefold the level in the street. The natural components used to manufacture the Starck with Biofa paints (raw materials from mineral and organic sources) respect human health. The exclusive colour range is a suggestion based on one of my most highly developed skills, an expertise in the meaning and physiological implications of colors. However, it is meant to be taken only as advice and not as a decorator's edict.
Produit: peinture Starck with Biofa, **références**: voir en page 45, références 1 à 30 **prix**: 1l - 55 F/8,29 Euros, 4l - 195 F/29,40 Euros, 10l - 450 F/67,85 Euros, **en 24h chez vous**: +149 F/22,47 Euros.

A

Wet Elegance Starck with K-Way. La ligne Wet Elegance est conçue pour rendre un pur service, mais de façon différente. Il m'a semblé en effet remarqu[...] une malédiction du vêtement "de sport", ayant la triste destinée de polluer les paysages avec des couleurs offensantes. Le "fun" ne m'a jamais fait rire. Il m[...] semblé aussi possible que nécessaire de proposer des vêtements parfaitement fonctionnels, mais dans un autre registre, se référant plutôt à une élégan[...] urbaine et moderne. Wet Elegance est une ligne au dessin classique, "nettoyé", d'un prix abordable, ayant les mêmes compétences pratiques que ses équiv[...] lents: légereté, imperméabilité, coupe-vent. Une matière de synthèse est, pour le moment, seule en mesure de satisfaire à ces critères. Avec K-Way, marq[...] emblématique, inventeur du coupe-vent, nous avons développé un tissu à reflets changeants, à la fois imperméable, respirant, et facile d'entretien. Nous [...] sommes pas condamnés à la vulgarité.

Starck with K-Way Wet Elegance. The Wet Elegance line was embarked upon to right a long-neglected wrong. I must not be the only one to have noticed th[...] casual clothing is beset by a curse, compelling it to pollute the scenery with offensive colors. Garish hues have never amused me. I also felt it was both pos[...] ble and necessary to make available completely functional clothing which takes its cue from an urban, modern concept of elegance. Wet Elegance is chara[...] terized by purity and classicism, at an affordable price range and with the same practical virtues as its peers: lightweight, waterproof, a windbreaker. Synthe[...] fibres are the only choice which fulfills these criteria at the moment. Working with K-Way, whose name is synonymous with windbreakers in France, we ha[...] developed a waterproof, air permeable fabric with a wet look finish, easy to maintain. We are not doomed to vulgarity.

Design: Philippe Starck, **produits:** ligne Wet Elegance Starck with K-Way, **fabricant:** K-Way, **date de conception:** 1997, **date de production:** 199[...]
A. Produit: Wet Lord Starck with K-Way, **description:** veste imperméable coupe-vent, trois boutons, mixte, trois poches passepoilées dont une poitrine, [...] fermé par bouton-pression, capuche, fournitures métal hypoallergeniques, composition 60% polyamide, 40% polyester, **références:** ext. gris/int. jau[...] 808.3096, ext. anthracite/ int.gris 808.3827, **tailles:** 1 (S), 2 (M), 4 (XL), 5 (XXL), **prix:** 790 F/119,12 Euros.

Tous les Starck with K-Way **en 24h chez vous:** +80 F/ 12,06 Eur[...]

ayak Starck with Rotomod. Dans le sport, on est passé du trois mâts à la planche à voile, de l'automobile aux patins à roulettes, de la paire de ski au mono-
i. Cette marche vers le minimum est l'évidence d'un progrès. Mais en même temps qu'ils se réduisaient, beaucoup de ces objets voyaient leur difficulté
emploi augmenter. Quoi de plus beau qu'un surfer dans les vagues? Quoi de plus difficile aussi? Ce mouvement de simplification a récemment touché le
yak. Avec la nouvelle génération "seat-on-top" – double avantage de ne plus enserrer la taille et d'être équipé d'un cockpit autovideur – les néophytes peu-
nt se permettre l'exploration du milieu aquatique en toute sécurité. Avec Rotomod, l'un des meilleurs fabricants du marché, nous avons décidé de ne pas
corer ce kayak de la trop commune panoplie de fluorescences: elles le transforment en injure visuelle, en contradiction avec l'intimité vis-à-vis du milieu
turel qu'il permet. Equilibré, très résistant, facile d'utilisation, d'un prix abordable, assez léger pour être porté sur l'épaule ou sur le toit d'une voiture.
ayak Starck with Rotomod. From the galleon to the windsurfer, from the automobile to the roller skate, from the ski to the snowboard: obviously, the
ture of transportation lies in minimalization. But many of these conveyances require greater skill to pilot as they are pared down to the bare essentials. A
rfer riding a wave is a thrilling sight, but not all of us can accomplish this feat. Recently, the kayak has also been simplified, and as a result the new seat-
-top generation is easier to paddle than its ancestors – the waist is no longer confined and the cockpit is self-draining. Neophytes can now explore the
uatic world safely. Rotomod, one of the leading manufacturers on the market, consented to forego decorating this model with the usual dayglo palette
at I find so displeasing. The kayak should blend in with the natural environment as the first step towards leading you to become acquain-ted with it. Sturdy,
lanced, and easy to paddle: it is well priced and lightweight enough to be carried on one shoulder or on a car roof.
oduit: Kayak Starck with Rotomod, fabricant: Rotomod, description: kayak multi-usage (en mer, rivière et torrent), insubmersible, autovideur (évacua-
n automatique de l'eau par 4 trous de vidange), siège réglable, cale-pieds intégrés, maniable et stable (coque type "aile de mouette", étravée sur toute
longueur), léger (18kg), empilable, cadenassable, sans entretien (P.E haute-densité, traité anti-UV), recyclable, livré avec pagaies, dimensions
30x0,78x0,34m, référence: 675.1784, prix: 3500 F/527,76 Euros, en 24h chez vous: +299 F/45,09 Euros.

A. TeddyBearBand. La mutiplication des jouets me paraît favoriser l'infidélité: l'enfant ne s'attache en définitive à aucun, zappant de l'un à l'autre d'autan
plus vite que les jouets sont nombreux. Il n'y a pas de raison pour que, plus tard, il se comporte différemment avec les gens, ami ou amant. Partisan d'u
amour unique, j'ai rêvé d'un jouet unique, une sorte d'entraînement à un attachement durable. Jouet surréaliste, TeddyBearBand fait aussi appel à l'imag
nation, bien plus loin que le simple ours en peluche. Il permet de placer l'amour et l'amitié en dehors du champ de la consommation.

TeddyBearBand. In my opinion, an overabundance of toys fosters infidelity. Instead of forming a lasting attachment to one toy, the child flits ever faste
from one to another, the greater the number of toys, the more frantic the pace. There is no reason that, later on, he or she should treat people, a friend o
a lover any differently. As an advocate of the one-true-love approach, I dreamt of a single toy that would serve as an apprenticeship for the lasting huma
relationships that await our children. A surreal toy, TeddyBearBand stimulates the imagination considerabily more than any mere plush bear. It removes lov
and friendship from the realm of disposable emotions.

Design: Philippe Starck, **éditeur**: Moulin Roty, **produit**: TeddyBearBand, **date de conception**: 1997, **date de production**: 1998, **description**: animal e
peluche à tête d'ours, dont 3 membres sont terminés par des têtes différentes, chien, chèvre, lapin, et membre inférieur droit comme une patte, hauteu
37cm, **tissu**: trame polyester, dessus coton, **bourrage**: 100% polyester, **référence**: 761.1897, **prix**: 275 F/41,47 Euros, **en 24h chez vous**: +80 F/12,06 Euro

A

B

B. Voiture à pédales. L'automobile est une chose ennuyeuse. Etrangement, les jouets qui la représentent n'essaient pas d'en changer les règles du je
ils se font le relais de l'erreur sémantique initiale. Pour éviter la petite auto qui ne serait qu'une simple caricature de la voiture inepte de papa, mon a
Ferdinand Amat de Vinçon m'a proposé cette essence d'automobile: la voiture de la mémoire collective. Cette voiture à pédales est malheureuseme
chère, et produite en série limitée. Mais, peut-être, sa qualité lui permet-elle aussi de servir d'exemple, pour ne pas acquérir la manie de changer plus ta
de voiture tous les ans. Quand une voiture est vraiment bonne, on peut l'aimer et la garder longtemps.

Pedalcar. Automobiles are a tiresome subject. Oddly, toys which represent them make no effort to improve on the rules of the game they merely echo t
initial semantic error. To offer an alternative to the expensive little caricature of Daddy's inept conveyance, my friend Ferdinand Amat de Vinçon suggest
this distillation of four-wheeled mythology, the automobile of our collective memory. Unfortunately, this pedalcar is expensive and produced as a limited e
tion. But perhaps its standards of quality will elevate it to the rank of revered archetype. Perhaps its owners will not become like those silly adults who pu
chase a new car every year. When an automobile is truly good, it can be loved and kept for a long time.

Produit: Voiture bleue, **fabricant**: Vilac, **description**: voiture à pédales, série limitée à 500 exemplaires, numérotée sur le volant, capot bois laqué ble
volant bois massif, siège réglable en matière plastique jaune, roues plastique, dimensions 1,20x1,055x0,50m, fabrication française (Jura), **référenc**
685.4800, **prix**: 2200 F/331,73 Euros, **en 24h chez vous**: +299 F/45,08 Euros.

God is dangerous Now

12   Architecture

68   Interiors

152   Furniture

228   Industrial Design

392   Magma

400   Words

422   Overview

446   A–Z

1989

1983

1983

1984

1984

1983

1987

1987

1978

1987

1991

1986

1984

1969

1980

1987

1986

1978

1978

1993

1987

1990

1994

1970

1983

1978

1983

1967

1978

1983

1978

1984

1986

1986

1987

1987

1992

1986

1978

1993

1993

1984

1982

1994

1984

19xx

1980

1969

1984

1981

1979

1967

1982

1984

1985

1994

1994

1967

1967

1983

1984

1984 · 1988 · 1984 · 1970 · 1969 · 1969 · 1996 · 1996 · 1970 · 1980 · 1983 · 1987 · 1987 · 1987 · 1985 · 1986 · 1967 · 1982 · 1996 · 1985–86 · 1983 · 1998 · 1987 · 1969 · 1983 · 1993–1994 · 1993–1994 · 1993–1994 · 1993–1994 · 1993 · 1978 · 1977 · 1978 · 1976

12 Architecture

68 Interiors

152 Furniture

228 Industrial Design

392 Magma

400 Words

422 Overview

446 A–Z

Starck recalls his youth spent beneath his father's drawing tables, hours filled sawing, cutting, glueing, sanding, taking apart bicycles, motorbikes and numerous other objects. →Hours, a life of taking to bits and rebuilding the things which surround him, recreating the world around him. →A few years and many prototypes later, the Italians entrusted him with our furniture, François Mitterrand, the French President called on him to change his life at the Elysée residence, the Café Costes earned the title "Le café", he set a new standard for hotels with the Royalton and the Paramount of New York, scattered throughout Japan architectural monsters designating him as a leader in expressionist architecture. His respect for the environment and human nature encourages France to hand him the projects to realize the Ecole Nationale Supérieure des Arts Décoratifs in Paris, the air traffic control tower for the airport of Bordeaux and a waste recycling plant in the Paris region. Abroad, he continues to jostle traditions and cultures within our great cities by decorating the Peninsula Hotel's restaurant in Hong Kong, the Delano Hotel in Miami and the Theatron restaurant in Mexico city and by creating an atmosphere of attraction, pleasure and meeting point. →Being an enthusiastic and honest citizen, he takes it upon himself to share his vision of subversiveness for a just world which he alone seems to own, yet which suits us so well. →He relentlessly changes our everyday life by sublimating our roots. He perpetuates sailing boats for Bénéteau, ennobles the humble toothbrush, reverses the process of squeezing lemons, reinvents our personal hygiene and our relationship with water and even manages to make our television sets more friendly by introducing his 'emotional style' in the electronic world of Thomson, by creating for each of the corporate brands a Sense, a Spirit with which everyone can identify, and a world guiding us towards the future. →But he also finds the time to change our noodles, ashtrays, lamps, door handles, cutlery, candlesticks, kettles, knives, vases, clocks, scooters, offices, beds, flasks, toys, in fact our lives. →The success of the Aprilia motorbike, launched to enthusiastic public acclaim, is further evidence of his well-conceived and on-target ideas. →The museums are not mistaken either: Paris, New York, Munich, London, Chicago and Tokyo have all devoted exhibitions in his honour. →He has been awarded Créateur de l'Année, Grand Prix pour le Design industriel, Oscar du design, and Officier des Arts et des Lettres. →Always and everywhere present, he seems to understand like no other our dreams and desires, leading us, enriching our lives with his unexpected, surprising yet evident creations. →Crazy and a genius, yet tremendously lucid, he creates incessantly, driven by necessity and urgency, for himself and for us all, touching us by his astute and intelligent work but also because it comes from his heart. → → → → →Seine Kindheit habe er unter den Zeichentischen seines Vaters verbracht, erinnert sich Starck. Stundenlang zerlegt er, schneidet aus, sägt, klebt zusammen und schmirgelt ab – alles, was ihm in die Finger kommt, auch Fahrräder und Motorräder. →Schon als Kind besteht sein Leben darin, die Dinge, die ihn umgeben, auseinanderzunehmen und so die ihn umgebende Welt neu zu gestalten. →Einige Jahre und viele Prototypen später lassen die Italiener von ihm Möbel entwerfen, bittet ihn der französische Präsident François Mitterrand, den Elysée-Palast umzugestalten und erringt das Café Costes den Titel »Le café«. Mit dem Royalton Hotel und dem Paramount Hotel in New York setzt er einen neuen Standard für Hotels; Japan überzieht er mit architektonischen Monstern, die ihn als Exponenten expressionistischer Architektur ausweisen. →Starcks Respekt vor der Umwelt und den Menschen ermutigt Frankreich, ihn mit Entwürfen zu der Ecole Nationale Supérieur des Arts Décoratifs in Paris, zum Kontrollturm für den Flughafen von Bordeaux und zu einer Müllverwertungsanlage in der Nähe von Paris zu beauftragen. →In den Metropolen der Welt bringt er Tradition und fest verwurzelte Kultur ins Wanken: Er dekoriert das Restaurant des Hotels Peninsula in Hongkong, das Hotel Delano in Miami und das Restaurant Theatron in Mexiko-Stadt: Begegnungsschauplätze zum Wohlfühlen und für die Sinne. →Als enthusiastischer und ehrlicher Weltbürger macht Starck es zu seiner Pflicht, seine subversive Version von einer gerechteren Welt an seine Mitmenschen weiterzugeben – eine Version, die sein geistiges Eigentum ist und doch so gut zu uns allen paßt. →Indem er unsere Wurzeln sublimiert, verändert er unermüdlich unseren Alltag. Er entwirft zeitlose Segelboote für Bénéteau, adelt eine Zahnbürste, kehrt das Zitronenauspressen einfach um, verwandelt unser Hygieneverhalten und unser Verhältnis zu Wasser. →Und es gelingt ihm sogar, daß wir unsere Fernsehgeräte sympathischer finden, indem er seinen »Emotional Style« in die elektronische Welt der Thomson-Gruppe einführt, jedem Produkt dieses Unternehmens Sinn und Geist verleiht, mit dem sich jeder gern identifiziert und sich in einer Welt wiederfindet, die in die Zukunft führt. →Aber Starck findet auch noch Zeit, unsere Nudeln, Aschenbecher, Lampen, Türgriffe, Bestecke, Kerzenleuchter, Kessel, Messer, Vasen, Uhren, Motorroller, Büros, Betten, Thermoskannen und unser Spielzeug – kurzum unser ganzes Leben zu verändern. →Wie durchdacht seine Ideen sind, beweist erneut der Erfolg seines Motorrads Aprilia, das enthusiastisch aufgenommen wurde. →Auch die Museen beweisen sicheres Gespür: Paris, New York, München, London, Chicago und Tokio – überall werden ihm Ausstellungen gewidmet. →Zu seinen Auszeichnungen zählen: Créateur de l'Année (Designer des Jahres in Frankreich), der Grand Prix pour le Design Industriel (der Große Preis für Industriedesign), den Oscar du design (den Oskar für Design) sowie Officier des Arts et des Lettres. →Immer und überall präsent, scheint Starck wie kein anderer unsere Träume und Sehnsüchte zu verstehen und reißt uns mit seinen unerwarteten, verblüffenden und immer überzeugenden Kreationen mit. →Verrückt und genial und hellsichtig wie kein zweiter, kreiert er unaufhörlich, als sei es eine Notwendigkeit für ihn selbst und die anderen. Er berührt uns mit seinem Schaffen, weil es ehrlich ist und intelligent, aber auch und vor allem, weil es von Herzen kommt. → → → → →Starck se rappelle avoir passé son enfance sous les tables à dessin de son père, d'heures passées à scier, découper, coller, poncer, décortiquer vélos, motos et autres objets. →Des heures, une vie à défaire et faire tout ce qui le touche, à refaire le monde qui l'entoure. →Quelques années et quelques prototypes plus tard, les Italiens lui confient notre mobilier, le Président Mitterrand lui demande de changer sa vie à l'Elysée, le café Costes devient «Le café», il fait du Royalton et du Paramount de New York, les nouveaux classiques de l'hôtellerie, il parsème le Japon de monstres architecturaux qui en font le chef de file de l'architecture expressionniste, son respect de l'environnement et des humains touche aussi la France qui lui confie la réalisation de l'Ecole Nationale Supérieure des Arts Décoratifs à Paris, la Tour de contrôle de l'Aéroport de Bordeaux et l'usine de retraitement de déchets en Région Parisienne. →A l'étranger, il continue de bousculer les traditions et les cultures des grandes métropoles en décorant le Restaurant du Peninsula Hôtel de Hong Kong , l'Hôtel Delano de Miami et le Theatron de Mexico, faisant aussitôt des endroits qu'on lui confie des hauts lieux d'attraction, de plaisir et de rencontres. →Citoyen enthousiaste et honnête, il se fait un devoir de nous faire partager sa vision subversive d'un monde plus juste qui seul lui appartient et qui pourtant nous va si bien. →Et il n'a de cesse de changer notre quotidien, en y sublimant toujours nos racines et nos sources profondes. Ainsi il retrouve l'éternel de la marine avec Bénéteau, anoblit la brosse à dents, presse les citrons mais à l'envers, réinvente notre hygiène et nos rapports avec l'eau, en arrive même à rendre nos télévisions amicales en faisant entrer son «emotional style» dans le monde électronique de Thomson, créant pour chaque grande marque du Groupe, un Sens, un Esprit, dans lequel chacun aime se retrouver, un Monde qui nous guide heureusement vers le Futur. →Mais il prend aussi le temps de changer nos pâtes, nos cendriers, nos lampes, nos brosses à dents, nos poignées de porte, nos couverts, nos bougeoirs, nos bouilloires, nos couteaux, nos vases, nos horloges, nos scooters, nos bureaux, nos lits, nos thermos, nos jouets, notre Vie enfin. →Le succès de sa moto Aprilia, nous prouve une fois encore la cohérence de ses choix par l'accueil enthousiaste de son public. →Les Musées ne s'y trompent pas, Paris, New York, Munich, Londres, Chicago, Kyoto, tous l'exposent et le consacrent. →Il est récompensé de tous les prix: Créateur de l'année, Grand Prix du Design Industriel, Oscar du Design, Officier des Arts et des Lettres, et bien d'autres. →Toujours et partout présent, il semble comprendre mieux que quiconque nos rêves et nos désirs, nous emportant dans son sillage et parsemant nos vies et nos villes de ses créations toujours inattendues, surprenantes et pourtant si évidentes. →Fou, génial mais aussi terriblement lucide, il crée sans répit, par nécessité, urgence, pour lui et les autres, nous touchant par son travail juste et intelligent, certes, mais aussi et surtout parce qu'il y met du cœur. →Ed Mae Cooper

Extract of a conversation with Elisabeth Laville (in August 1998), originally published in a special issue of *La Lettre d'Utopies* / "Responsible Design"

We have to replace beauty, which is a cultural concept, with goodness, which is a humanist concept

Philippe Starck spent a Saturday morning answering our questions in the peace and calm of his house in Formentera (Spain) – a house "in the middle of nowhere, without water or electricity, facing the Mediterranean", where he goes to "give thanks to God until the end of time for portables" – meaning both telephones and computers, thanks to which he can work there just as efficiently as if he were in his Paris offices. The result is what he calls "management through absence." There, he can remain completely detached and think creatively when making decisions, because of the distance between him and the "fever" and the "backroom problems" which are handled by his small and "extremely competent" team in Paris.

In your opinion, what is the role of the designer today?

In the 1950s, one of the fathers of design, Raymond Loewy, invented a slogan which was responsible both for his own success and, in part, for that of the design movement: "ugliness doesn't sell well." At that time, he may have been right, but I'm afraid that this formula was already structurally flawed. We have to escape from this flaw, we have to kill the word of the father... We have to understand that "ugliness doesn't sell well" means that design is simply the slave of industry and production, that its role is to help things sell. Structurally, that is no longer what we do. Today, the problem is not to produce more so you can sell more. The fundamental question is that of the product's right to exist. And it is the designer's right and duty, in the first place, to question the legitimacy of the product, and that is how he too comes to exist. Depending on what answer he comes up with, one of the most positive things a designer can do is refuse to do anything. This isn't always easy. He should refuse, nevertheless, when the object already exists and functions perfectly well. Simply to repeat it would be a venal act, and one which would have serious consequences, impoverishing the wealth of the Earth, and impoverishing and dulling the minds of people, because afterwards his act will be picked up and carried further by those services which browbeat people until they buy something. I mean advertising, and the press in general...

How then should one judge of an object's right to exist?

The essential thing to do is to test it in relation to a number of more or less strict criteria.

The first quite strict criterion is to do nothing which could cause harm to man. This is a rather simplistic criterion, but we must respect it nevertheless, and sometimes that means losing a lot of money. So we don't work for the arms industry, we don't work for hard spirits, we don't work for tobacco, we don't work for religion, and we don't work for anything which involves money from dubious sources, which is getting more and more complicated. It's quite possible that we could end up accepting dirty money which has been laundered through one kind of business or another. I had to refuse a fabulous contract in East Berlin, because of such doubts, and in fact, now, in all our contracts, we have a clause which says that our clients must declare the sources of their financing. If it turns out that they lied to us, the contract is automatically void. So those are the most immediate demands, the necessary moral rules, which are just obvious.

After that, you have to test the object in relation to another set of parameters which aim to justify its existence. To begin with, the product must provide a new service, offer something more interesting than what is there already, establish a new skill... otherwise, you might just as well use an object that exists already. Next, it must perform its function completely, with as much honesty as possible. This honesty is difficult to identify, because often it is not what it seems. Objects serve other purposes than those for which they appear to be destined, so you have to know how to read between the lines, you have to know how to read in both our unconscious and in the objects' unconscious. ... Then, you have to try and perform the function purely, with as few preconceived ideas as possible, which means, as a rule, using the least possible quantity of matter. This is where I always mention the example of a client who asked for a boat, and he was very happy with the advice of his designer, who suggested he try swimming and in this way led him to rediscover the pleasures of swimming. Today, we have the means to redirect the efforts of research and industry to produce tools which would allow you, instead of having 20 per cent functionality against 80 per cent useless matter (which as a rule is only there to serve the greed of the producer), to invert the process and have 80 per cent functionality. To achieve this, designers have to stop thinking of their solutions in terms of matter. It is essential for designers, when faced with a question, to be extremely open and say: "the right answer is a biological answer, not an industrial answer; the right answer is a semantic answer, not a material answer..." Then the designer who stares at his paper and his pencil is no longer just the accomplice of systematic production, he is a conductor who has to bring certain skills to bear in relation to certain needs. This determination to get rid of what is useless and replace it with what is honest is based on a strong principle, which we can call "dematerialisation". The object, the non-object of tomorrow, will be like a star in the sky which is in a state of perpetual implosion, that is, its volume is constantly decreasing, even as its mass increases – its mass of skills, its mass of honesty and its mass of emotion. The only way forward for the productive system is through dematerialisation. ... Meanwhile, there is something essential that we must attend to provisionally, in parallel: we must reposition everything around us, politically, socially, sexually and economically. This is easy. It doesn't require any substantial means, but just our awareness and determination.

On the political level, we must avoid making objects which represent aggression, violence, fascism, let's say, forms of darkness. ... This requires a great deal of reflection on the political meaning of what we do: we have to clean our objects of all these barbaric signs and load them instead with positive, constructive signs which can indicate another way forward...

The second parameter is social or financial, and is related to the first.

Objects should not serve as a means of representing money so that people can humiliate their neighbours. Much of today's production does nothing else. That is, its meaning is, "I've earned lots of money, mine is bigger than yours, and you can just fuck off." This is a big problem, because you cannot build a civilisation on such negativity.

The third parameter is sex, which is again related to the first point, since everything has to do with politics. Today, 80 per cent of objects are unnecessarily macho. Yet it is plain:

The intelligence of a truly modern society must be feminine.

This is due to a series of structural differences, which are grounded in the protection of the species, the value of continuity, and in something which I find more difficult to explain – a sort of pragmatism which leads someone to do many different things simultaneously, rather than sacrificing everything to one big idea, which appropriates and perverts everything. So it is very interesting to ask these questions of every object we meet. Often, the answer is quite obvious and quite shocking, when you keep your eyes open. Apart from a machine pistol, I can't think of many objects which actually need to be extravagantly masculine!

The next point is economic, and concerns how affordable these products are.

It is absolutely essential to "dis-elitify" quality objects, so as to make the best things available to the greatest number of people. If an idea is right, and if it can be repeated over and over again, it would be an act of theft not to repeat it. This means we have to work on restoring dignity to the word "popular". We have to work on the power that comes from multiplication, on the increase in quality that comes from multiplication. And to this end – but this is already one of your hobbyhorses – we should not put our faith in craftsmanship, but in the moralisation of large businesses.

Is that what your role was at Thomson?

That was my main task when I was artistic director at Thomson for four years: to make the company virtuous. Not because there was a desire there to do evil, but because they had simply forgotten their purpose in life – to be of service, to use their skills to be of service. It is essential to try to play the role of a friendly "enemy within". That is, to catch the interest of these big companies so that they make money available, and research facilities, and distribution networks, for this return to what is the origin of all their activities – to serve others. It even means changing the words they use. One of the things I did at Thomson was to change their name. Thomson used to be called TCE, Thomson Consumer Electronic, and I asked them: who wants to be a "consumer of electronics?" At the time, I was lucky to work with an extraordinary managing director, Alain Prestat, who understood what I was getting at straightaway. We chose the name, Thomson Multimedia, because he was betting on the technological success of multimedia, and I wanted to talk about the multiple channels such a company must use to express itself, if it wants to act morally. For what's the use of making beautiful television sets if all you can watch on them is crap... The other important thing I did was that I outlawed the word "consumer" in all company meetings, and insisted it be replaced by the words "my friend", "my wife", "my daughter", "my mother", or "myself." It doesn't sound the same at all, if you say: "It doesn't matter, it's shit, but the consumers will make do with it," or if you start over again and say: "It's shit, but it doesn't matter, my daughter will make do with it." ... All of a sudden, you can't get away with it any more. So there is an enormous task to be done with this kind of symbolic repositioning, using just one word. The other thing I did at Thomson was to invent the slogan "Thomson: from technology to love," and again, that completely repositioned the problem. Because now we were saying that technology wasn't an end in itself, but just a means – and that the real goal, the final goal, was what had always been there, the original priority, humanity, whose fundamental criterion is love.

That connects back to your idea of the friendly object, the good object...

Yes, this takes us back more or less to the role of the designer. You're not designing the object for the sake of the object, you don't care whether it's beautiful or not. We have to replace beauty, which is a cultural concept, with goodness, which is a humanist concept. The object must be of good quality, it must satisfy one of the key modern parameters, which is to be long-lived, and we'll come

back to that. But above all it must be good for the person who is going to live with it – by which I mean, it mustn't hide the person behind logos, or oppress him or her by the admiration it provokes. Instead it must allow the person to blossom, to be him or herself, and to be happier with it than without it. Saying that an object must bring out the best in someone already eliminates 70 per cent of contemporary production, which turns people into clowns: fake Harley Davidsons which turn people into fake bikers, over-labelled sunglasses which turn people into coatstands for ridiculous brands... People disguise themselves so that they don't have to exist. And it is essential that people begin to exist again, otherwise, they will disappear. We have to fight against the way in which people are turned into an audience, into spectators, by working continually to restore them to their proper place, as actors.

After that, of course, there is ecology.

We have to talk to the big companies which are now moral actors, so that they make sure their production is not damaging to man, that the object is not a cause of harm in their lives.

This obviously means getting rid of recycling, which is just a marketing gimmick... Recycling was invented by the ecologists, but in the end, all it does is enable us to go on producing and consuming wastefully. A good product is a product which lasts. When it has lasted 10, 20, 30 years, then whether it is recyclable, whether it is actually recycled, in a sense is not important. But to recycle useless objects every year is a completely crazy waste of matter and energy. I am not against recycling, I am against its being used as a universal panacea. Recycling is a sticking plaster, a way of repairing a mistake, nothing more. It's a false solution, a false problem, a kind of ecological practical joke, of a kind that is proliferating nowadays: like electrically-powered cars, which are just a way of moving the exhaust pipe away from the car and towards the nuclear power plants. ...

You were talking a little earlier about the need to make products affordable. Is that why you are working on the Good Goods catalogue with Carrefour and La Redoute – because they are trying to democratise the best kind of product?

One of the few victories I've won in my career is to have succeeded in conferring a certain nobility on the idea of multiplication, that is, on the word "popular." I raised the status of contempt. Before, a toothbrush would be hidden in the bottom of a drawer. Then, overnight, people started giving toothbrushes for Christmas, they started showing them to their friends. The other thing I have achieved is to have brought prices down, and made them affordable. Over the space of ten years, I managed, despite all the resistance, to halve the price of my objects just about every year or two. One of my first successes, the Café Costes chair, started out at about 4,000 francs... Today, we make chairs for 300 francs, maybe even 200. ... We're even collaborating with Vitra to see if we can find a way to hire out furniture or buy it back again. We've been thinking about this idea for five or six years, and the problem is that today we don't know how to do it. We don't know how to oblige someone to bring back a chair in exchange for less than 50 francs, which very soon will be the price of the chair itself. ... This kind of scheme is necessarily for the super-mass market, but the people who make up that super-mass market aren't yet sufficiently educated for this. And there's also a problem of price. How much do you rent a chair for, when the chair's worth 50 francs? One franc a month? As you see, there are a number of real obstacles there. So it's better for us to use a style, a non-style, which will survive through time. Take the little Dr. No chair, for example: it's comfortable, you can stack it, it's more or less indestructible, with all the problems that represents, and you could keep it for 20 years... and in 20 years time, you'll find it at the bottom of the garden, someone will go and pick it up and melt it down. But for now, it's no use our trying to make a big push on this issue, we just don't have the means to do it. The supermarkets are a necessary part of what I do. Good Goods came out in 1998, and at the same time we were presenting our Seven Eleven operation in Japan. This was one of the biggest single operations in the history of design. Seven Eleven is a chain of convenience stores which are open 24 hours round the clock. They have 8,000 shops in Japan, 30,000 throughout Asia and I don't know how many in the US. They've given me more or less all their objects to design – yoghurt pots, razors, underpants, pencils, everything. They are the biggest buyer in the world, so this will really allow us to go to scale, to offer the best to everyone. We know already that 10 million copies of each object will be manufactured each year, and that means... I don't think any of these objects costs more than 10 or 12 francs. So that's really one in the face for the elitist notion of design. For me, this is something essential, it's almost like achieving my ultimate goal. After this, I don't know what more I can do, except keep going, and try to show that I can make better yoghurt pots, better underpants...

And Good Goods?

This is a project which has been close to my heart for many years. For two years I put an enormous amount of work into it, and for the first time in my life, I can even say that while I don't regret it, I wouldn't choose to do it again. It cost me a fortune in terms of lost earnings through all the time it consumed. I'm trying to move towards making objects which are honest, objects for non-consumers, for "modern rebels" who are fed up with marketing and advertising trying to make them believe that they absolutely have to change their R5 for an R6, their 4:3 television for one with a 16:9 screen... For me, these people represent a new unspoken political force. ... That's what interests me: these non-consumers, catalysed by the catalogue, will be establishing rules for what I call the "moral market," which is more or less what we've just described. People will get the catalogue, with a little message from me telling them something which is quite revolutionary in the world of commerce, that is, that it isn't worth buying these products, and that it's more important for them to read the catalogue, and read between the lines. In Good Goods, there are some interesting products, but they don't pretend to be the kind of non-product which I'm aiming for eventually, they're just there to kickstart the process. And what is important is that with each object there is a short explanation, not as long as I would have liked, because we didn't have space, but an attempt to explain why, and symmetrically, why not: why not other things, why we don't want these other things any more ...

Today, you can use your reputation to try and put these messages across... But in the Good Goods catalogue, you say that you're trying to "correct the course of a history in which I was doubtless an accomplice myself." Does that mean that, in relation to the criteria you've talked about, the Starck objects in this catalogue are those to which you now feel closest?

You know, I've always been the same, I've always pursued the same idea. Except in the beginning, because when you're young, you work for yourself in order to survive, and you do what you can. I'm 49 years old now, I have certain means at my disposition, and I'd be an idiot if I hadn't thought my strategy through, and I'd be dishonest if I didn't try to stick to it. So I admit that I've done what I could, that there have been high points and low points, but I have always proceeded honestly. Now, I can't say that everything is perfect, but I have the means to be more rigorous. You know, to begin with, what mattered was to assert myself, because I had to build up this power. When you're a French design-

er... you must never forget that there's no such thing as a French designer!

Extract of a conversation with Sophie Tasma Anargyros, March 1996, organised by VIA (Valorisation de l'Industrie de l'Ameublement)

The Myth of Progress

The idea of world evolution depends on the idea of progress. The invention of this idea sums up the difference between Man and animal life in the sense that it contains the deliberate intention of improving the species.

Unless he is reaching out to the unknown, Man does not consider himself to have any reality. In order to crystallise this idea, Man invented a concept: that of God. God is a model of progress in the absolute, but at the same time an ambiguous model. Inhuman by definition, and human since He is a human idea. The result of the infinite distance which Man has placed between himself and God is that the same distance must be traversed in the other direction: moving towards God. This idea, which is extraordinarily dynamic, also defines the shape of a dream: in His image, to become ultra-powerful, omnipresent, to vanquish mysteries.

Man attains his model

The means of becoming are on one hand material and tools, and on the other hand intelligence and knowledge. Little by little, Man drew closer to his model, slowly at first, until the 18th century, then ever more rapidly during the 19th and 20th centuries. The first major step: the invention of the machine. From the beginning of the 20th century until the present day, a dazzling moment, a state of admiration for the machine. I note in passing the occurrence of a proportionally inverse movement: the idea of improving life, and as a consequence equality, liberty and fraternity, is not attained, and the word is weak. Then, at the dawn of the 21st century, the possibility of attaining the model is glimpsed, with tools which have become dematerialised, computers, which bring to Man the capacity for untold knowledge with the internet or what the internet will become, which enables collective thought, parallel to the system of powers which have until now controlled the contents, and finally the speed of movement. The movement of people in space, but above all the movement of thoughts, that is to say the immediacy of communication. A bit further, but still very close, genetics today brings us within reach of the creation of artificial life. The pieces of the puzzle begin to fall into place, displaying a model projected as unattainable. There remains the problem of size. It would seem that the epoch when all the fantasies have almost become reality is also one of loss. As he progresses down these roads, Man has lost on the way what we might call an ideal. Perhaps this represents one of the explanations for non-consumption. Mankind no longer has the urge to consume the material. The material without its double, the idea, which provides all its meaning, is a phenomenon emptied of its content.

The 21st century will be immaterial and human

Real immateriality – micro-processors, information, processes of whatever kind – must, as a matter of urgency, have a human corollary. The 21st century will not be mystical, it will be immaterial and human. If it is not, the decline that we are experiencing today will continue.

With regard to the human factor, it is necessary to return to the unconscious source of the idea of progress as the improvement of everyone's life, happiness and fulfilment.

I shall use a very simple image to illustrate this idea. It is New Year's Day, a rather special one, a sort of Super New Year's Day, the New Year's Day of the third millennium. Everyone knows what happens the day before New Year's Day. We all look back over the previous year and say to ourselves: "I shall try to be better." It is in this ideal of a 'good resolution' that humanity may cross the millennium, or lose itself there. That is where the first priority lies, in humanity. If mankind continues to cling to materiality, that is the possession of material objects, if the concept of matter is not replaced by that of love, how will it be possible to survive in a world where Man has become omnipresent, ultra-powerful and in which the issues of power are no longer represented materially?

Progress or pre-history?

This is the most serious issue, the simplest but the most serious. Thousands of years have passed, yet Man has not managed to attain love. He has acquired, and lost, only material things. If I think about it in even more basic terms: the origin of love resides in that which is known as the maternal instinct, which is nothing less than the desire to protect the species. The species is delicate. If Man loses the notion of love, in the sense of species, one will return at an incredible speed to a pre-historical state in which the individual works without a plan of civilisation, without a social plan. I even think that the greatest danger is to forget the very existence of love. Why is it that the most 'comfortable' societies are those most prone to suicide, that is to say severed from the survival instinct?

In my opinion a major line of thought for all those who produce objects, signs or meaning resides in the realisation of the disembodiment of the material in favour of the human and its most beautiful invention: love. It is imperative that producers reflect on the non-object of tomorrow.

The non-object

What is the Man of tomorrow? I shall attempt to describe him. Artificial intelligence already exists and before long biological computers with neural nodes will also be in existence. Even death is in retreat. Man will soon be face to face with himself – transcended. With biological computers we arrive at the disappearance of matter, the disappearance of objects. So far, we have produced and refined the structure, the form and the function of objects. At Thomson, research is already being carried out on visual and mental commands. There is no longer any relation between the gesture and the object. The command is implemented directly by the mind.

We are going behind the mirror because the entire system of representing humanity through objects will disappear. The human being of tomorrow will be naked (this is an image), without the interference of matter between him and the world, inscribed in a biorhythm, blessed with almost boundless power. Every service will reside in a word or a thought.

He will be able to communicate with the whole world. If he wants to know anything, he connects himself to the network in a few seconds and he immediately has at his disposal millions of replies. When one realises that the further knowledge advances, the further violence retreats, it is possible to believe that given the imperative condition of the construction of civilisation, communication will be a factor in world peace. It will become difficult to organise a war, because Man will have the ability to check the information he is given. Great lies will no longer be possible unless the lie is total. This will be the reign of manipulation, chaos and counter-information. The internet, besides much else, must

become a tool of peace and self-control. According to this schema, Man becomes his own territory. He has ceased to desire to conquer the earth, which has been the cause of wars since the beginning of time – because his power is no longer a matter of territorial issues and borders. Moreover, the notion of frontiers will be understood in new terms. Man will no longer practically use his real territory because he will live in a virtual territory, one which will be constructed, codified and regulated like a genuine territory. It will be necessary only to connect in order to have access to the presence of the other person, his image, his thoughts, his knowledge.

The house of tomorrow

The house of the tomorrow's Man will be reduced to an empty envelope: the temperature will be controlled from the floor, the light will be an electro-luminescence provided by windows of liquid crystals, sound and pictures will come from the walls. Man will become an affective being. He will produce his own system of signs. In this space, one will witness a complete dissociation of functional services and the senses. This will be.

The reign of the Poetic

Signs, relieved of all functional notions, will attain their highest level of purity and efficacy, and in this sense, will come close to art, while, paradoxically, the body will return to a natural state, being relieved of all the objects which intervene between Man and his acts. Of course, the corollary of such a usage of the tools of communication largely integrated into the body resides in the confusion between real and virtual, and the psychological danger in the desire for disembodiment. According to this scenario, people will no longer move about. The profession of decorator will become that of a programmer of images. Everyone will invent an appearance with a synthesised image. The means of transport will decrease, roads will become paths again. The town outskirts logic will be reversed. The town will no longer be the centre, since it will no longer be necessary to perform acts in the city, the place of an outdated concentration of powers. The town will become a place of chaos.

Violence: who imagines the future?

Dictatorship will be in the hands of those who control the paths of communication. They will have a power of life or death since the economy of societies will be based on a system of virtual exchange. To make someone disappear, all that will be necessary is to disconnect them. There is no violence there. Violence as a direct physical attack is replaced by disappearance, neglect, indifference. (This phenomenon is already known to

us in another form: a kind of total anaesthetic such that we can chat here, in my office, while in Bosnia, Chechenia, Rwanda and elsewhere massacres are occurring just as gratuitously and with the same indifference as if we were living in the 15th century, unenlightened, and without having ever developed concepts such as democracy or the Rights of Man.)

All this (apart, alas, from my last remark) is only a hypothesis. But it permits us to realise how much we lack the tools to think about it, how much this new society – which is coming, is almost upon us already, whose first signs we can already decipher – is ill-omened if Man does not address as a matter of urgency the philosophical and political problems which it foreshadows.

Man is a mutant

This hypothesis brings to light something which Man has a great deal of difficulty in accepting, namely his mutant essence. If we examine how things developed across millions of years, we see that we started out as bacteria, then amphibians and animals before becoming men. On the other hand, what happens today occurs much more quickly. Marketing and consumer experts are well aware of the phenomenon of attachment to former practices. A large part of food production is no longer the result of 'natural' processes, but we continue to inject colourants so that products resemble those of our grandparents. The phenomenon can be observed in many domains, and designers are necessarily and repeatedly confronted by the discrepancy between reality and the image. The reality of their production or the mechanisms of their appearance, that is to say their signs.

Survival or Civilisation?

There will be a long period of transition, translation and adaptation. But it is essential to look things in the face. The problems of the 21st century, as we know only too well, will be those of survival. Today, as a result of instantaneous media coverage, the West has already witnessed without lifting a finger the genocide which has taken place in former Yugoslavia. Why? For economic reasons, of course. It is impossible to say today, as was said about the Holocaust, that 'we didn't know about it'. The West is also abandoning Africa. If we do not concern ourselves with Africa, an entire continent will disappear. The famine of 2020 is already predicted. Today, at this very moment, there are 800 million under-nourished people. How can those who act in the name of economies ignore that equilibrium is now world-wide? That all the mutations we have been discussing here will completely alter the stakes. That we have to

show solidarity on a world-wide scale. If not
for reasons of morality or civilisation, then
simply for the sake of survival of the species?
Nobody is pasting together again the pieces
of this immense puzzle. A global vision does
not exist. There are no proposals.
We live in a period of non-consciousness,
without a vision or a project.
Fundamentally, I am obsessed by that. And
on my own modest level, I am trying to pon-
der it out. But everyone should be ponder-
ing, asking themselves questions about life,
money, desire, war, themselves.

The profession of
designer is one
which is very
closely linked to
these changes.
The designer can
and should partici-
pate in the search
for meaning, in the
construction of a
civilised world.

Auszug aus einem Gespräch mit Elisabeth Laville (im August 1998), veröffentlicht in einer Sonderausgabe von *La Lettre d'Utopies* / »Verantwortliches Design«

An die Stelle des wesentlich kulturellen Schönen muß das wesentlich humanistische Gute treten

Philippe Starck beantwortete unsere Fragen an einem Samstagvormittag in der Stille seines Hauses auf Formentera (Spanien): ein Haus »irgendwo im Niemandsland, ohne Wasser und ohne Strom, mit Blick aufs Mittelmeer«, wo er »Gott auf ewig dafür dankt, daß es tragbare Geräte gibt« (Handy und Laptop), die ihm ein genauso effizientes Arbeiten ermöglichen, als wäre er in seinen Pariser Büros. Dank diesem »Management in Abwesenheit« trifft er Entscheidungen kreativ und mit kühlem Kopf und hält sich fern vom »Fieber« und »Gebrodel« – darum kümmert sich sein kleines und »ungemein kompetentes« Team in Paris.

Welche Aufgabe hat für Sie ein Designer heute?

Einer der Pioniere des Designs, Raymond Loewy, hat in den fünfziger Jahren einen Slogan geprägt, der ihm persönlich und zum Teil auch der gesamten Designbewegung Erfolg gebracht hat: »Häßlichkeit verkauft sich schlecht.« Zu seiner Zeit hatte er damit vielleicht recht, doch lag im Kern der Aussage schon ein Fehler, den wir heute unbedingt abstellen müssen ... »Häßlichkeit verkauft sich schlecht« bedeutet ja im Grunde, daß das Design der Industrie und Produktion als bloßer Erfüllungsgehilfe dient, damit sich Waren besser verkaufen. Damit ist uns aber im Ansatz nicht mehr geholfen: Heute geht es nicht mehr darum, mehr zu produzieren, um mehr zu verkaufen. Vordringlich stellt sich vielmehr die grundsätzliche Frage, mit welchem Recht ein Produkt überhaupt existiert. Es ist das Recht und die Aufgabe des Designers, nach der Legitimität des Produktes zu fragen, darauf fußt seine wahre Existenz. Und je nachdem, wie die Antwort ausfällt, gehört zu den besten Dingen, die ein Designer tun kann, nein zu sagen – was aber nicht immer leichtfällt. Nein sagen, weil das Produkt bereits existiert und ganz ausgezeichnet funktioniert, so daß seine Wiederholung lediglich eine Frage der Verkäuflichkeit wäre. Und zwar mit schwerwiegenden Folgen, was sowohl die Plünderung der Bodenschätze als auch die Abstumpfung und Verarmung des menschlichen Intellekts anbelangt. Denn der Tätigkeit des Designers folgt die Arbeit derjenigen, die die Leute so lange verblöden, bis sie kaufen – ich spreche von der Werbung und ganz allgemein von der Presse ...

Wie läßt sich denn die Existenzberechtigung eines Objektes beurteilen?

Grundsätzlich muß es einen Katalog von mehr oder weniger strengen Kriterien erfüllen.

Das erste strenge Kriterium lautet, nichts zu tun, was den Menschen schaden kann. Das ist ein sehr schlichtes Gebot, aber man muß es trotzdem erst einmal einhalten, was manchmal herbe finanzielle Einbußen mit sich bringt: Es bedeutet, nicht für die Waffenindustrie zu arbeiten, nicht für harte Alkoholika, nicht für die Tabakindustrie, nicht für die Religion und für kein Projekt, das womöglich auf zweifelhafter Finanzierung beruht. Letzteres wird immer schwieriger. Schmutziges Geld, das durch irgendwelche Geschäfte gewaschen wurde, kann uns durchaus wiederbegegnen. Weil ich da meine Zweifel hatte, habe ich einmal ein überwältigendes Angebot aus Ostberlin abgelehnt. Übrigens enthalten unsere Verträge jetzt eine Klausel, die jeden Kunden verpflichtet, seine Geldquellen

offenzulegen – sollte sich herausstellen, daß er gelogen hat, wird der Vertrag automatisch nichtig. Soweit also die unmittelbaren Forderungen, die obligatorischen moralischen Regeln, die auf der Hand liegen.

Damit ein Objekt existieren darf, muß es aber noch weitere Kriterien erfüllen. Zunächst muß das Produkt etwas Neues bringen, es soll etwas Interessantes, bislang Unbekanntes leisten ... sonst kann man gleich auf schon Bestehendes zurückgreifen. Dann muß es seinen Zweck auch wirklich erfüllen, mit größtmöglicher Aufrichtigkeit, was schwer zu überprüfen ist, denn oft ist der Zweck ein anderer, als man glaubt. Etliche Produkte dienen in Wahrheit nicht dem Zweck, den man vordergründig zu erkennen meint. Deshalb kommt es darauf an, zwischen den Zeilen zu lesen, in unserem eigenen Unbewußten und in dem der Objekte. (...) Schließlich muß man den Zweck zu klären versuchen, und zwar mit möglichst wenig vorgefaßten Ideen, das heißt meistens, mit möglichst wenig Material. Hier führe ich immer mein kleines Beispiel von dem Kunden an, der ein Boot in Auftrag gibt. Als der Designer ihm rät, es doch mit Schwimmen zu versuchen, ist er hochzufrieden, weil er aufgrund dieser Empfehlung etwas wiederentdeckt, was ihm Spaß macht. Man könnte Forschung und Industrie so umstellen, daß das heutige Verhältnis von 20 Prozent Nutzen zu 80 Prozent Ballast (der meist nur der Profitmaximierung des Herstellers dient) umgekehrt würde zu 80 Prozent Nutzenanteil. Das setzt voraus, daß der Designer aufhört, die Lösung im Material zu suchen. Entscheidend ist, daß er unvoreingenommen an die Frage herangeht und etwa sagt: Hier hilft keine industrielle Lösung, sondern eine biologische, dort keine materielle, sondern eine semantische ... Dann nämlich ist der Designer nicht mehr der Komplize eines systematischen Produktionsbetriebs, der mit dem Bleistift vor einem Stück Papier sitzt, sondern jemand, der das Heft selbst in die Hand nimmt und bestimmten Bedürfnissen bestimmten Kompetenzen entgegenbringt. Man muß sich klarmachen, daß der Wunsch, unnützen Ballast abzuwerfen und ihn durch ehrliche Leistung zu ersetzen, auf einer wichtigen Entwicklungstendenz beruht, nämlich der zur Dematerialisation. Das Objekt oder, besser gesagt, das Nicht-Objekt von morgen befindet sich wie ein Stern am Himmel in dauernder Implosion: So stetig sein Volumen abnimmt, so stetig nimmt seine Masse zu – die Masse an Leistung, Aufrichtigkeit und Gefühl. Die Produktion kann sich nur in Richtung Dematerialisierung entwickeln. (...) Bis dahin kommen wir um eine vorläufige, aber unausweichlich mit diesem Prozeß verknüpfte Aufgabe nicht herum: unsere Umwelt politisch, sozial, sexuell und ökonomisch neu zu positionieren. Diese Arbeit ist einfach und erfordert keinen großen Aufwand, bloß Bewußtwerdung und Stehvermögen.

Die politische Positionierung: vermeiden, daß die Objekte Aggressivität, Gewalt, Faschismus, sagen wir, finstere Tendenzen vermitteln. (...) Das bedeutet, eine umfassende Rechenschaft abzulegen über den politischen Zweck unseres Tuns: Wir müssen die Objekte von den barbarischen Zeichen befreien und sie mit positiven, konstruktiven Zeichen aufladen. Nur so können wir einen anderen Weg aufzeigen ...

Die zweite Maßgabe ist die gesellschaftliche oder finanzielle, und sie hängt mit der ersten zusammen: Die Objekte dürfen keine Selbstdarstellung des Geldes werden, mit dem Ziel, die Mitmenschen zu demütigen. Ein Großteil der heutigen Produkte ist auf nichts anderes angelegt, als zu symbolisieren: »Ich habe Geld verdient, meiner ist dicker als deiner, und du kannst mich mal.« Dies ist sehr bedenklich, denn keine Zivilisation läßt sich auf Negativem aufbauen.

Der dritte Parameter ist die Sexualität. Auch sie hat mit dem ersten Punkt zu tun, denn mit der Politik hängt alles zusammen: Heute sind 80 Prozent aller Produkte völlig überflüssigerweise machistisch. Dabei steht fest:

Die moderne Intelligenz ist weiblich.

Und zwar deshalb, weil das Verhalten der Frauen in vieler Hinsicht strukturell anders ist, basierend auf dem Schutz der Gattung, der Sicherung des Fortbestands und auch auf etwas, das ich noch nicht richtig erklären kann: einer Art Pragmatismus, der verschiedene Handlungsweisen gleichzeitig zuläßt und großen Ideen, die sich vereinnahmen und pervertieren lassen, aus dem Weg geht. Deshalb ist es sehr wichtig, sich zu jedem Objekt Fragen zu stellen. Bei unverstelltem Blick ist die Antwort oft klar und schockierend: Von einer Maschinenpistole abgesehen, wüßte ich kaum einen Gegenstand, der unbedingt überwältigend männlich sein müßte!

Der nächste Punkt ist der ökonomische, er betrifft die Erschwinglichkeit der Produkte: Die Qualitätsprodukte müssen dringend »ent-elitisiert« werden, um möglichst viele mit dem Besten zu versorgen.

Wenn eine Idee richtig und vervielfältigbar ist, ist es Diebstahl, sie nicht zu vervielfältigen. Es bedarf also einer Aufwertung des Begriffs »populär«, einer Verbesserung der Vervielfältigungsmöglichkeiten und der Qualität, die Vervielfältigung liefern kann. Und dafür – aber für diese These haben Sie ja schon vehement gestritten – darf man nicht allzusehr auf das Handwerk bauen, sondern eher auf das Einsetzen eines moralischen Verantwortungsgefühls bei den Großunternehmen.

Und diese Rolle haben Sie bei Thomson übernommen?

Das war meine Haupttätigkeit während meiner vierjährigen Arbeit als Art-Direktor bei Thomson: das Unternehmen, das nicht willentlich Böses im Schilde führte, aber ganz einfach den Grund seines Daseins vergessen hatte, zu bestimmten Tugenden zu bekehren – sich nützlich zu machen und die eigenen Kompetenzen für eine Dienstleistung einzusetzen. Man muß dann so etwas wie einen freundlichen inneren Feind spielen, damit man die großen Firmen dafür gewinnt, ihr Fachwissen, ihre finanziellen Mittel, Forschungs- und Vertriebsmöglichkeiten verfügbar zu machen und zum Ausgangspunkt aller Dinge zurückzukehren, zur Dienstleistung. Das beinhaltet auch einen anderen Sprachgebrauch, weshalb ich übrigens bei Thomson unter anderem auf eine Namensänderung gedrungen habe. Thomson nannte sich TCE, Thomson Consumer Electronic. Ich habe gefragt: Wer will ein »Elektronik-Konsument« sein? Damals hatte ich das Glück, einen außergewöhnlichen Vorstand zu haben, Alain Prestat, dem dies sofort einleuchtete. Wir entschieden uns für den Namen Thomson Multimedia, weil Prestat auf den Erfolg der Multimedia-Techniken setzte und ich deutlich machen wollte, daß eine moralisch verfaßte Gesellschaft mehrere Ausdrucksträger benötigt. Schließlich ist es nicht der Mühe wert, schöne Fernsehapparate zu bauen, wenn darin nur Mist läuft ... Darüber hinaus haben wir das Wort »Verbraucher« aus den Besprechungen verbannt und verlangt, es durch »mein Freund«, »meine Frau«, »meine Tochter«, »meine Mutter« oder »ich« zu ersetzen. Es ergibt nämlich einen ganz anderen Sinn, wenn man, statt zu erklären: »Nicht schlimm, das Ding ist zwar Dreck, aber die Verbraucher werden sich damit schon zufriedengeben«, neu ansetzt und sagt: »Nicht schlimm, das Ding ist zwar Dreck, aber meine Tochter wird sich damit zufriedengeben.« Plötzlich kommt das gar nicht mehr so gut an. Mit einem Wort läßt sich also ungeheuer viel bewirken, und seien es auch nur symbolische Verschiebungen. Außerdem habe ich den Thomson-Slogan geprägt. Er lautet: »Thomson: von der Technologie zur Liebe« und verlagerte das Problem ebenfalls auf eine völlig andere Ebene, weil er klarstellte, daß Techno-logie kein Selbstzweck, sondern ein Mittel ist, und daß es schließlich seit jeher in erster Linie auf das Menschliche ankommt, das einer so fundamentalen Empfindung wie der Liebe fähig ist.

Das führt uns wieder zu Ihrer Idee von einem freundschaftlichen, einem guten Objekt ...

Richtig, wir kehren damit praktisch zur Rolle des Designers zurück. Man entwirft das Objekt nicht um des Objektes willen, man pfeift darauf, ob es schön ist. Daß es gut ist, das ist das Entscheidende. An die Stelle des wesentlich kulturellen Schönen muß das wesentlich humanistische Gute treten. Selbstverständlich soll das Objekt von guter Qualität sein und eines der zeitgemäßesten Merkmale überhaupt, nämlich Langlebigkeit aufweisen (dazu kommen wir noch). Vor allem aber soll es gut für diejenigen sein, die mit ihm leben: Das heißt, es soll sie nicht hinter Logos verstecken und sie nicht dem Druck des Bewundernmüssens aussetzen, den Objekte ausüben können. Das Produkt soll dem Menschen erlauben, sich zu entfalten, er selbst zu sein und glücklicher zu werden. Unter der Voraussetzung, daß ein Produkt dem Menschen zu seiner Entfaltung verhelfen soll, kann man schon einmal 70 Prozent der derzeitigen Produktion wegwerfen, weil sie nämlich die Leute zu Kaspern macht. Falsche Harley Davidsons verwandeln die Leute in falsche Biker, mit Labels aufgemotzte Brillen verwandeln sie in Reklameschilder für Marken, die einem egal sind ... Die Menschen verkleiden sich, um nicht zu existieren. Es kommt aber darauf an, daß die Menschen wieder existieren, weil sie sonst verschwinden werden. Wir müssen fortwährend gegen eine Vorstellung ankämpfen, die Menschen zu Publikum, zu Zuschauern machen will, und sie wieder an ihren Platz als Handelnde stellen.

Dann gibt es natürlich noch das Problem der Ökologie.

Die moralisch gewordenen Großunternehmen müssen davon überzeugt werden, daß die Produktion den Menschen nicht schädigen, das Objekt sein Leben nicht beeinträchtigen darf.

Der Marketing-Gimmick Recycling hat dabei natürlich nichts zu suchen. Von den Ökologen erfunden, sorgt Recycling letzten Endes dafür, daß wir heute nutzlos weiterproduzieren und -konsumieren können. Ein gutes Produkt ist ein haltbares Produkt: Wenn es zehn, zwanzig, dreißig Jahre gehalten hat, darf es einem im Zweifelsfall egal sein, ob es wiederverwertbar ist und wiederverwertet wird. Aber jahraus, jahrein nutzlose Dinge zu recyceln, ist eine wahnsinnige Vergeudung von Material und Energie. Ich bin nicht gegen Recycling, aber gegen den Versuch, es zum Allheilmittel zu stilisieren. Recycling ist ein Notbehelf, das nachträgliche Ausbügeln eines Fehlers, und sonst nichts. Es ist eine Scheinlösung, ein falsches Problem, ein ökologischer Schmus, wie es ihn heute überall gibt: etwa der Elektroantrieb bei Autos, der bloß den Auspuff in die Atomkraftwerke verlegt. (...)

Sie sprachen vorhin von der Erschwinglichkeit der Produkte: Ist das der Grund, warum Sie an Ihrem Katalog Good Goods arbeiten und mit den Kaufhausketten Carrefour und La Redoute kooperieren, die sich die Demokratisierung der besten Produkte zum Ziel gesetzt haben?

Einer der wenigen Erfolge, die ich in meiner Laufbahn errungen habe, war die Aufwertung der Vervielfältigung, mit anderen Worten des Begriffs »populär«, die Nobilitierung des Verachteten. Früher wurde eine Zahnbürste im hintersten Eck einer Schublade versteckt, und von einem Tag auf den anderen schenkte man sie sich plötzlich zu Weihnachten. Sie wurde vorzeigbar. Mein zweiter Erfolg war es, die Preise zu brechen und Dinge erschwinglich zu machen: Im Verlauf eines Jahrzehnts habe ich es gegen alle und jeden durchgesetzt, die Preise meiner Objekte alle ein bis zwei Jahre praktisch zu halbieren. Einer meiner ersten Erfolge, der Stuhl für das Café Costes, kostete damals 4000 Francs ... Heute arbeiten wir an Stühlen für 300, vielleicht sogar 200 Francs. (...) Mit Vitra überlegen wir sogar, wie man Möbel vermieten oder zurücknehmen könnte. Daran arbeiten wir jetzt seit mindestens fünf bis sechs Jahren, das Problem ist nur, daß das derzeit nicht machbar ist. Wir wissen nicht, wie wir jemanden verpflichten können, gegen ein Entgelt von weniger als 50 Francs einen Stuhl zurückzubringen, was in Kürze der Preis sein wird, den er dafür bezahlt hat. (...) Diese Überlegung bezieht sich zwangsläufig auf den absoluten Massenmarkt, aber die Zielgruppe dieses Marktes ist dafür noch nicht aufgeklärt genug. Auch gibt es das Gebührenproblem: Für wieviel vermieten Sie einen Stuhl, der 50 Francs kostet? Einen Franc im Monat? Da tun sich einige Sackgassen auf. Besser also einen Stil bzw. Nicht-Stil entwickeln, der zeitresistent ist. Nehmen Sie zum Beispiel den kleinen Stuhl Dr. No: Er ist bequem, stapelbar, praktisch unverwüstlich, was wiederum das Problem mit sich bringt, daß man ihn zwanzig Jahre lang behält. Nach zwanzig Jahren findet man ihn in einer Ecke des Gartens wieder, jemand sammelt ihn auf, und er wird eingeschmolzen. Aber vorerst brauchen wir keine großen Geschütze aufzufahren, denn uns fehlen die Mittel, das oben erwähnte Projekt durchzuführen.

Großdistribution ist für mich unumgänglich. Der Katalog Good Goods kam 1998 heraus, und gleichzeitig präsentierten wir in Japan Seven Eleven, eine der größten Aktionen in der Geschichte des Designs. Seven Eleven, eine Kette durchgehend geöffneter *convenient stores* (8 000 in Japan, 30 000 in Asien und ich weiß nicht mehr wie viele in den USA), hat mir im Grunde die Gestaltung sämtlicher Artikel übertragen: Joghurts, Rasierer, Slips, Buntstifte, alles was Sie wollen. Sie ist der größte Auftraggeber der Welt, mit dem man wirklich Großes in Bewegung setzen kann, und zwar zum Besten aller. Wir wissen schon jetzt, daß jedes Objekt eine Auflage von 10 Millionen Stück pro Jahr haben wird. Ich glaube nicht, daß eines davon mehr als zehn oder zwölf Francs kostet – eine Ohrfeige für das elitäre Design. Das ist für mich das Wesentliche, fast ein Endziel. Was mir danach zu tun bleibt, weiß ich noch nicht so recht. Höchstens, weiterzuarbeiten und zu beweisen, daß man noch bessere Joghurts, noch bessere Slips machen kann ...

Und Good Goods?

Das ist ein Projekt, das mir seit Jahren am Herzen liegt und in das ich zwei Jahre lang enorm viel Mühe investiert habe. Ich würde sogar zum ersten Mal in meinem Leben behaupten, daß ich es nicht bereue, aber stünde es mir erneut bevor, ich würde es nicht noch einmal machen. Die Zeit, die ich in dieses Projekt gesteckt habe, hat mich ein Vermögen an Verdienstausfall gekostet. Ich versuche, eine Bresche für aufrichtige Objekte zu schlagen, Objekte für Nicht-Konsumenten, für »moderne Rebellen«, die es leid sind, daß Marketing und Werbung ihnen weismachen wollen, sie müßten unbedingt ihren R 5 gegen einen R 6 eintauschen, oder ihren 4/3-Fernseher gegen einen 16/9-Fernseher ... Diese Leute stellen für mich eine neue, bislang unbekannte politische Kraft dar. (...) Deshalb liegt mir daran, daß sie den Katalog als Katalysator benutzen, um Regeln aufzustellen, die ich die des *moral market* nenne, also in etwa das, was ich gerade beschrieben habe. Die Menschen werden den Katalog mit einer kleinen Notiz von mir bekommen, die ihnen etwas in der Geschäftswelt ziemlich Revolutionäres mitteilt, nämlich, daß sie die Produkte gar nicht kaufen müssen, sondern daß es wichtiger ist, im Katalog zwischen den Zeilen zu lesen. Im Good-Goods-Katalog gibt es interessante Produkte, die aber nicht den Anspruch erheben, Anti-Produkte in dem von mir angestrebten Sinn zu sein. Sie sind nur dazu da, die Sache ins Rollen zu bringen. Wichtig ist, daß jedes Produkt ein klein wenig erklärt wird – aus Platzmangel leider nicht so ausführlich, wie ich es wollte: Wir versuchen ver-

ständlich zu machen, warum, und umgekehrt, warum nicht; warum so und nicht anders, und warum wir dieses andere nicht mehr wollen. (...)

Heute benutzen Sie Ihren Ruf dazu, diese Botschaften unter die Leute zu bringen ... Trotzdem sagen Sie im Good-Goods-Katalog, Sie wollten »ein Unrecht wiedergutmachen, daß ich wahrscheinlich selbst mitverschuldet habe«. Heißt das, daß Sie hinsichtlich des Kriterienkatalogs, von dem wir sprachen, hinter den Starck-Objekten aus diesem Katalog stärker stehen als hinter anderen?

Wissen Sie, ich bin immer derselbe geblieben, mit derselben Idee im Kopf. Nur daß man anfangs, wenn man jung ist, arbeitet um zu überleben und jeden Auftrag annimmt. Jetzt bin ich 49 und habe gewisse Mittel zur Verfügung. Hätte ich meine Strategie nicht erst einmal in Konzepte gefaßt, wäre ich ein Trottel, und hielte ich mich nicht an sie, wäre ich ein Schwindler. Ich gebe also zu, daß ich getan habe, was ich tun konnte, mit Höhen und Tiefen, aber immer mit einer gewissen Aufrichtigkeit. Nicht, daß jetzt alles perfekt wäre, aber ich kann mir strengere Maßstäbe leisten. Wissen Sie, es kam ja zunächst darauf an, meinen Unterhalt zu bestreiten, und diese Fähigkeit mußte ich entwickeln. Wenn man ein französischer Designer ist ... ach was – lassen Sie uns nicht vergessen: Einen französischen Designer gibt es gar nicht!

Auszug aus einem Gespräch mit Sophie
Tasma Anargyros, organisiert vom Verband
VIA (Valorisation de l'Industrie de l'Ameuble-
ment) im März 1996

Der Mythos vom Fortschritt

Die Vorstellung einer sich ständig wandelnden Welt ist mit der Idee des Fortschritts verquickt. Seit ihrem Aufkommen markiert diese Idee den Unterschied zwischen Mensch und Tier durch ihre Absicht, die Gattung Mensch verbessern zu wollen.

Der Mensch empfindet sich selbst nicht als wirklich, solange er nicht nach dem Unbekannten strebt. Um diese Idee herauszukristallisieren, hat er sich ein Konzept erdacht, und das ist Gott. Gott ist das absolute Modell jeglichen Fortschritts, aber auch ein schwer bestimmbares: einerseits nicht menschlich per definitionem, andererseits jedoch menschlich, da der menschlichen Vorstellung entsprungen. Aus dieser unendlichen Distanz, die der Mensch zwischen sich und Gott geschaffen hat, ergibt sich der unendlich lange Weg zurück, zu einer Annäherung an Gott. Diese außerordentlich dynamische Idee äußert sich auch in dem Wunschtraum, ebenso übermächtig, allgegenwärtig und allwissend zu werden wie das göttliche Modell.

Der Mensch erreicht sein Modell

Die Mittel, die der Mensch einsetzt, um so zu werden wie sein Modell, sind zum einen Werkstoffe und Werkzeuge, zum anderen Intelligenz und Wissen. Nach und nach nähert er sich seinem Modell an. Bis zum 18. Jahrhundert geschieht das relativ langsam, beschleunigt sich aber rapide im Verlauf des 19. und 20. Jahrhunderts. Der erste große Schritt ist die Mechanisierung. Anfang des 20. Jahrhunderts ist man überwältigt von der Maschine, und dieser Zustand der Bewunderung dauert bis heute an. Am Rande sei vermerkt, daß sich gleichzeitig eine gegenläufige Bewegung vollzieht: Die Idee eines besseren Lebens und damit auch die Ideen von Gleichheit, Freiheit und Brüderlichkeit sind nicht verwirklicht, ganz im Gegenteil – und hier untertreibe ich. Am Horizont des 21. Jahrhunderts zeichnet sich nun die Möglichkeit ab, das Modell zu erreichen. Einerseits mit Werkzeugen, die sich entstofflicht haben, mittels Computern also, die dem Menschen über Internet oder das, was Internet einmal sein wird, eine unermeßliche Wissensmenge liefern werden. Sie ermöglicht das Entstehen eines gemeinsamen Denkens, parallel zu den Machtsystemen, die bislang die Inhalte dieses Denkens bestimmten. Anderseits durch die Geschwindigkeit, mit der sich die Menschen durch den Raum bewegen können, vor allem jedoch durch die Geschwindigkeit, mit der menschliches Denken durch den Raum reist, die Unmittelbarkeit der Kommunikation. Gleichzeitig nähern wir uns heute in der Genetik der Schöpfung künstlichen Lebens. Die einzelnen Puzzleteile beginnen, sich aneinanderzufügen, die Verwirklichung des als unerreichbar konzipierten Modells zeichnet sich ab. Ein nicht unerhebliches Problem bleibt allerdings bestehen. Es sieht ganz so aus, als sei diese Epoche, in der nahezu alle Phantasievorstellungen Wirklichkeit geworden sind, auch eine Epoche des Verlusts. Seinem Modell entgegenstrebend, hat der Mensch unterwegs etwas verloren, das man als ein Ideal bezeichnen könnte. Vielleicht ist das eine Erklärung dafür, daß die Menschen keine Lust mehr haben, Materie zu konsumieren. Die Materie ohne ihr Double – die Idee, durch die sie erst ihre ganze Bedeutung erhält – ist eine ihres Inhalts beraubte Hülse.

Das 21. Jahrhundert wird immateriell und menschlich sein

Die bereits bestehende Immaterialität der Mikroprozessoren beispielsweise, der Nachrichtenübertragung und aller sonstigen Prozesse muß sich, und das mit aller Dringlichkeit, aus dem Menschlichen heraus entwickeln. Das 21. Jahrhundert wird nicht mystisch sein, sondern immateriell und menschlich. Sollte das nicht geschehen, wird der Verfall, den wir heute erleben, fortschreiten.

Was das Menschliche betrifft, so müssen wir zu der im Unbewußten liegenden Quelle des Fortschrittsgedankens zurückkehren: zum Wunsch nach einem besseren Leben für jeden einzelnen, nach Glück und Entfaltung. Ich werde ein einfaches Bild benutzen, um diesen Gedanken zu illustrieren: Wir bewegen uns auf ein ganz besonderes Neujahrsfest zu, auf eine Art Super-Neujahr, die Wende zum dritten Jahrtausend. Ein jeder von uns erinnert sich noch an vergangene Silvesterabende. Man zieht Bilanz und beschließt, ein besserer Mensch zu werden. Entweder die Menschheit wappnet sich mit diesem guten Vorsatz für den Übergang ins dritte Jahrtausend, oder sie wird darin verlorengehen. Das Menschliche hat die absolute Priorität. Wenn der Mensch jedoch der Idee der Materie verhaftet bleibt, sich nicht von ihr zu lösen vermag, wenn das Konzept Materie nicht durch das Konzept Liebe ersetzt wird, wie soll man dann noch in einer Welt überleben, in der der Mensch allgegenwärtig und übermächtig geworden ist und in der das Kräftespiel materiell nicht mehr zum Ausdruck kommt?

Fortschritt oder Vorgeschichte

Es stimmt äußerst bedenklich, daß es dem Menschen im Verlauf vieler Jahrtausende nicht gelungen ist, sich etwas so Einfaches wie die Liebe zu eigen zu machen. Sich zu eigen gemacht und verloren hat er lediglich die Materie. Wenn ich die Sache gedanklich noch einfacher angehe, sage ich: Der Ursprung der Liebe beruht in dem, was wir als mütterlichen Instinkt bezeichnen und was nichts anderes ist als das Verlangen, die Gattung zu schützen. Und diese Gattung ist nun einmal gefährdet. Wenn dem Menschen die Bedeutung der Liebe zur Wahrung der Gattung abhanden kommt, landen wir im Handumdrehen wieder in der Vorgeschichte, in einer Zeit, in der das Leben des Individuums ohne zivilisatorisches oder gesellschaftliches Projekt ablief. Ich glaube sogar, daß die größte Gefahr darin besteht, zu vergessen, daß es so etwas wie die Liebe überhaupt gibt. Warum sind denn die »bequemsten« Gesellschaften auch zugleich die suizidärsten, die den Überlebensinstinkt verloren haben? Meinem Empfinden nach bewegen sich die Überlegungen all derer, die Objekte, Zeichen und Sinn produzieren, um eine gemeinsame Achse: das Bewußtsein, daß die Materie als Bedeutungsträger ausgedient hat – zugunsten des Menschlichen und seiner schönsten Erfindung, der Liebe. Das zwingt die Produzenten, sich über das Nicht-Objekt von morgen Gedanken zu machen.

Das Nicht-Objekt

Wie sieht der Mensch von morgen aus? Ich werde versuchen, ihn zu beschreiben. Wir befinden uns bereits im Zeitalter der künstlichen Intelligenz und werden bald schon über »biologische«, d. h. auf der Grundlage neuronaler Netze gebaute Rechner verfügen. Selbst der Tod weicht zurück. In kurzer Zeit wird der Mensch sich selbst gegenüberstehen. Transzendiert.

Mit den biologischen Rechnern löst sich die Bedeutung der Materie und damit der Objekte auf. Bei der Produktion von Objekten ging es bislang darum, ihre Struktur, Form und Funktion zu verfeinern. Bei Thomson experimentiert man aber jetzt schon mit Steuerungstechniken auf visueller und mentaler Basis. Da gibt es keine Verbindung mehr zwischen Geste und Objekt. Das Ergebnis wird direkt von der Vorstellung gesteuert.

Von der anderen Seite des Spiegels aus gesehen, verschwindet das ganze System des Menschen, sich durch Objekte darzustellen. Der Mensch von morgen wird nackt sein – bildlich gesprochen. Ohne Einmischung der Materie zwischen sich selbst und die Welt, gebunden an seinen Biorhythmus und mit einer nahezu unendlichen Macht versehen. Alle Dienstleistungen werden in sprachlichem oder gedanklichem Handeln bestehen. Der Mensch von morgen kommuniziert weltweit. Wenn er eine Frage hat, benötigt er nur ein paar Sekunden, um sie auf dem Netz in Umlauf zu bringen, und verfügt quasi sofort über Millionen von Antworten. Vermehrtes Wissen führt bekanntermaßen zu einer Verminderung von Gewalttätigkeit. Unter der Voraussetzung eines echten Willens zum Aufbau einer neuen Kultur kann die Kommunikation als ein Faktor zur Stiftung eines zukünftigen Weltfriedens betrachtet werden. Es wird dann nämlich schwierig, einen kriegerischen Einsatz zu rechtfertigen, weil jedermann jederzeit alle Informationen überprüfen kann. Die großen Lügen werden dann nicht mehr möglich sein. Oder aber die Lüge wird zum System, und damit wäre die totale Herrschaft von Manipulation, Chaos und bewußter Falschinformation gegeben. Internet muß nicht zuletzt zu einem Werkzeug des Friedens und der Selbstkontrolle werden. In diesem Fall würde das Territorium des Menschen in ihm selbst liegen. Damit würde er aufhören, ständig neue Territorien erobern zu wollen, und damit würde auch endlich der Grund hinfällig, aus dem heraus seit Urzeiten Kriege geführt werden. Der Mensch muß seine Macht dann nicht mehr länger bei Gebiets- oder Grenzstreitigkeiten einsetzen. Überhaupt wird sich der Begriff der Grenze völlig wandeln. Statt sein reales Territorium wird der Mensch fast nur noch ein virtuelles benutzen, das jedoch genau wie ein tatsächlich vorhandenes eigene Strukturen, Normen und Regeln entwickeln wird. Man wird sich lediglich ans Netz anzuschließen brauchen, um Zugang zur Präsenz des anderen, zu seinem Bild, seinem Denken und seinem Wissen zu erhalten.

Das Haus von morgen

Der Mensch von morgen wird ein Haus bewohnen, das auf eine leere Hülle reduziert ist. Die Wärmeregulierung erfolgt über den Fußboden, das Licht fällt in Form von Elektro-Lumineszenz über Scheiben aus Flüssigkristallen ein, Ton und Bild kommen aus der Wand. Der Mensch wird sich zu einem emotionalen Wesen entwickeln, das sein eigenes Zeichensystem erfinden muß. Damit vollzieht sich die totale Trennung zwischen der Funktion bzw. Leistung der Zeichen und ihrer Bedeutung. Die Herrschaft des Poetischen bricht an.

Die von jeglicher Funktion entbundenen Zeichen erreichen ihre allerhöchste Reinheit und Wirksamkeit und gehören in dieser Hinsicht zur Kunst; von den Objekten befreit, die bislang zwischen ihm und seinem Handeln standen, gewinnt der menschliche Körper hingegen paradoxerweise seine ursprüngliche Natürlichkeit zurück. Selbstverständlich wird der Einsatz der zu einem Großteil in den Körper integrierten Kommunikationswerkzeuge die Verwechslung zwischen Realem und Virtuellem mit sich bringen sowie die Gefahr für die Psyche, sich der Wirklichkeit entziehen zu wollen. In diesem Szenario kann jeder ständig am gleichen Ort bleiben. Aus dem Beruf des Innenausstatters wird der des Bilderprogrammierers. Mit Hilfe von Computerbildern entwirft jeder Mensch den Rahmen, in dem er auftreten möchte. Die Zahl der Verkehrsmittel nimmt ab, die Straßen verwandeln sich in Wege zurück. Das Verhältnis zwischen Stadt und Peripherie kehrt sich um. Die Stadt verliert ihre Stellung als Zentrum, in dem alle Machtlinien zusammenlaufen, da die Akte öffentlichen Lebens sich nicht länger innerhalb ihrer Grenzen verkörpern müssen. Außerhalb der Städte leben die Stämme der Mächtigen, in den Städten die von der Gesellschaft Ausgeschlossenen. Die Stadt wird zu einem Ort des Chaos.

Gewalt: Wer entwirft die Zukunft?

Die Diktatur geht von denjenigen aus, die die Kontrolle über die Kommunikation innehaben. Damit können sie in einer Gesellschaft, deren Wirtschaft auf einem System virtuellen Austauschs basiert, über Leben und Tod entscheiden. Es genügt, das Abonnement eines Teilnehmers zu löschen, um ihn verschwinden zu lassen. Physische Gewalt gibt es nicht. Sie wird durch das Auslöschen ersetzt, durch das Vergessen, nicht so sehr durch Nichtwissen wie durch Gleichgültigkeit. (Dieses Phänomen ist uns in einer anderen Form schon bekannt: als ein der Vollnarkose ähnlicher Zustand, der es uns erlaubt, uns in aller Ruhe hier in meinem Büro zu unterhalten, während sich in Bosnien, Tschetschenien, Ruanda oder anderswo Massaker ereignen, deren Sinnlosigkeit uns genauso gleichgültig läßt, als wenn wir im 15. Jahrhundert lebten. Als wären wir uns dessen nicht bewußt und als hätten wir Konzepte wie die Demokratie oder die Menschenrechte nie erarbeitet.) Abgesehen von meiner letzten, leider auf Erfahrung beruhenden Bemerkung, ist das alles bis jetzt lediglich eine Hypothese. Sie macht aber deutlich, wie sehr es uns an Werkzeugen zu einer Reflexion über die Zukunft mangelt und welche dunklen Zeiten diese im Kommen begriffene neue Gesellschaft, deren Vorzeichen schon spürbar sind, der Menschheit verheißt, wenn sie sich nicht dringend mit den daraus erwachsenden philosophischen und politischen Problemen auseinandersetzt.

Der Mensch – ein Mutant

Diese Hypothese läßt auch etwas erkennen, das der Mensch nur ungern akzeptiert: daß er der Mutation unterworfen ist. Betrachten wir die Dinge nämlich nach Jahrmillionen, dann sehen wir, daß wir als Bakterien begonnen und uns über Lurche und Säugetiere zum Menschen fortentwickelt haben. Nun wird in der Zukunft alles viel schneller gehen. Die Fachleute, die den Markt und das Verbraucherverhalten studieren, kennen das Phänomen des Festhaltens am Althergebrachten. Ein Großteil der Nahrungsmittel wird heute nicht mehr »natürlich« erzeugt. Damit sie aber trotzdem wie zu Großmutters Zeiten aussehen, setzt man ihnen weiterhin Farbstoffe zu. Dieses Phänomen erlebt man in vielen anderen Bereichen. Auch die Designer werden natürlich ständig mit dem Abstand zwischen Realität und Vorstellung konfrontiert, mit der Realität der Produktion oder der Mechanismen und ihrer äußeren Erscheinung, d. h. ihren Zeichen.

Überleben oder Zivilisation

Es wird also eine lange Zeit des Übergangs, der Übertragung und Anpassung geben. Aber man muß den Dingen ins Gesicht sehen. Wir wissen genau, daß das Hauptproblem des 21. Jahrhunderts das Überleben sein wird. Heute hat der Westen – die simultane Nachrichtenübertragung ist schon längst keine Zukunft mehr – den Völkermord in Ex-Jugoslawien live miterlebt. Ohne sich zu rühren. Warum? Ganz offensichtlich aus wirtschaftlichen Gründen. Es kann heute niemand mehr behaupten, wie das nach dem Holocaust vorkam, er habe »von nichts gewußt«. Der Westen ist ebenfalls im Begriff, Afrika aufzugeben. Wenn wir uns nicht um Afrika kümmern, dann geht ein ganzer Kontinent unter. Die Hungersnot des Jahres 2020 ist schon vorprogrammiert. Heute, in diesem Augenblick, leiden 800 Millionen Menschen an Unterernährung. Wie können diejenigen, die im Namen einzelner Volkswirtschaften handeln, noch länger ignorieren, daß das wirtschaftliche Gleichgewicht heute global betrachtet werden muß, daß die erwähnten Mutationen die Problemstellungen grundsätzlich ändern werden und daß wir weltweit solidarisch handeln müssen? Und selbst wenn dies nicht aus moralischen oder zivilisatorischen Gründen geschehen sollte, dann zumindest, um die menschliche Gattung zu erhalten. Niemand scheint die Teile dieses riesigen Puzzles zusammenlegen zu wollen, es gibt keine globale Zukunftsvision, nicht einmal Ansätze dazu.

Wir leben in einer Zeit mangelnden Bewußtseins, ohne Vision und ohne Projekt.

Das beschäftigt mich am meisten. Und in meinem kleinen Maßstab versuche ich nachzudenken. Jeder von uns muß unbedingt nachdenken und sich Fragen stellen über das Leben, das Geld, das Verlangen, den Krieg und sich selbst.

Das Metier des Designers gehört zu denen, die in enger Berührung zu diesen Entwicklungen stehen. Der Designer kann – oder vielmehr muß – sich an der Suche nach dem Sinn und dem Aufbau einer neuen weltweiten Zivilisation beteiligen.

Extrait d'une conversation avec Elisabeth Laville (en août 1998), initialement publiée dans *La Lettre d'Utopies* / Spécial « Design Responsable »

Il faut remplacer le beau d'essence culturelle par le bon d'essence humaniste

Philippe Starck a répondu à nos questions, un samedi matin, au calme dans sa maison de Formentera (Espagne) : une maison « au milieu de nulle part, sans eau ni électricité, face à la Méditerranée », et d'où il « remercie Dieu jusqu'à la fin des jours pour les portables » (téléphone et ordinateur) qui lui permettent de travailler aussi efficacement que s'il était dans ses bureaux parisiens – un « management par l'absence » qui, selon lui, permet d'être complètement froid et créatif pour les décisions en restant détaché des problèmes de « fièvre » et de « cuisine » que sa petite équipe « extraordinairement compétente » gère à Paris.

Quel est selon vous le rôle du designer, aujourd'hui ?

Un des pères du design, Raymond Lœwy, dans les années 50, a inventé un slogan qui a fait son succès et une partie du succès du design : « La laideur se vend mal. » A son époque, il avait peut-être raison mais hélas, déjà, ça portait un vice structurel dont il faut absolument sortir aujourd'hui en tuant la parole du père... Il faut bien comprendre que « la laideur se vend mal » signifie que le design n'est qu'un complice de l'industrie et de la production afin que les choses se vendent mieux. Structurellement, ce n'est plus le propos : aujourd'hui le problème n'est pas de produire plus pour vendre plus, la question fondamentale est d'abord celle de la légitimité des produits à exister. L'acte légitime du designer est d'abord la question sur la légitimité du produit, c'est ça qui lui donne sa vraie existence. Et suivant la réponse qu'il donnera à cette question, l'un des actes les plus positifs que le designer puisse faire, c'est le refus – ce qui n'est pas toujours facile. Refus parce que l'objet existe déjà et fonctionne extrêmement bien – le répéter ne serait qu'un acte vénal porteur de conséquences graves en termes d'appauvrissement des richesses de la Terre, en termes d'abrutissement et d'appauvrissement des gens puisqu'après c'est relayé par des services qui abrutissent les gens jusqu'à temps qu'ils achètent – je parle de la publicité, de la presse en général...

Comment statuer, alors, sur cette légitimité de l'objet à exister ?

Il est fondamental de le faire passer à travers plusieurs grilles d'exigence, strictes ou plus malléables. La première grille stricte est de ne rien faire qui puisse aider à des choses néfastes pour l'homme. Cette grille-là est simpliste, mais il faut quand même la respecter et quelquefois cela représente de grosses pertes financières : c'est ne pas travailler pour l'armement, ne pas travailler pour les alcools durs, ne pas travailler pour le tabac, ne pas travailler pour la religion et ne pas travailler pour tout ce qui peut provenir de financement douteux, ce qui devient de plus en plus compliqué. L'argent sale qui est blanchi dans des affaires peut tout à fait nous rejoindre : je me suis vu refuser un marché sidérant à Berlin-Est pour une raison de doute et d'ailleurs, maintenant, nous avons dans nos contrats une clause selon laquelle tous nos clients doivent dire quelle est leur source de financement – et s'il s'avérait que ces gens avaient menti, le contrat serait automatiquement cassé. Donc ça, c'est les grilles d'exigence immédiates, les règles morales obligatoires, qui tombent sous le sens. Après, on doit faire passer l'objet à travers

une autre grille de paramètres qui vont en excuser l'existence. Le produit doit d'abord amener un service nouveau, apporter quelque chose de plus intéressant, une compétence nouvelle... sinon, autant se retourner vers des objets déjà existants. Ensuite, il doit rendre profondément son service, avec le plus d'honnêteté possible : l'honnêteté du service est difficile à déchiffrer, car souvent ce n'est pas celui qu'on croit. Des objets servent à autre chose, réellement, que l'aspect qu'ils représentent, donc il faut savoir lire entre les lignes, il faut savoir lire à la fois dans notre inconscient et dans l'inconscient des objets. (...) Après, il va falloir essayer de rendre le service pur, avec le minimum d'idées préconçues c'est-à-dire en général le minimum de matière – c'est là que je cite toujours mon petit exemple du client qui a demandé un bateau et se trouve très satisfait des conseils du designer qui lui recommande d'essayer la nage et lui en fait redécouvrir les plaisirs. Il est possible désormais d'orienter la recherche et l'industrie vers des outils qui permettraient, au lieu d'avoir comme aujourd'hui 20 pour cent de service pour 80 pour cent de matière inutile (qui en général ne sert qu'à la vénalité du producteur), d'inverser le processus pour avoir 80 pour cent de service. Pour cela, il est fondamental que le designer cesse de penser la réponse à travers la matière. Il est fondamental que, devant une question, il soit extrêmement ouvert et qu'il puisse dire : la réponse est une réponse biologique et non pas industrielle, la réponse est une réponse sémantique et non pas matérielle... Dans ce cas-là, le designer n'est plus, en face d'un papier et d'un crayon, le complice d'une production systématique mais se retrouve en chef d'orchestre, mettant en face de certains besoins certaines compétences. Il faut comprendre que cette volonté de faire disparaître l'inutilité au profit de l'honnêteté est basée sur un axe fort qui s'appelle la dématérialisation. L'objet, le non-objet de demain matin, est, à l'exemple d'une étoile dans le ciel, en perpétuelle implosion, c'est-à-dire que son volume décroît en permanence au profit de sa masse – de sa masse de compétences, de sa masse d'honnêteté et de sa masse d'affectivité. Le seul axe possible de la production est la dématérialisation. (...) En attendant, il y a un travail provisoire mais parallèle dont on ne peut faire l'économie : le repositionnement politique, social, sexuel et économique de ce qui nous entoure. C'est un travail facile, qui ne demande pas de gros moyens mais simplement une prise de conscience et de la ténacité.

Le positionnement politique : éviter que les objets soient représentatifs de l'agressivité, la violence, le fascisme... on va dire d'obscurités. (...) C'est tout un travail sur le sens politique de ce que l'on fait : il est fondamental de nettoyer les objets des signes barbares et de les charger de signes positifs, constructifs, pour montrer une autre voie... Le deuxième paramètre est le paramètre social ou financier, qui est en rapport avec le premier : Les objets n'ont pas à devenir des moyens de représentation de l'argent afin d'humilier son voisin. Une grande part de la production ne sert qu'à ça, c'est-à-dire « j'ai gagné de l'argent, j'en ai une plus grosse que toi et je t'emmerde ». C'est très grave, car on ne bâtit pas une civilisation sur du négatif. Le troisième paramètre est le sexe, qui a encore un rapport avec le premier point puisque tout a rapport avec la politique : aujourd'hui 80 pour cent des objets sont inutilement machistes. Il est clair :

L'intelligence moderne est féminine,

à cause d'une série de fonctionnements structurels différents, basés sur la protection de l'espèce, sur le continuum, et sur quelque chose que j'ai plus de mal à expliquer encore : une sorte de pragmatisme qui donne une simultanéité d'actions et évite la grande idée, celle qui se récupère et qui se pervertit. Donc il est très intéressant de se poser des questions sur chaque objet. La réponse est assez souvent claire et choquante quand on a l'œil ouvert là-dessus : excepté un pistolet mitrailleur, je vois peu d'objets qui ont besoin d'être outrageusement virils ! Le point suivant est le point économique, qui touche à l'abordabilité des produits : Il est fondamental de « dés-élitiser » les objets de qualité pour donner ce qu'il y a de mieux au maximum de gens.

Si l'idée est juste et multipliable, ne pas la multiplier est un vol. D'où un travail sur l'anoblissement du mot populaire, sur le pouvoir que donne la multiplication, sur l'augmentation de qualité que donne la multiplication. Et pour cela – mais ça c'est déjà un cheval de bataille pour vous – il ne faut pas trop croire dans l'artisanat mais dans la moralisation des grandes entreprises. C'est le rôle que vous avez joué chez Thomson ?

Cela a été mon principal travail de directeur artistique pendant 4 ans chez Thomson, pour rendre vertueuses des sociétés qui n'avaient pas de volonté de méchanceté, mais qui avaient simplement oublié leur raison d'être : rendre service, mettre leurs compétences au profit d'un service. Il est fonda-

mental de jouer une sorte d'ennemi intérieur amical, c'est-à-dire d'arriver à intéresser les grandes sociétés afin qu'elles donnent les savoir-faire, les moyens financiers, la recherche, la distribution... en revenant à l'origine des choses qui est le service. Cela implique même un autre vocabulaire, et d'ailleurs une des choses que j'avais faite chez Thomson était de changer le nom. Thomson s'appelait TCE, Thomson Consumer Electronic, et j'avais posé la question : qui veut être un « consommateur d'électronique » ? A l'époque j'avais eu la chance d'avoir un président extraordinaire, Alain Prestat, qui avait compris à la seconde. On avait choisi le mot Thomson Multimédia, parce que lui pariait sur le succès des technologies du multimédia et moi je voulais parler des multiples vecteurs d'expression qu'une société morale doit avoir. Car ce n'est pas la peine de faire des beaux téléviseurs si on y voit de la merde... L'autre point important, c'est d'avoir interdit le mot « consommateur » dans les réunions et d'avoir exigé qu'il soit remplacé par « mon ami », « ma femme », « ma fille », « ma mère » ou « moi-même ». La phrase n'est plus du tout la même quand on dit : « C'est pas grave, c'est une merde, mais les consommateurs s'en contenteront » et si on recommence en disant : « C'est une merde, mais c'est pas grave, ma fille s'en contentera »... Tout d'un coup ça passe mal. Il y a donc un travail gigantesque à faire, ne serait-ce que sur des repositionnements symboliques, avec un mot. L'autre chose que j'ai faite chez Thomson, c'était le slogan, qui était « Thomson : de la technologie à l'amour », et qui là encore repositionnait complètement le problème en disant que la technologie n'est pas une fin en soi, c'est un moyen – et que le but réel et final, c'est ce qui a toujours été, c'est la priorité, c'est l'humain, avec un paramètre fondamental qui est l'amour.

On rejoint ici votre idée d'un objet ami, d'un objet bon...

Oui, là on en revient quasiment au rôle du designer, on ne dessine pas l'objet pour l'objet, on se fout qu'il soit beau, il est fondamental qu'il soit bon ; il faut remplacer le beau d'essence culturelle par le bon d'essence humaniste. L'objet doit être bon qualitativement évidemment, avec un des paramètres les plus modernes qui est la longévité, on y reviendra, mais surtout il doit être bon pour la personne qui va vivre avec – ça veut dire qu'il ne doit pas la cacher par des logos, ni l'opprimer par l'admiration que l'on peut porter aux objets, il doit permettre à la personne de s'épanouir, d'être elle-même et d'être plus heureuse avec. Dire qu'un produit doit épanouir la personne,

cela enlève déjà 70 pour cent de la production actuelle qui transforme les gens en clowns : les fausses Harley Davidson transforment les gens en faux *bikers*, les lunettes griffées énormément transforment les gens en des portemanteaux de marques dont on se moque... Les gens se déguisent pour ne pas exister. Et il est fondamental que les gens ré-existent parce que sinon ils disparaîtront. Il faut combattre l'idée de la transformation des gens en public, en spectateurs, par un travail continuel pour les remettre à leur place d'acteurs.

Après, évidemment, il y a l'écologie.

On doit parler aux grandes sociétés devenues morales afin que l'élaboration n'ait pas de nuisance pour l'homme, que l'objet ne soit pas une nuisance dans sa vie, en enlevant évidemment le gimmick marketing du recyclage... Le recyclage, inventé par les écologistes, est finalement ce qui permet de continuer aujourd'hui à produire et à consommer inutilement. Un bon produit est un produit qui dure : quand il a duré dix, vingt, trente ans, qu'il soit recyclable, recyclé, à la limite on s'en fout un petit peu. Mais recycler tous les ans des objets inutiles est une dépense de matière et d'énergie folle. Je ne suis pas contre le recyclage, je suis contre l'idée d'en faire une panacée universelle : le recyclage est un pansement, la réparation d'une erreur, pas autre chose. C'est une fausse solution, un faux problème, une tarte à la crème écologique comme il en existe beaucoup aujourd'hui – comme l'énergie électrique pour les voitures, qui n'est qu'un déplacement du tuyau d'échappement vers les centrales nucléaires. (...)

Vous parliez d'accessibilité des produits tout à l'heure : est-ce que c'est pour ça que vous travaillez, sur le catalogue Good Goods, avec Carrefour et La Redoute, parce qu'ils ont cette volonté de démocratiser les meilleurs produits ?

L'une des rares victoires de ma carrière est d'avoir anobli la multiplication, autrement dit d'avoir anobli le mot « populaire », anobli le mépris. Avant, une brosse à dents se cachait au fond d'un tiroir, et du jour au lendemain les gens se sont offert ça pour Noël et tout d'un coup on se le montrait. L'autre chose, c'est d'avoir rendu abordable, d'avoir cassé les prix : en une décennie, j'ai réussi, envers et contre tous, à presque casser le prix de mes objets par deux tous les ans ou tous les deux ans. L'un de mes premiers objets à succès, le siège du Café Costes, valait à l'époque dans les 4000 francs... Aujourd'hui on est sur des chaises à 300, peut-être même 200 francs. (...) On est même sur des réflexions, avec Vitra, sur la location ou sur la reprise du mobilier. Cela fait au moins 5–6 ans qu'on est dessus, le problème c'est qu'aujourd'hui on ne sait pas le faire. On ne sait pas comment obliger quelqu'un à ramener une chaise contre moins de 50 francs, qui sera bientôt le prix qu'il l'aura payée. (...) Ce propos-là est forcément du super mass-market, or les populations du super mass-market ne sont pas encore assez éduquées pour ça. Et il y a le problème du prix : combien vous louez une chaise qui vaut 50 francs ? Un franc par mois ? On s'aperçoit qu'on est dans quelques impasses. Donc il vaut mieux adopter un style, un non-style à l'épreuve du temps : prenez la petite chaise Dr No, qui est confortable, qui s'empile, qui est quasiment indestructible, avec justement le problème que cela représente, eh bien on va la garder vingt ans... et dans vingt ans, on va la retrouver au bout d'un jardin, quelqu'un va la ramasser et on ira la faire fondre. Mais c'est pas la peine de sortir une grosse machine de guerre pour l'instant, on n'a pas les moyens de le faire. La grande distribution, pour moi, est obligatoire. Good Goods est sorti en 1998 et, à la même époque, on a présenté au Japon l'opération Seven Eleven, qui a été l'une des plus grosses opérations de l'histoire du design, puisque cette chaîne de *convenient stores* ouverts 24h/24 (8000 au Japon, 30 000 sur l'Asie et je ne sais plus combien sur les USA) m'a en gros donné tous les objets de la boutique – yaourts, rasoirs, culottes, crayons, tout ce que vous voulez : c'est le plus gros donneur d'ordres du monde, alors ça permet de passer réellement, en vraie grandeur, au mieux pour tout le monde. On sait déjà que chaque objet va être édité à 10 millions de pièces chacun dans l'année, et ça permet... je ne crois pas qu'il y ait d'objet qui coûte plus que dix ou douze francs. C'est une claque définitive au design élitiste. Pour moi, c'est fondamental, c'est presque une finalité : après je ne vois pas ce que je vais pouvoir faire, sauf continuer, montrer qu'on peut faire des yaourts mieux, des culottes mieux...

Et Good Goods ?

C'est un projet qui me tient à cœur depuis des années, qui a été un travail gigantesque pendant deux ans, pour la première fois de ma vie je dirais même que je ne le regrette pas mais que, si c'était à faire je ne le referais pas, ça m'a coûté des fortunes de manque à gagner par le temps que ça m'a pris. J'essaie d'ouvrir une voie vers des objets honnêtes, des objets pour des non-consommateurs, des «rebelles modernes» qui en ont marre que le marketing et la pub essaient de leur faire croire qu'il faut absolument changer leur R5 pour une R6, leur télévision 4/3 pour une 16/9... Ces gens-là pour moi représentent une nouvelle force

politique non-dite. (...) C'est ça qui m'intéresse : ces non-consommateurs installant, à travers ce catalyseur qui est le catalogue, des règles que j'appelle le *moral market*, qui est à peu près ce qu'on vient de décrire. Les gens vont recevoir le catalogue, avec un petit mot de moi qui leur dit quelque chose d'assez révolutionnaire dans le monde du commerce, à savoir que ce n'est pas la peine qu'ils achètent les produits et qu'il est plus important de lire le catalogue entre les lignes. Dans Good Goods, il y a des produits qui sont intéressants, mais qui n'ont en aucun cas la prétention d'être des non-produits comme j'en ai l'ambition, ils sont simplement là pour amorcer la pompe. Et c'est important, chaque objet est un petit peu expliqué, hélas pas autant que je le voulais par manque de place : on essaie de faire comprendre pourquoi, et symétriquement de faire comprendre pourquoi pas, pourquoi pas l'autre, pourquoi on ne veut plus de l'autre.

Aujourd'hui vous utilisez votre notoriété pour faire passer ces messages-là... Pourtant dans le catalogue Good Goods, vous dites vouloir «corriger une histoire dont j'ai sûrement été moi-même complice». Est-ce que cela veut dire que les objets Starck du catalogue sont, par rapport à ces grilles de critères dont on a parlé, ceux que vous revendiquez plus que d'autres ?

Vous savez, j'ai toujours été le même, sur la même idée. Sauf qu'au début, quand on est jeune, on travaille pour soi, pour survivre, et on fait ce qu'on peut. Moi j'ai 49 ans aujourd'hui, j'ai les moyens, si je n'avais pas d'abord conceptualisé ma stratégie je serais un imbécile et si je ne la respectais pas je serais un malhonnête. Donc je reconnais que j'ai fait ce que j'ai pu, qu'il y a des hauts et des bas mais que j'ai toujours fait avec une certaine honnêteté ; maintenant je ne dis pas que c'est parfait, mais j'ai les moyens d'avoir plus de rigueur. Vous savez, l'important c'était d'abord d'exister, parce qu'il a fallu construire ce pouvoir. Quand on est un designer français... n'oublions pas que ça n'existe pas, un designer français !

Extrait d'une Conversation avec Sophie Tasma Anargyros, mars 1996, organisée par la VIA (Valorisation de l'Industrie de l'Ameublement).

Le mythe du progrès
L'idée de l'évolution du monde tourne autour de l'idée de progrès. L'invention de cette idée résume la différence entre l'homme et l'animal en ce sens qu'elle contient l'intention délibérée d'améliorer l'espèce.

Sinon, s'il ne tend pas vers l'inconnu, l'Homme estime qu'il n'a pas de réalité. Pour cristalliser cette idée, l'Homme a inventé un concept : celui de Dieu. Dieu est un modèle de progrès dans l'absolu, et en même temps un modèle ambigu. Inhumain par définition, et humain puisqu'il est une idée humaine. De cette distance infinie que l'Homme a mis entre lui et Dieu résulte ensuite un chemin inverse à parcourir : se rapprocher de Dieu. Cette idée extraordinairement motrice établit aussi une forme de rêve : à son image, devenir surpuissant, omniprésent, vaincre les mystères.

L'Homme atteint son modèle

Les moyens de ce devenir sont d'une part la matière, l'outil, d'autre part, l'intelligence, la connaissance. Peu à peu, l'Homme se rapproche du modèle, encore lentement jusqu'au XVIIIème siècle, puis dans un processus d'accélération aux XIX et XXème siècles. Le premier très grand pas : la création de la machine. Moment d'intense éblouissement, le début du XXème siècle jusqu'à aujourd'hui vit dans cet état d'admiration de la machine. Je note au passage qu'un mouvement inversement proportionnel se produit : l'idée de l'amélioration de la vie et par conséquent de l'égalité, de la liberté et de la fraternité n'est pas atteinte, au contraire, et le mot est faible. Et puis à l'aube du XXIème siècle, on voit poindre la possibilité d'atteindre le modèle, avec les outils qui se sont dématérialisés, les ordinateurs, qui apportent à l'Homme une capacité de connaissance incommensurable, avec internet ou ce que va devenir internet, qui va permettre une pensée commune, parallèle au système des pouvoirs qui en détenait jusqu'alors le contenu, et enfin la vitesse de déplacement. Déplacement des hommes dans l'espace, mais surtout déplacement de la pensée, c'est-à-dire l'immédiateté de la communication. Un peu plus loin, mais très proche cependant, on touche aujourd'hui avec la génétique à la création de la vie artificielle. Les morceaux du puzzle commencent à se rassembler et à figurer ce modèle projeté comme inaccessible. Demeure un problème de taille. Il semblerait que l'époque où tous ces fantasmes sont pratiquement devenus des réalités est aussi celle de la perte. En avançant sur ces chemins-là, l'Homme a perdu au passage ce qu'on peut appeler un idéal. Peut-être est-ce une des explications de la non-consommation. Les Hommes n'ont plus envie de consommer de la matière. La matière sans son double, l'idée, qui lui donne tout son sens, est un phénomène vidé de son contenu.

Le XXIème siècle sera immatériel et humain

L'immatérialité réelle – des microprocesseurs, de l'information, des processus quels qu'ils soient – doit, et c'est de toute urgence, être corollaire d'humain. Le XXIème siècle ne sera pas mystique, il sera immatériel et humain. S'il ne l'est pas, la déliquescence que nous connaissons aujourd'hui va continuer. Pour ce qui est de l'humain : il faut revenir à la source inconsciente de l'idée de progrès qui est l'amélioration de la vie pour chacun, le bonheur et l'épanouissement.

Je vais utiliser une image très simple pour illustrer cette idée : on arrive à un jour de l'An un peu particulier, une sorte de super jour de l'An, le jour de l'An du troisième millénaire. Tout le monde peut se souvenir de ce qui se passe le lendemain d'un jour de l'An. A chaque fois, chacun fait le bilan et se dit : je vais essayer d'être meilleur. C'est dans cette idée de « bonne résolution » que l'humanité peut passer le millénaire, ou alors s'y perdre. La priorité absolue est là : l'humain. Si l'Homme reste dans l'idée de la matière, c'est-à-dire de la possession de la matière, si le concept de matière n'est pas remplacé par celui d'amour, comment survivre dans un monde où l'Homme est devenu omniprésent, surpuissant et où les enjeux du pouvoir ne sont plus représentés matériellement ?

Progrès ou préhistoire ?

C'est la chose la plus grave. La chose la plus simple mais la plus grave. En plusieurs milliers d'années, l'Homme n'a pas réussi à acquérir l'amour. Il n'a acquis, et perdu, que de la matière. Si je réfléchis encore plus simplement : l'origine de l'amour réside dans ce qu'on appelle l'instinct maternel, qui n'est pas autre chose que le désir de protection de l'espèce. Et l'espèce est fragile. Si l'Homme perd la notion d'amour, au sens de l'espèce, on va revenir à une vitesse ahurissante aux temps de la préhistoire, où l'individu fonctionne, sans projet de civilisation, sans projet social. Je pense même que le plus grand danger, ce serait d'oublier jusqu'à l'existence même de l'amour. Pourquoi les sociétés les plus « confortables » sont-elles les plus suicidaires, c'est-à-dire coupées de l'instinct de survie ?

A mon sens un grand axe de réflexion pour tous ceux qui produisent, des objets, des signes et du sens, réside dans la prise de conscience de la désincarnation déjà matière au profit de l'humain et de sa plus belle invention, l'Amour. Les producteurs doivent impérativement réfléchir au non-objet de demain.

Le non-objet

L'Homme de demain, qui est-ce ? Je vais essayer de le décrire. On est déjà dans le monde de l'intelligence artificielle et on va arriver très vite aux ordinateurs biologiques et aux jonctions neuronales. Même la mort recule. Dans assez peu de temps, l'Homme va se trouver face à lui-même. Transcendé. Avec les ordinateurs biologiques, on est dans la disparition de la matière, la disparition des objets. Jusqu'à présent, on a produit et affiné la structure, la forme et la fonction des objets. Chez Thomson, on étudie déjà des commandes visuelles et mentales. Il n'y a plus de liaisons entre le geste et l'objet. La commande se fait directement de la pensée à l'agi.

On traverse le miroir parce que tout le système de représentation de l'Homme au travers des objets va disparaître. L'Homme de demain sera nu (c'est une image), sans interférence de la matière entre lui et le monde, inscrit dans un biorythme, doué d'une puissance presque infinie. Tous les services résideront dans un acte de parole et de pensée.

Il pourra communiquer avec le monde entier. Sur une question qu'il se pose, il se connecte en quelques secondes sur le réseau et il dispose de millions de réponses immédiates. Quand on sait que plus la connaissance avance, plus la violence recule, on peut considérer qu'à l'impérative condition d'une construction de civilisation, la communication sera un facteur de paix mondiale. Il deviendra difficile de diriger un conflit, parce que les hommes auront la possibilité de vérifier l'information. Les grands mensonges ne seront plus possibles ou alors le mensonge sera total, ce sera le règne de la manipulation, du chaos et de la contre-information. Internet, entre autres, doit devenir un outil de paix et d'auto-contrôle. Dans ce schéma, l'Homme devient son propre territoire. Il cesse de vouloir conquérir de la terre, qui est la cause des guerres depuis la nuit des temps – parce que son pouvoir ne se joue plus sur des questions de territoires et de frontières. D'ailleurs, la notion de frontières va se poser en des termes nouveaux. L'Homme n'utilisera presque plus son territoire réel parce qu'il va vivre dans un territoire virtuel, qui va se construire, se codifier, se réglementer comme un vrai territoire. Il suffira de se connecter pour avoir accès à la présence de l'autre, son image, sa pensée, sa connaissance.

La maison de demain

La maison de l'Homme de demain se réduira à une enveloppe vide : la régulation thermique viendra du sol, la lumière sera de l'électro-luminescence par des vitres à cristaux liquides, le son et l'image viendront des murs. L'Homme deviendra un être affectif. Il devra produire lui-même son système de signes. Dans cet espace, on assiste à une dissociation totale entre les fonctions-services et le sens.

Ce sera le règne du poétique. Les signes, délivrés de toute notion de fonction, atteignent leur plus haut niveau de pureté et d'efficacité, et en ce sens, relèvent de l'art, tandis que le corps, paradoxalement, redevient naturel, délivré de tous les objets qui s'interposent entre lui et ses actes.

Bien sûr, le corollaire d'un tel usage d'outils de communication pour une grande part intégrés au corps, réside dans la confusion entre réel et virtuel, et le danger psychique, dans le désir de désincarnation.

Dans ce scénario, les gens ne se déplacent plus. Le métier de décorateur devient celui d'un programmateur d'images. Chacun s'invente une apparence avec l'image de synthèse. Les moyens de locomotion décroissant, les routes redeviennent des chemins. La logique ville-périphérie s'inverse. La ville n'est plus le centre puisqu'il n'est plus nécessaire d'incarner les actes dans la cité, lieu de concentration périmé des pouvoirs. Hors des villes les tribus puissantes. Dans la ville les exclus. La ville devient le lieu du chaos.

La violence : qui pense le futur ?

La dictature vient de ceux qui détiennent les voies de communication. Ils détiennent un droit de vie ou de mort puisque l'économie des sociétés est basée sur un système d'échange virtuel. Il suffit de désabonner pour faire disparaître. Il n'y pas de violence. La violence comme atteinte directe à l'intégrité physique est remplacée par la dispari-

tion, l'oubli, plus que l'indifférence : l'ignorance. (Nous connaissons déjà ce phénomène sous une autre forme, une espèce d'anesthésie totale qui fait que nous pouvons discuter tranquillement ici, dans mon bureau, tandis qu'en Bosnie, en Tchétchénie au Rwanda et ailleurs, se perpètrent des massacres, dans la même gratuité et la même indifférence que si nous vivions au XVème siècle, sans le savoir, et sans avoir élaboré des concepts comme la démocratie ou les droits de l'Homme).

Tout ceci (hormis malheureusement ma dernière remarque), n'est qu'une hypothèse. Mais elle permet de voir combien nous manquons d'outils de réflexion, combien cette société nouvelle qui arrive, et elle arrive déjà maintenant, on peut en lire les signes avant-coureurs, présage de temps sombres si les hommes ne se préoccupent pas de toute urgence des problèmes philosophiques et politiques qu'elle annonce.

L'Homme est un mutant

Cette hypothèse met en évidence une chose que l'homme a beaucoup de mal à accepter, qui est son essence mutante. Si on regarde les choses en millions d'années, on voit qu'on a commencé bactéries puis batraciens animaux avant de devenir hommes. En revanche, ce qui se passe aujourd'hui va aller beaucoup plus vite. Les spécialistes de marketing et de consommation connaissent bien ce phénomène d'attachement aux formes anciennes. Une grande partie de la production alimentaire n'est plus le résultat d'un processus dit « naturel », mais on continue d'injecter des colorants pour qu'elle ressemble à celle de nos grands-parents. Ce phénomène se vérifie dans beaucoup de domaines, et les designers sont forcément et constamment confrontés à ce décalage entre la réalité et l'image. La réalité de la production ou des mécanismes et leur apparence, c'est-à-dire leurs signes.

Survie ou civilisation ?

Il y aura donc une longue période de transition, de traduction et d'adaptation. Mais il faut regarder les choses en face. Les problèmes du XXIème siècle, on le sait très bien, vont être des problèmes de survie. Aujourd'hui, et déjà par le fait de l'information immédiate, l'Occident a assisté sans bouger au génocide dans l'ex-Yougoslavie. Pourquoi ? Pour des raisons économiques, évidemment. On ne peut plus dire aujourd'hui comme on l'a dit pour l'Holocauste qu'on « ne savait pas ». L'Occident est aussi en train d'abandonner l'Afrique. Si on ne s'occupe pas de l'Afrique, c'est un continent entier qui va disparaître. La famine de 2020 est déjà annoncée. Aujourd'hui, en ce moment même, il y a 800 millions de gens sous-alimentés. Comment ceux qui agissent au nom des économies peuvent-ils ignorer que l'équilibre est aujourd'hui mondial ? Que toutes les mutations dont nous venons de parler vont totalement modifier les enjeux ? Que nous devons être solidaires à l'échelle mondiale ? Et quand bien même ne serait-ce pas pour des raisons morales, ou de civilisation, pour des raisons de maintien de l'espèce humaine ? Personne ne recolle les morceaux de cet immense puzzle. Il n'y a pas de vision globale. Pas de propositions. Nous vivons une époque de non-conscience, sans vision ni projet.

Je suis essentiellement obsédé par ça. Et à ma toute petite échelle, j'essaie de réfléchir. Mais tout le monde doit absolument réfléchir, s'interroger sur la vie, sur l'argent, sur le désir, sur la guerre, sur soi-même.

Le métier de designer est un des métiers qui touchent de très près à ces évolutions et il peut, il doit participer à la recherche du sens, à la reconstruction d'un monde civilisé.

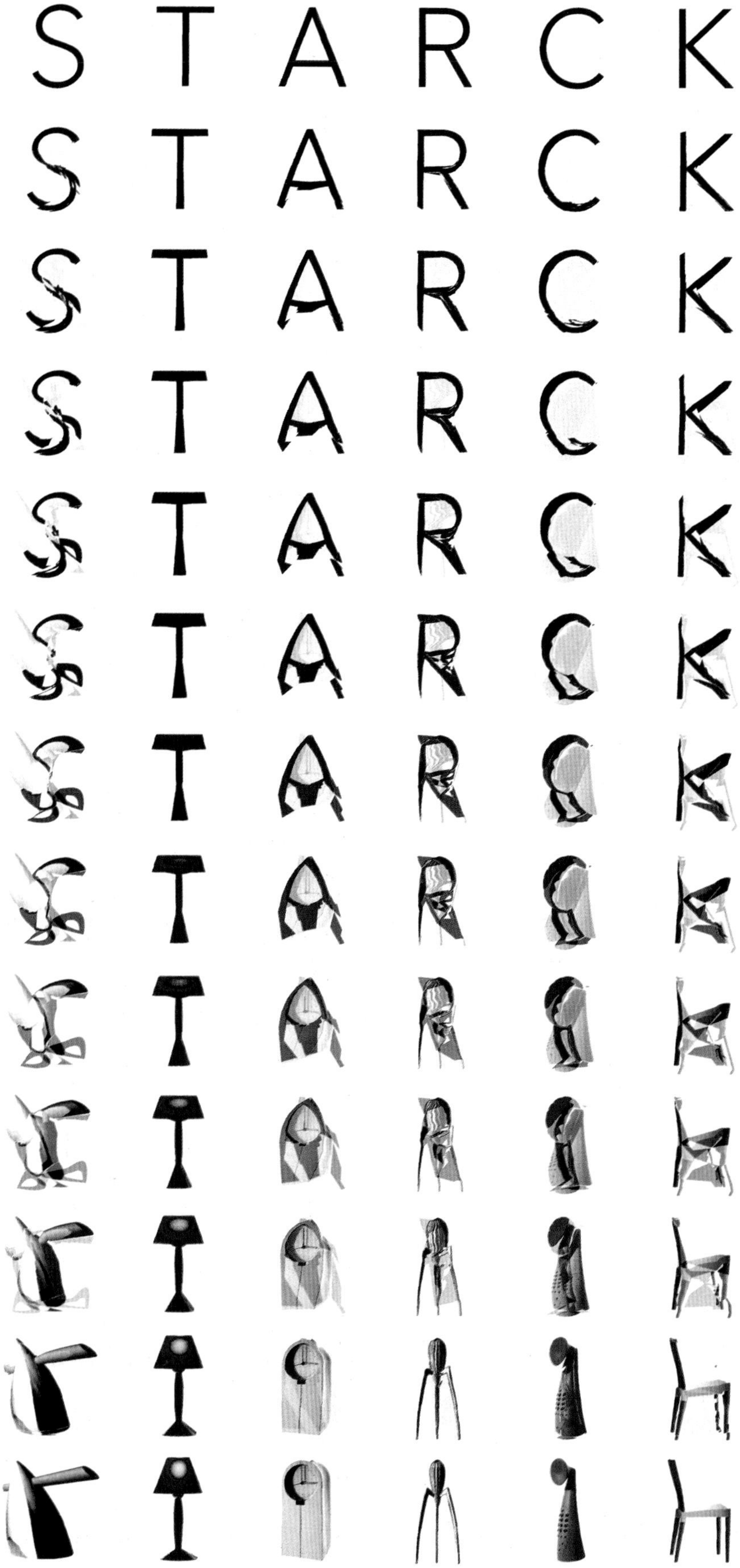
S T A R C K

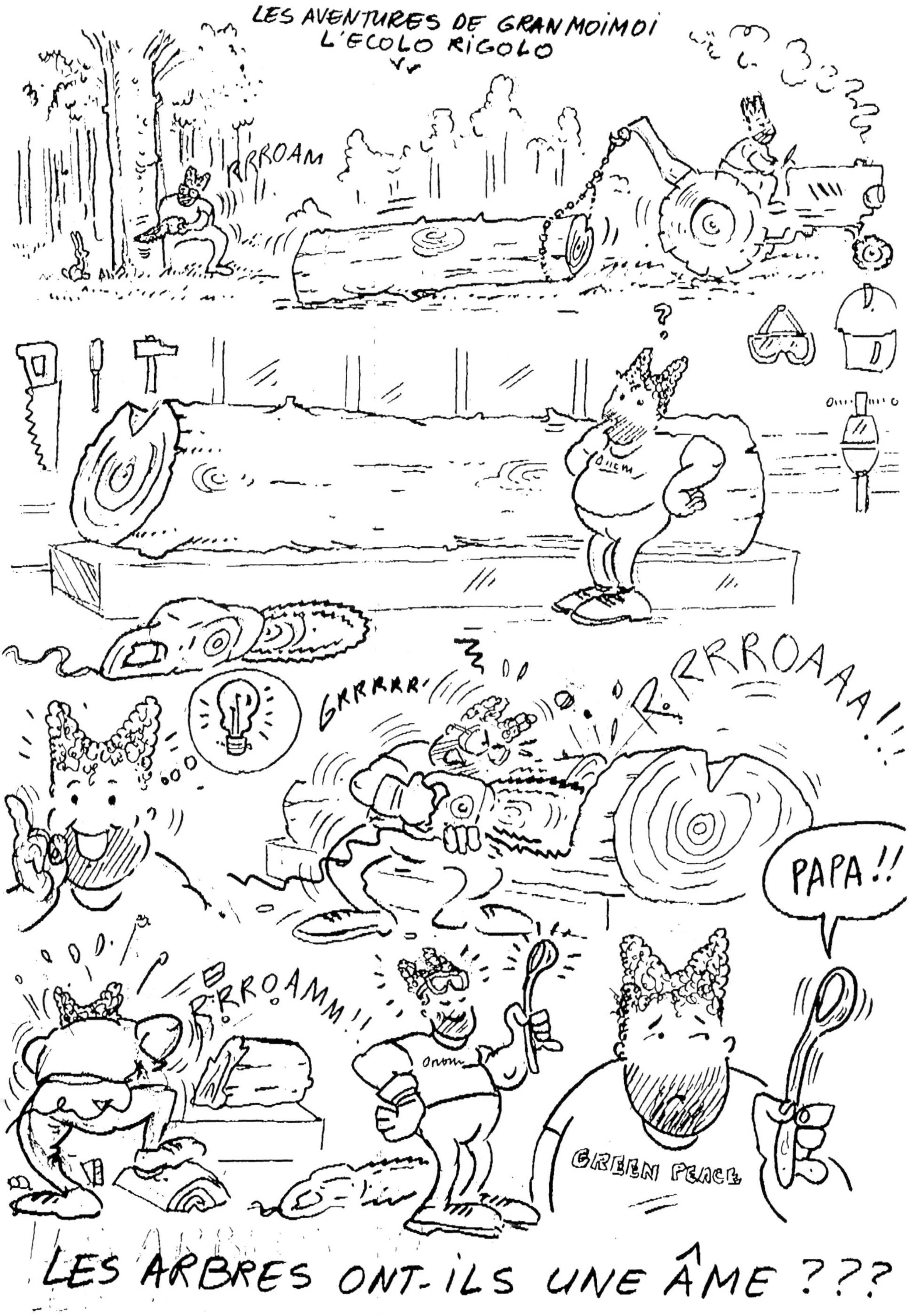

LES AVENTURES DE GRANMOIMOI
L'ECOLO RIGOLO
RRROAM
?
GRRRRR
RRRRROAAA!!
PAPA!!
RRROAMM!!
GREEN PEACE
LES ARBRES ONT-ILS UNE ÂME ???

12 Architecture

68 Interiors

152 Furniture

228 Industrial Design

392 Magma

400 Words

422 Overview

446 A–Z

"I must be photographed with the chair..." | »Man muß mich mit dem Stuhl fotografieren,...« | « ...il faut me photographier avec la chaise...»
Photo: Malick Sidibé

Photo: Gueorgui Pinkhassov/Magnum

"...with my radio..." | »...mit meinem Radio...« | « ...avec mon poste radio... »
Photo: Malick Sidibé

Starck & Ara Starck

"...doing the twist." | »...Twist tanzend.« | « ...en position de twist. »
Photo: Malick Sidibé

Ganesh by | von | par Jean-Baptiste Mondino

Larousse
Page | Seite 1636

Architecture
Architektur

Starck House (3 Suisses) 1994
Timber House | Holzhaus | Maison en bois
Mail order sale | Versandhausverkauf | Vente par correspondance
3 Suisses
Photo: Jacques Dirand

Philippe Starck and inflatable structure | und aufblasbares Objekt | et structure gonflable
1969

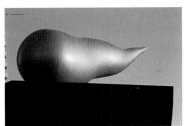

Asahi Beer Hall 1990
Azumabashi 1-25-4-79, Sunida-Ku, Tokyo 150, Japan

Asahi breweries | Asahi Brauerei | Brasserie Asahi

The flame on the roof | Die Flamme auf dem Dach | La flamme sur le toit

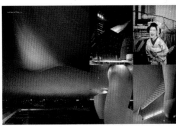

Asahi Beer Hall 1990
Detail of the flame | Detail der Flamme | Détail de la flamme

View of the building at night | Außenansicht bei Nacht | Vue d'ensemble la nuit
Geisha in front of the building | Geisha vor dem Gebäude | Geisha devant le bâtiment
Detail of a column | Detail einer Säule | Détail d'un pilier
White marble staircase | Treppe aus weißem Marmor | Escalier en marbre blanc
Photos: Alberto Venzago/ Nacása & Partners Inc.

Le Baron Vert 1992
Yanimachi 9-5-1, Chuo-Ku, Osaka, Japan

Office building | Bürogebäude | Immeuble de bureaux

View of the building (rear) | Gebäudeansicht (Rückseite) | Vue du bâtiment (face arrière)
Detail of the building | Gebäudedetail | Détail du bâtiment
View of the building (front) | Gebäudeansicht (Vorderseite) | Vue du bâtiment (face avant)
Photos: Hiroyuki Hirai/ Nacása & Partners Inc.

Nani Nani 1989
Shirokane Dai 4-273-42, Minato-Ku, Tokyo, Japan

Biomorphic building with a floor area of 959 m², including restaurant, showroom and offices in the centre of Tokyo, for the Rikugo group of companies | Biomorphes Gebäude von 959 m² Grundfläche mit Restaurant, Aus-

stellungsraum und Büros im Zentrum von Tokio im Auftrag des Rikugo-Konzerns | Immeuble biomorphique d'une surface-plancher de 959 m² comprenant un restaurant, un show-room et des bureaux dans le centre de Tokyo pour le compte du groupe Rikugo
Photos: T. Waki, Shokokusha Ou/Shigro Ogawa, Shinkenchi

Formentera House 1995
Formentera, Spain

Private house | Privathaus | Maison particulière

Formentera House 1995

Private house | Privathaus |
Maison particulière

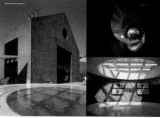

titres tracasseries administratives, un carnet de notes
vierge pour noter ses propres
expériences, un marteau,
symbole de l'intervention personnelle dans la maison, un
drapeau français pour le faîte
de la maison. Les plans de la
maison, qui peuvent être per-
sonnalisés, ont été réalisés
par Patrick Bouchain, concep-
teur et par L. Juliene et J. M.

Mandon, architectes. Il faut
bien évidemment faire appel
à des spécialistes pour con-
crétiser le projet, obtenir les
autorisations administratives
et adapter le projet au terrain
et à l'environnement régional.
3 Suisses
Photos: Jacques Dirand

Placido Arango Jr. House 1996
Madrid, Spain

Private house | Privathaus |
Maison particulière
Exterior | Außenansicht |
Extérieur

Staircase | Treppenhaus |
Escalier
Swimming pool | Swimming-
pool | Piscine
Photos: Cuauhtli Gutierrez

Citizenship is avant-garde

Zivilcourage ist avantgardistisch

Le civisme est d'avant-garde

Starck House (3 Suisses) 1994
Timber House | Holzhaus |
Maison en bois
Mail order sale | Versand-
hausverkauf | Vente par cor-
respondance
Starck House kit | Bausatz für
das Starck-Haus | Le coffret
de la maison Starck

The wooden box contains the
general plan of the house and
its components on a scale of
1:50, with and without canopy,
with additional 150 m² floor
space (ground floor, first
floor, roof, two sections and
all four façades), detailed
plans on a scale of 1:50 for the
ground woodwork, principles
of woodworking (beams and
joists, insulation, flooring and
parquet), roofing woodwork,
exterior construction work
(windows on the four façades
and plans for electrical wiring,
heating and plumbing), a site
checklist, a video showing the
various stages of construction, commented by Philippe
Starck, a step-by-step site

management notebook, a
blank notebook for the client's own comments, a hammer to symbolize the labour
of building a house and a
French flag for the topping
out ceremony.
The plans for the house,
which can be customized,
were drawn up by designer
Patrick Bouchain and archi-
tects L. Juliene and J. M. Mandon. Needless to say, imple-
mentation of the project calls
for skilled workers, official
planning permission and
adaptation to the site and
local conditions |
Der Holzkoffer enthält die
Konstruktionspläne und Bau-
teile im Maßstab 1:50, mit
oder ohne zusätzlicher 150 m²
großer überdachter Veranda
(Erdgeschoß, erster Stock,
Dach; zwei Schnitte und vier
Fassaden), die detaillierten
Pläne im Maßstab 1:50 für die
Gerüstverankerung im Boden,
die wichtigsten Holzarbeiten
(Wand- und Deckenbalken,
Isolierung, Fußböden und Par-

kett), Dachdeckarbeiten,
äußere Konstruktionsarbeiten
(Fenster an den vier Fassaden, Schaltpläne für Strom,
Heizungs- und Wasserrohre),
eine Baumappe, eine Video-
kassette, auf der Philippe Starck die einzelnen Bauab-
schnitte des Hauses kom-
mentiert, ein Notizheft, in
dem die Entstehung und Ent-
wicklung des Projekts, die
Wahl des Ortes und die kleinen Schikanen der Behörden
festgehalten sind, ein leeres
Notizbuch für die Nieder-
schrift der eigenen Erfahrun-
gen, einen Hammer als Sym-
bol für den persönlichen Einsatz beim Hausbau und eine
französische Nationalflagge
für den Dachfirst. Die Pläne
für das Haus, die noch indivi-
duell geändert werden können, wurden von dem Desi-
gner Patrick Bouchain und
den Architekten L. Juliene und
J. M. Mandon ausgearbeitet.
Natürlich müssen Fachleute
mit der Verwirklichung des
Projekts, der Einholung be-

hördlicher Genehmigungen
und seiner Anpassung an die
örtlichen Voraussetzungen
und die landschaftliche Um-
gebung beauftragt werden |
Ce coffret en bois contient les
plans généraux au 1/50 de la
maison dans les formules,
avec ou sans auvent, d'une
surface de 150 m² supplé-
mentaire (rez-de-chaussée,
étage, toiture, 2 coupes et élé-
vation des 4 façades), les
plans spécifiques au 1/50 de
l'implantation de la charpente
au sol, les principes de charpente (poutres, solivages, iso-
lants, plancher et parquet), la
charpente toiture-couverture,
les menuiseries extérieures
(fenêtres des 4 façades et les
schémas de principe pour
l'électricité, le chauffage et la
plomberie), un classeur de
chantier, une vidéo montrant
les étapes de la construction
de la maison commentée par
Philippe Starck, le carnet de
notes qui explique les étapes
de la gestation du projet, le
choix de l'endroit et les pe-

Le Moult House 1985–1987
29, rue Pierre Poli, 92130 Issy-
les-Moulineaux, France

Private house | Privathaus |
Maison particulière
On a Parisian island in the
Seine, not Saint-Louis but
Saint-Germain, near the for-
mer Renault factory, Philippe
Starck has undertaken the de-
sign of a house of remarkable
proportions: 5.6 m wide and
70 m long | Auf einer Pariser
Seine-Insel – nicht Saint-
Louis, sondern Saint-Germain

– unweit der früheren
Renault-Werke hat Philippe
Starck ein Haus von unge-
wöhnlichen Dimensionen ge-
baut: 5,60 m breit und 70 m
lang | Sur une île parisienne
de la Seine, non pas Saint-
Louis mais Saint-Germain,
près de l'ancienne usine
Renault, Philippe Starck a
aménagé une maison aux
dimensions surprenantes :
5,6 m de large x 70 m long
View of the house | Ansicht
des Hauses | Vue de la mai-
son

Le Moult House 1985–1987

View at night | Ansicht bei
Nacht | Vue la nuit

Pamela and | und | et Bruno
Le Moult
Staircase | Treppe | Escalier
Office | Büro | Bureau

Groningen Museum 1993
Museumeiland 1, Postbus 90,
9700 ME Groningen, The
Netherlands

Museum of Modern Art |
Museum für Moderne Kunst |
Musée d'art moderne
Architects | Architekten | Ar-
chitectes : P. Starck, A. Mendini, Coop Himmelblau,
M. De Lucchi

Exterior | Außenansicht | Ex-
térieur
Exhibition room | Austel-
lungsraum | Salle d'exposi-
tion
*Photos: Ralph Richter/Archi-
tekturphoto*

**Manifesto by | Manifest von |
Manifeste de Philippe Starck**
1982

roningen Museum 1993
xhibition room with globe |
ustellungsraum mit Weltku-
el | Salle d'exposition avec
obe terrestre
*hoto: Ralph Richter/Archi-
kturphoto*

Laguiole factory 1987
Z.A. Route d' Aubrac,
12210 Laguiole, France

Cutlery factory at Laguiole |
Messerfabrik in Laguiole |
Coutellerie à Laguiole

Star's Door 1992
Parc de Bercy, Paris, France
Drawings | Entwurfszeichnun-
gen | Dessins de projet

We must mutate

Wir müssen mutieren

Mutons

Tour de Contrôle 1993
Control tower for the Bor-
deaux-Mérignac airport | Kon-
trollturm für den Flughafen
Bordeaux-Mérignac | Tour de

contrôle de l'aéroport de
Bordeaux-Mérignac
Competition entry in cooper-
ation with Luc Arsène-Henry Jr. |
Wettbewerbsentwurf mit Luc
Arsène-Henry Jr. | Projet de
concours en collaboration avec
Luc Arsène-Henry Jr.
Layouts, sections, elevations |
Grundrisse, Schnitte, Aufrisse |
Plans, coupes, vues

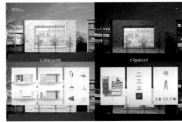

oondog (project) 1990
partment building design
t the Rikugo group of com-
anies, Tokyo | Entwurf eines
ohngebäudes für den
kugo-Konzern, Tokio | Ma-
uette pour un immeuble
habitation pour le compte
u groupe Rikugo, Tokyo

Computer graphics | Compu-
tergrafiken | Infographies

Maison de France, Venice 1990
Design for the French pavilion
at the Venice Biennale | Ent-
wurf für den Pavillon Frank-
reichs auf der Biennale in Ve-
nedig | Maquette du pavillon de
France à la Biennale de Venise
Model, east façade with open
door | Modell, Ostfassade mit
geöffneter Tür | Maquette, vue
façade est porte ouverte
Model, west and north façades

with open doors | Modell,
West- und Nordfassade mit ge-
öffneten Türen | Maquette, vue
façade ouest et nord portes
ouvertes
Bronze model | Bronzemodell |
Maquette en bronze

Vitry 2001
Incineration plant | Müllver-
brennungsanlage | Usine
d'incinération des déchets
Drawings | Entwurfszeichnun-
gen | Dessins de projet
Reproductions: Hervé Ternisien

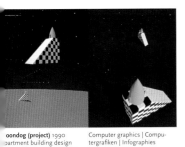

ole des Beaux-Arts 1991
ompetition entry for the de-
gn of the Ecole des Beaux-
ts of Paris city in cooperation
th Luc Arsène-Henry Jr. |
ettbewerb für den Bau der
ochschule für bildende Kün-
e der Stadt Paris in Zusam-
enarbeit mit Luc Arsène-
enry Jr. | Concours pour la
nstruction de l'Ecole des
eaux-Arts de la ville de Paris
collaboration avec Luc
sène-Henry Jr.
çade design | Entwurf der
ssade | Dessin de la façade

Floor plans and section of the
second building | Grundrisse
und Schnitt des zweiten Ge-
bäudes | Plans et coupe du
second bâtiment
Façades, ground floor plan
and section | Fassaden,
Grundriß des Erdgeschosses
und Schnitt | Façades, plan du
rez-de-chaussée et coupe
Floor plan and section of the
first building | Grundrisse und
Schnitt des ersten Gebäudes |
Plans et coupe du premier
bâtiment
Perspectival view and façades |
Perspektivische Gesamtan-
sicht und Fassaden | Vue de
l'ensemble et des façades en
perspective

**ENSAD
(Ecole Nationale Supérieure
des Arts décoratifs)** 1993
rue d'Ulm, Paris, France

Competition entry for rede-
signing the school in cooperation with Luc Arsène-Henry
Jr. | Wettbewerbsentwurf für
die Neugestaltung der Hoch-
schule in Zusammenarbeit mit
Luc Arsène-Henry Jr. | Con-

cours pour redessiner l'école en
collaboration avec Luc Arsène-
Henry Jr.
*Computer graphics | Computer-
grafiken | Infographies: DEIS*

Darkness grows

Die Dunkelheit verdichtet sich

L'obscurité s'épaissit

ENSAD 1998
Façade in the evening |
Fassade am Abend | Façade le
soir
Photo: Jean-Marie Monthiers

ENSAD 1998
Façade in the daytime |
Fassade bei Tag | Façade le jour

Washbasin | Waschbecken |
Lavabo
Corridor | Korridor | Couloir
Studio | Werkstatt | Atelier
Staircase | Treppenhaus |
Escalier
Photos: Jean-Marie Monthiers

Rue Starck (project) 1991
rue Pierre Poli, 92130 Issy-les-
Moulineaux, France
Drawing | Zeichnung | Dessin

Starck House (project) 1991
Drawing | Zeichnung | Dessin

**Condominiums (project), Los
Angeles** 1992
Drawing | Zeichnung | Dessin

**Condominiums (project), Los
Angeles** 1992
Drawing | Zeichnung | Dessin

Angle (project), Antwerp 1991
Façade design | Fassadenent-
wurf | Projet de façade
Reproductions: Hervé Ternisien

Philippe Starck, Hans Hollein and others | und andere | et autres

Interiors
Innenarchitektur
Intérieurs

Café Costes 1984 (closed | geschlossen | fermé en 1994) 4-6, rue Berger, place des Innocents, Paris, France
Photo: Jacques Dirand

Les Bains-Douches 1978 7, rue du Bourg-l'Abbé, Paris, France

Nightclub | Nachtklub | Night-club
Photo: Anthony Oliver

La Main Bleue 1976 Centre Commercial de la Mairie de Montreuil, 93100 Montreuil

Nightclub | Nachtklub | Night-club

François Mitterrand 1991
Photo: Leo Erken/Agence Vu

Palais de l'Elysée 1983–1984 55-56, rue du Faubourg-St-Honoré, Paris, France

President's apartment | Präsidentenwohnung | Appartement présidentiel

Café Costes 1984 (closed | geschlossen | fermé en 1994) 4-6, rue Berger, place des Innocents, Paris, France

View of the stairs | Blick auf die Treppe | Vue sur l'escalier
Photo: Stéphane Couturier

Row of chairs | Stuhlreihe | Rangée de chaises
Photo: Guy Bouchet

Waiter | Ober | Garçon Gallery | Galerie
Photos: Jaques Dirand

Café Costes 1984 Outside the café | Vor dem Café | Devant le café Detail | Détail Costes Logo | Logo des Café Costes | Logo du Café Costes

First floor | Erster Stock | Premier étage
Photos: Jacques Dirand

Royalton Hotel 1988 44 West 44th Street, New York 10036, NY, USA

Candleholder | Kerzenhalter | Chandelier
Ian Schrager Hotels

Royalton Hotel 1988 Corridor | Korridor | Couloir Lobby | Eingangshalle | Hall d'entrée

Candleholder | Kerzenhalter | Chandelier
Washbasin in a hotel bathroom | Waschbecken im Bad eines Hotelzimmers | Lavabo dans la salle de bains d'une chambre de l'hôtel
Entrance | Eingang | Entrée
Ian Schrager Hotels
Photos: Tom Vack

Royalton Hotel 1988 Lobby | Eingangshalle | Hall d'entrée

Vase in the lobby | Vase in der Eingangshalle | Vase dans le hall d'entrée
Restaurant
Lobby | Eingangshalle | Hall d'entrée
Ian Schrager Hotels
Photos: Tom Vack

Paramount Hotel 1990 235 West 46th Street, New York 10036, NY, USA

Entrance (detail) | Eingangsbereich (Detail) | Entrée (détail) Cladding (detail) | Eckschoner (Detail) | Protège-coin (détail) Staircase in the lobby | Treppe in der Eingangshalle | Escaliers dans le hall d'entrée Lounge chair in the lobby by

Marc Newson | Stuhl in der Eingangshalle von Marc Newson | Chaise dans le hall d'entrée, par Marc Newson Protective cladding, matt-finish cast aluminium | Eckschoner, mattiertes Gußaluminium | Protège-coin, aluminium coulé dépoli
Ian Schrager Hotels
Photos: Tom Vack

Paramount Hotel 1990 Distorting mirror in the lobby | Vexierspiegel in der Eingangshalle | Miroir déformant dans le hall d'entrée Mahogany postcard display in the lobby | Postkartenständer aus Mahagoni in der Eingangshalle | Présentoir de cartes postales en acajou dans le hall d'entrée

Public toilets | Öffentliche Toiletten | Toilettes publiques Weather forecast in the lift lobby | Wettervorhersage in der Fahrstuhlhalle | Prévisions météorologiques dans l'ascenseur Washbasin | Waschbecken | Lavabo
Ian Schrager Hotels
Photos: Tom Vack

ra 1997

Fax from Ara to Philippe
Starck | Fax von Ara an
Phlilippe Starck | Fax d'Ara
pour Philippe Starck 1999

Hotel Mondrian 1996
8440 Sunset Boulevard, West
Hollywood CA 90069, USA

Lobby | Eingangshalle | Hall
d'entrée
Ian Schrager Hotels
Photo: Todd Eberle

Drawing by | Zeichnung von |
Dessin par Jean-Baptiste
Mondino

Hotel Mondrian 1996
Terrace | Terrasse
Photo: Todd Eberle

Ian Schrager and | und | et
Philippe Starck, 1996

Lift lobby | Blick auf die
Fahrstühle | Ascenseurs
Room | Zimmer | Chambre
Cocopazzo
Ian Schrager Hotels
Photos: Todd Eberle

otel St Martins Lane 1999
 St Martins Lane, London
 2N 4HX, Great Britain

obby | Eingangshalle | Hall
 entrée
ght Bar | Licht-Bar | Bar lu-
ière

Philippe Starck and | und | et
Ian Schrager
Photo: Jean-Baptiste Mondino

Fish Bar | Fisch-Bar | Bar à
poissons
Asia de Cuba restaurant | Asia
de Cuba-Restaurant | Restau-
rant Asia de Cuba
Ian Schrager Hotels

Photos: Richard Davies

Starck Club 1982
703 McKinney, Dallas,
Texas 75202, USA

Nightclub | Nachtklub |
Night-club
Photo: Anthony Oliver

Photo: André Kertész

**Love is an endangered
species**

**Die Liebe ist eine vom
Aussterben bedrohte Art**

**L'amour est une espèce
en voie de disparition**

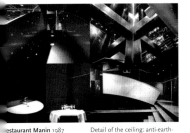

estaurant Manin 1987
22-12 Jingudae, Shibuya-Ku,
kyo, Japan

ntrance (detail) | Eingang
etail) | Entrée (détail)
ashroom (detail) | Wasch-
um (Detail) | Lavabo (détail)
ble in the restaurant | Tisch
 Restaurant | Table dans le
staurant

Detail of the ceiling: anti-earth-
quake system | Deckendetail:
Sicherheitskonstruktion gegen
Erdbebenerschütterung | Détail
du plafond : Dispositif de sécurité contre les secousses
sismiques
Bridge to the underground res-
taurant | Brücke zu dem unter-
irdisch gelegenen Restaurant |
Passerelle conduisant au restaurant souterrain

Boutique Hugo Boss 1991
2, place des Victoires, Paris,
France

Drawer handle | Schubladen-
griff | Poignée de tiroir
Photo: Jacques Dirand

Boutique Hugo Boss 1991
Staircase | Treppe | Escalier

Table in the shop | Tisch im
Laden | Table dans la boutique
Shop Interior | Inneneinrich-
tung | Intérieur
Staircase | Treppe | Escalier
Photos: Jacques Dirand

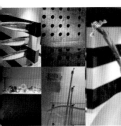

uzzle 1987
e Princesse et rue Balzac,
aris, France

eneral store, snack bar and
ghtclub | Lebensmittella-
en, Imbiß und Nachtklub |
picerie, snack-bar et night-
ub

Interiors (details) | Innen-
raumdetails | Intérieurs
(détails)
Wire flower holder | Blumen-
halter aus Draht | Porte-fleurs
en fil de fer

Salon Coppola 1992
Corso Garibaldi 110, Milan,
Italy

Hairdressing salon | Friseur-
salon | Salon de coiffure
Entrance stairs | Eingangs-
treppe | Escalier d'entrée

Interior | Innenraum | Intérieur
Detail | Détail
Entrance | Eingang | Entrée

We are God

Wir sind Gott

Nous sommes Dieu

Restaurant Teatriz 1990
Hermosilla 15, Madrid, Spain

WC door (details) | WC-Tür
(Details) | Porte des W.C.
(détails)

Restaurant Teatriz 1990
Pillar in the entrance hall |
Säule in der Eingangshalle |
Pilier dans le hall d'entrée

Corridor leading to toilets |
Gang zu den Toiletten | Cou-
loir menant aux toilettes
Washbasin | Waschbecken |
Lavabo
Corridor with illuminated wall
panelling | Korridor mit be-
leuchteten Wandtafeln | Cou-
loir avec tableaux muraux
éclairés
Interior | Innenraum | Intérieur
Photos: Jordi Sarra

Restaurant Teatriz 1990
Bar (detail | Detail | détail)
Ceiling decoration | Decken-
gestaltung | Décoration du
plafond
Floor design, based on a pain-
ting by Giorgio de Chirico |
Fußbodengestaltung nach einem Gemälde von Giorgio de
Chirico | Décoration du plan-
cher d'après un tableau de
Giorgio de Chirico

View of the restaurant | Blick
in das Restaurant | Vue du
restaurant
View of the bar, luminous onyx
before a large mirror | Blick
auf die Bar mit beleuchtetem
Onyx vor einem großem Spie-
gel | Vue du bar, avec onyx il-
luminé de l'intérieur et placé
devant une grande glace

Restaurant Teatriz 1990
View from the restaurant into
the bar | Blick vom Restaurant
auf die Bar | Vue du restaurant
sur le bar

Floor in the basement (detail) |
Fußboden im Untergeschoß
(Detail) | Plancher du salon au
sous-sol (détail)
Detail | Détail

Café Mystique 1988
6-27-8 Jingumae, Shibuja-Ku,
Tokyo, Japan

Detail of the wall | Wanddetail |
Détail du mur
Entrance | Eingang | Entrée

Detail | Détail
View of the restaurant | Blick
in das Restaurant | Vue du
restaurant

La Cigale 1988
120, bd. Rochechouart,
75018 Paris, France

Concert Hall | Konzertsaal |
Salle de concert
Entrance | Eingang | Entrée
Seating (detail) | Sitze (De-
tail) | Sièges (détail)

Ceiling in the Concert Hall
(detail) | Decke im Konzert-
saal (Detail) | Plafond de la
salle de concert (détail)
Entrance | Eingang | Entrée

Restaurant Theatron 1985
Paseo de la Reforma, 50 Calle
Bosques de Chapultepec,
11560 Mexico City DF, Mexico

Entrance | Eingang | Entrée
Photo: Stéphane Couturier

Restaurant Theatron 1985
Staircase | Treppe | Escalier
Entrance | Eingang | Entrée
Washbasin in the toilets |
Waschbecken in den Toiletten |
Lavabo dans les toilettes

Staircase | Treppe | Escalier
Disco 'Crazy Box'
View of the restaurant | Blick
in das Restaurant | Vue du
restaurant
Photos: Stéphane Couturier

Restaurant Theatron 1985
Entrance | Eingang | Entrée
Photo: Stéphane Couturier

Delano Hotel 1995
1685 Collins Avenue, 33139
Miami Beach, Florida, USA

Lobby | Eingangshalle | Hall
d'entrée
Ian Schrager Hotels

Delano Hotel 1995
Public phone | Öffentlicher
Fernsprecher | Cabine télé-
phonique

Fitness centre | Fitneßcenter |
Centre de mise en forme
View of the exterior | Außen-
ansicht | Vue de l'extérieur
Bungalows in front of the
swimming pool | Bungalows
vor dem Swimming-pool |
Bungalows devant la piscine
Ian Schrager Hotels

Delano Hotel 1995
Lobby | Eingangshalle | Hall
d'entrée

Lobby with furniture by Ray
and Charles Eames | Eingangs-
halle mit Möbeln von Ray und
Charles Eames | Hall d'entrée
avec meubles par Ray et
Charles Eames
Lobby (detail) | Eingangshalle
(Detail) | Hall d'entrée (détail)
View of the restaurant | Blick
in das Restaurant | Vue du
restaurant
Ian Schrager Hotels

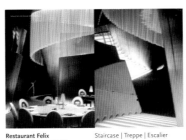

Delano Hotel 1995
View of the exterior | Außen-
ansicht | Vue de l'extérieur
Garden | Garten | Jardin
Dinner table | Eßtisch | Table
dressée
Entrance | Eingang | Entrée
Eat-in kitchen | Eßküche |
Cuisine-salle à manger

Bathroom | Badezimmer |
Salle de bains
Photo: Michael Mundy

Detail apple holder | Detail
Apfelhalter | Détail porte-
pomme
Restaurant
Ian Schrager Hotels

Photos: Todd Eberle

Restaurant Felix
in the Peninsula Hotel 1994
Salisbury Road, Kowloon,
Hong Kong

View of the restaurant | Blick
in das Restaurant | Vue du
restaurant

Staircase | Treppe | Escalier

Restaurant Felix
in the Peninsula Hotel 1994
View of the restaurant | Blick
in das Restaurant | Vue du
restaurant

Peninsula Hotel 1994
Oyster Bar | Austernbar | Bar
huîtres
Ian Schrager Hotels

Peninsula Hotel 1994
Public toilets | Öffentliche Toi-
letten | Toilettes publiques
View of the restaurant | Blick
in das Restaurant | Vue du
restaurant

Bar
W.W. Stool
Lift (detail) | Fahrstuhl (De-
tail) | Ascenseur (détail)
Staircase (detail) | Treppe
(Detail) | Escalier (détail)
Ian Schrager Hotels

Asia de Cuba Restaurant 1997
237, Madison Avenue, New
York, USA

View of the restaurant | Blick
in das Restaurant | Vue du
restaurant
First floor lounge | Salon im
Erdgeschoß | Salon du rez-de-
chaussée
Rum bar | Rum-Bar | Rum Bar
View of the restaurant | Blick

in das Restaurant | Vue du
restaurant
Ian Schrager Hotels
Photos: Todd Eberle

Drawing by | Zeichnung von |
Dessin par Jean-Baptiste
Mondino

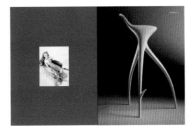

Everything
as a Birth a Life a Death

Alles hat einen Anfang,
ein Sein, ein Ende

out a un début,
une existence, une fin

Furniture
Möbeldesign
Meubles

Ceci n'est pas une brouette 1996
Armchair | Lehnstuhl | Fauteuil
Ashwood frame. Seat and back in
pale pink satin | Rahmen aus
Eschenholz. Rücken- und
Sitzflächen mit blaßrosafarbe-
nem Satinbezug | Structure en
frêne naturel. Siège et dossier
garnis satin rose pâle
140 x 43 x 84 cm
XO
Photo: Tom Vack

W.W. Stool 1990
Stool | Hocker | Tabouret
Sand-blasted cast aluminium,
lacquered | Sandgestrahltes
Gußaluminium, lackiert | Alu-
minium moulé traité au jet de
sable, laqué
97 x 56 x 53 cm
Vitra
Photo: Andreas Sütterlin/Vitra

Louis XX 1992
Chair | Stuhl | Chaise
Polypropylene, aluminium |
Polypropylen, Aluminium |
Polypropylène, aluminium
44.5 x 59 x 60 cm
Vitra
Photo: Andreas Sütterlin/Vitra

Président M. 1984
Table designed for President
Mitterrand's private study at
the Elysée Palace | Tisch, ent-
worfen für Präsident Mitter-
rands privates Arbeitszimmer
im Elysée-Palast | Table réalisée
pour le bureau du Président
Mitterrand à l'Elysée
Square table | Quadratischer
Tisch | Table carrée :
73 x 136 x 136 cm

Rectangular table | Rechteckiger
Tisch | Table rectangulaire :
73 x 170 x 120 cm
Round table | Runder Tisch | Table
ronde : H: 73.5 cm, ø: 150 cm
Baleri
Photo: Marco Schillaci

Pieces of the table | Einzelteile
des Tisches | Pièces détachées
Baleri
Photo: Carlo Orsi

Coque 1999
Computergraphics | Comput-
ergrafiken | Infographies

Richard III 1985
Armchair | Sessel | Fauteuil
Polyurethane, painted with
polyurethane enamel, cushion
in polyurethane and dacron,
woollen cloth or leather |
Polyurethan, Polyurethan-
Emailfarbe, Kissen aus Polyurethan und Dralon, Bezug
aus Wolle oder Leder | Po-
lyuréthane, peint à l'émail polyuréthane, coussin en po-

lyuréthane et dacron, garni-
ture laine ou cuir
92 x 93 x 82 cm
Baleri

We must share

Wir müssen teilen

Partageons

Miss Trip 1996
Take-apart chair | Zerlegbarer
Stuhl | Chaise démontable
Polypropylene, laminated
back, solid beechwood legs |
Polypropylen, laminiertes
Rückenteil, massive Buchen-
holzbeine | Polypropylène,
dossier en multiplis de hêtre,
pieds en hêtre tourné massif
40 x 42 x 85 cm
Kartell

Prince Aha 1996
Composite stool | Komposit-
Hocker | Tabouret composé
Coloured polypropylene | Far-
biges Polypropylen | Polypro-
pylène teinté
30 x 43 cm
Kartell

Photos: Fabrizio Bergamo

Dr. No 1996
Stackable chair | Stapelbarer
Stuhl | Chaise empilable
Coloured polypropylene, aluminium, epoxy polyester or
natural finish | Farbiges
Polypropylen, Aluminium, mit
oder ohne Polyesterbeschich-
tung | Polypropylène teinté,
aluminium, finition laquage
époxy ou naturel.

54.5 x 51.5 x 80 cm
Kartell
Photos: Fabrizio Bergamo

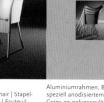

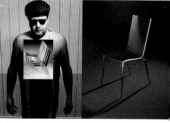

We are mutants

Wir sind Mutanten

Nous sommes des mutants

**Saint Esprit, Napoléon and
Attila** 1999
Stools and table | Hocker und
Tisch | Tabourets et table
Polypropylene | Polypropylen |
Polypropylène
Stool: H: 46 cm, ø: 40 cm,
Table: H: 46 cm, ø: 35 cm
Kartell

La Marie 1998
Stackable monoblock chair |
Stapelbarer Monoblock-Stuhl |
Chaise monobloc, empilable
Transparent polycarbonate |
Transparentes Polycarbonat |
Polycarbonate transparent
50 x 52.5 x 87.5 cm
Kartell

**Philippe Starck and | und | et
La Marie** 1999
*Photo: Karl Lagerfeld/
Deutsche Vogue*

**Philippe Starck and | und | et
Dr. Glob** 1990
Stackable chair | Stapelbarer
Stuhl | Chaise empilable
Tubular steel, polypropylene |
Stahlrohr, Polypropylen | Tube
d'acier, polypropylène
48 x 47.5 x 73 cm
Kartell

Lola Mundo 1988
Table-cum-chair | Tisch-Stuhl |
Table-chaise
Legs in polished cast aluminium. Tops in ashwood with
ebony finish. Hinge in black
coloured chromium-plated
steel. Studs in coloured rub-
ber | Beine aus poliertem
Gußaluminium. Holzflächen
aus ebenholzgetönter Esche.
Scharniere aus schwarzem
verchromten Stahl. Nägel-
köpfe aus farbigem Gummi |
Pieds en aluminium poli.
Dessus frêne, finition ébène.
Charnières en acier chromé
noir. Clous en caoutchouc
coloré
48.5 x 33.5 x 53 cm
Driade
Photo: Tom Vack

We have to allow for the fall
of Western civilisation

Wir müssen den Verfall des
Westens einkalkulieren

Gérons la décadence de
l'Occident

Lord Yo 1994
Stackable armchair | Stapel-
barer Lehnstuhl | Fauteuil
empilable
Body in polypropylene available in dark green, light green,
light yellow, ivory and pink.
Frame in aluminium: legs in
special anodised metal | Kor-
pus aus Polypropylen, erhältlich in Dunkelgrün, Hellgrün,
Hellgelb, Elfenbein und Rosa.

Aluminiumrahmen, Beine aus
speziell anodisiertem Metall |
Corps en polypropylène disponible dans les coloris : vert
foncé, vert clair, jaune clair,
ivoire et rose. Structure en
aluminium, pieds en métal
anodisé
94.5 x 64 x 66 cm
Driade
Photos: Tom Vack

Olly Tango 1994
Stackable chair | Stapelbarer
Stuhl | Chaise empilable
Body in curved plywood. Light
walnut wood or ebonized
finishing, or lacquered in the
following colours: grey, light
green, light yellow, ivory.
Chromium-plated metal legs |
Korpus aus geformten Sperr-
holz mit hell bzw. schwarz ge-
beiztem Walnußfurnier oder

lackiert in den Farben Grau,
Hellgrün, Hellgelb oder Elfenbein. Beine aus verchromtem
Metall | Corps en contre-plaqué.
Finition en bois de noyer clair
ou ébène, ou laquée dans les
couleurs : gris, vert pâle, jaune
pâle, ivoire. Pieds en métal
chromé
90 x 42 x 58 cm
Driade
Photos: Tom Vack

Asahy 1991
Armchair | Lehnstuhl | Fauteuil
Cherrywood and pearwood,
eather, polyurethane foam |
Kirsch- und Birnbaumholz,
Lederbezug, Schaumstoffpol-
sterung | Bois de cerisier et de
poirier, cuir, mousse de nylon
91.5 x 45 x 55.5 cm
Driade

Paramount 1991
Armchair | Lehnstuhl | Fauteuil
Cherrywood and pearwood,
eather, polyurethane foam |
Kirsch- und Birnbaumholz,
Lederbezug, Schaumstoffpol-
sterung | Bois de cerisier et de
poirier, cuir, mousse de nylon
95 x 67 x 71.5 cm
Driade

Vicieuse 1992
Height-adjustable table |
Höhenverstellbarer Tisch |
Table à hauteur réglable
Cast aluminium, polished
frame with central screw for
height adjustment. Top in
multilayered wood with diafos
laminate finish | Gestell aus
poliertem Gußaluminium mit
zentraler Schraube zur Höhen-
einstellung. Tischplatte aus
Schichtholz mit laminierter
Oberfläche | Aluminium coulé,
cadre poli avec vis de réglage
en hauteur. Dessus bois multiplis, finition lamellée
H: 50–73 cm, ø: 40 cm
Driade

Boom Rang 1992
Stackable chair | Stapelbarer
Stuhl | Chaise empilable
Frame in stiff polyurethane with
steel inserts. Available in the following versions: seat light grey
and back salmon pink, seat dark
grey and back light grey | Rah-
men aus gehärtetem Polyurethan
mit Stahleinlagen. Erhältlich in
den folgenden Versionen: hell-
grüner Sitz mit lachsfarbenem
Rücken oder dunkelgrauer Sitz
mit hellgrauem Rücken | Cadre
en polyuréthane rigide, inser-
tions acier. Disponible dans les
versions suivantes : siège gris
clair, dossier saumon ; siège gris
foncé, dossier gris clair
79 x 35.5 x 49 cm
Driade

Boom Rang 1992
Photo: Tom Vack

Asahy 1991

Paramount 1991

Royalton 1991
Chair and bench | Stuhl und
Bank | Chaise et banc
Cherrywood, pearwood, alu-
minium | Kirschholz, Birnbaum-
holz, Aluminium | Bois de
cerisier et de poirier, aluminium
Chair | Stuhl | Chaise :
69 x 46 x 42 cm
Bench | Bank | Banc :
69 x 138 x 42 cm
Driade
Photo: Tom Vack

**Achille Castiglioni and
Philippe Starck**
Photo: Ramak Fazel

Big Nothing 1997
High-backed two-seater sofa |
Hohes zweisitziges Sofa | Haut
canapé à deux places
Removable cover in cotton or
velvet | Abnehmbarer Bezug
aus Baumwolle oder Samt |
Housse amovible en coton ou
velours
170 x 84 x 93 cm
Driade
Photo: Emilio Tremolada

Cam El Eon 1999
Stackable chair | Stapelbarer
Stuhl | Chaise empilable
Aluminium frame, polypropylene seat. Available in ivory,
beige, orange and dark grey.
Also suitable for outdoor use |
Rahmen aus Aluminium, Sitz-
schale aus Polypropylen. Erhältlich in Elfenbein, Beige,
Orange und Dunkelgrau. Auch
für den Außenbereich geeignet
| Structure en aluminium, coque
en polypropylène. Existant dans
les tons : ivoire, beige, orange
et gris foncé. Utilisable aussi à
l'extérieur
55 x 59 x 76 cm
Driade
Photo: Tom Vack

Lola Mundo 1988

Titos Apostos 1985
Folding table | Klapptisch |
Table pliante
Epoxy, tubular steel, sheet
steel | Epoxyd, Stahlrohr,
Stahlblech | Epoxy, tube
d'acier, tôle d'acier
H: 71 cm, ø: 85 cm
Driade

J. (Série Lang) 1987
Armchair | Lehnstuhl | Fauteuil
Tubular steel, aluminium,
leather, padding | Stahlrohr,
Aluminium, Leder, Polsterung |
Tube d'acier, aluminium, cuir,
rembourrage
86 x 60 x 66 cm
Driade

Costes 1984
Armchair | Lehnstuhl | Fauteuil
Epoxy, tubular steel, padded
leather seat, mahogany |
Epoxyd, Stahlrohr, gepolsterter
Ledersitz, Mahagoni | Epoxy,
tube d'acier, siège en cuir
rembourré, acajou
80 x 47.5 x 55 cm
Driade

Costes Alluminio 1988
Armchair | Lehnstuhl | Fauteuil
Tubular aluminium, sheet
aluminium | Aluminiumrohr
und -blech | Tube d'alu-
minium, tôle d'aluminium
74.5 x 46.5 x 56.7 cm
Driade

Pratfall 1985
Armchair | Lehnstuhl | Fauteuil
Tubular steel, leather seat,
black laquered or mahogany
finish | Stahlrohr, Ledersitz,
Rückenlehne aus Holz,
schwarz lackiert oder mit Ma-
hagonifunier | Tube d'acier,
siège cuir, finition laque noire
ou acajou
86 x 61.5 x 78 cm
Driade

J. (Série Lang) 1991
Table | Tisch
Cast aluminium, glass or
wood | Aluminium coulé, Glas
oder Holz | Aluminium coulé,
verre ou bois
Square version | Quadra-
tische Version | Version
carrée : 72.5 x 135 x 135 cm
Rectangular version | Recht-
eckige Version | Version rec-
tangulaire : 72.5 x 90 x 210 cm
Round version | Runde Ver-
sion | Version ronde :
H: 72.5 cm, ø: 130 cm
Driade

Colucci 1986
Stool and container | Hocker-
Behälter | Tabouret-récipient
Aluminium, red or blue | Alu-
minium, rot oder blau | Alu-
minium, rouge ou bleu
H: 45 cm, ø: 38 cm
Driade

Tippy Jackson 1985
Folding table | Klapptisch |
Table pliante
Epoxy, tubular steel, sheet
steel | Epoxyd, Stahlrohr, Stahl-
blech | Epoxy, tube d'acier, tôle
d'acier
H: 71 cm, ø: 120 cm
Driade

Sarapis 1986
Stool | Hocker | Tabouret
Epoxy, tubular steel | Epoxyd,
Stahlrohr | Epoxy, tube d'acier
85.5/105 x 35 x 45.4 cm
Driade

Von Vogelsang 1985
Stackable chair | Stapelbarer

Stuhl | Chaise empilable
Tubular steel, sheet steel |
Stahlrohr, Stahlblech | Tube
d'acier, tôle d'acier
71.5 x 54 x 45.5 cm
Driade

Titos Apostos 1985

Romantica 1987
Stackable chair | Stapelbarer
Stuhl | Chaise empilable
Aluminium
85.4 x 42.7 x 62.5 cm
Driade

Dick Deck 1989
Chair | Stuhl | Chaise
Beechwood | Buchenholz |
Bois de hêtre
91 x 35.5 x 62 cm
Driade

Costes Alluminio 1988

Bob Dubois 1987
Chair | Stuhl | Chaise
Cherrywood, pearwood, wicker |
Kirsch- und Birnbaumholz,
Korbgeflecht | Bois de cerisier,
bois de poirier, assise cannée
91.5 x 39 x 54 cm
Driade

Tessa Nature 1989
Chair | Stuhl | Chaise
Beechwood, pearwood, wicker |
Buchen- und Birnbaumholz,
Korbgeflecht | Bois de hêtre,
bois de poirier, assise cannée
74 x 48 x 52.5 cm
Driade

Cameleon 1992
Table | Tisch
Multi-layered wood frame,
pearwood finish with connect-
ing parts in cast aluminium.
Glass top with sand-blasted
parts and bevelled edges |
Gestell aus Schichtholz, Bir-
nenholzfurnier. Verbindungs-
stücke aus Gußaluminium.
Glasplatte mit sandge-
strahlten Bereichen und ab-
geschrägten Kanten | Cadre en
bois multiplis, finition poirier,
liaisons en aluminium moulé.
Dessus verre avec parties
décapées au jet de sable et
coins biseautés
Square version | Quadra-
tische Version | Version
carrée : 723 x 130 x 130 cm
Rectangular version | Recht-
eckige Version | Version rec-
tangulaire : 73 x 100 x 210 cm
Round version | Runde Ver-
sion | Version ronde :
H: 73 cm, ø: 140 cm
Driade

Placide of the Wood 1989
Chair | Stuhl | Chaise
Cherrywood, pearwood |
Kirschbaum- und Birn-
baumholz | Bois de cerisier,
bois de poirier
91.5 x 44 x 56.5 cm
Driade

Photos: Tom Vack

Royalton Couch 1991
Couch with one armrest | Sofa
mit einer Armlehne | Canapé
avec accoudoir unique
Steel, polyurethane foam, aluminium, pearwood, cotton
fabric, velvet | Stahl, Schaum-
stoff, Aluminium, Birnbaum-
holz, Baumwollstoff, Samt |
Acier, mousse de nylon,
aluminium, bois de poirier,
coton, velours
113 x 207 x 100 cm
Driade

Royalton Couch 1991
Couch with two armrests |
Sofa mit zwei Armlehnen |
Canapé avec deux accoudoirs
Steel, polyurethane foam, aluminium, pearwood, cotton
fabric, velvet | Stahl, Schaum-
stoff, Aluminium, Birnbaum-
holz, Baumwollstoff, Samt |
Acier, mousse de nylon,
aluminium, bois de poirier,
coton, velours
113 x 207 x 100 cm
Driade

Royalton Long Chair 1991
Long chair | Liegesofa | Divan
Steel, polyurethane foam, cast
aluminium | Stahl, Schaum-
stoff, Gußaluminium | Acier,
mousse de nylon, aluminium
coulé
93 x 89 x 173 cm
Driade

Royalton Armchair 1991
Armchair | Sessel | Fauteuil
Steel, cotton fabric, velvet,
polyurethane foam, pearwood,
aluminium | Stahl, Baumwoll-
stoff, Samt, Schaumstoff, Birn-
baumholz, Aluminium | Acier,
coton, velours, mousse de nylon, bois de poirier, aluminium
113 x 98 x 100 cm
Driade

Pouf | Hocker | Tabouret
Steel, cotton fabric, polyur-
ethane foam, aluminium |
Stahl, Baumwollstoff, Schaum-
stoff, Aluminium | Acier, coton,
mousse de nylon, aluminium
45 x 60 x 60 cm
Driade

Asahy 1991
Armchair | Lehnstuhl | Fauteuil
Cherrywood and pearwood,
leather, polyurethane foam |
Kirsch- und Birnbaumholz,
Lederbezug, Schaumstoffpol-
sterung | Bois de cerisier et de
poirier, cuir, mousse de nylon
91.5 x 45 x 55.5 cm
Driade

Paramount 1991
Armchair | Lehnstuhl | Fauteuil
Cherrywood and pearwood,
leather, polyurethane foam |
Kirsch- und Birnbaumholz,
Lederbezug, Schaumstoffpol-
sterung | Bois de cerisier et de
poirier, cuir, mousse de nylon
95 x 67 x 71.5 cm
Driade

Le paravent de l'autre 1992
Screen | Paravent
Pearwood, glass, polished cast
aluminium | Birnbaumholz,
Glas, Gußaluminium | Bois de
poirier, verre, aluminium coulé
190 x 150 x 3 cm
Driade

Royalton Bed 1992
Bed | Bett | Lit
Steel frame with board in laminar
wood. Cotton wool padding, removable cover in velvet. Head-
board with a removable cover in
white piqué. Front feet in cast
aluminium, back feet in black
plastic | Stahlrahmen, Preßholz-
platte, Baumwollpolsterung,
abziehbarer Kopfbezug aus
white Piqué. Vordere Beine aus
Gußaluminium, hintere Beine
aus schwarzem Plastik | Cadre
acier, panneau aggloméré. Rembourrage laine de coton, couver-
ture amovible en velours. Dosse-
ret amovible en piqué blanc.
Pieds avant en aluminium
moulé, pieds arrière en plastique
noir
49/175 x 175 x 210 cm
Driade

Royalton 1988
Chair | Stuhl | Chaise
Wooden seat with mahogany or
ebony finish. Back and armrests
in curved plywood. Front legs in
mahogany or ebony. Rear legs in
cast aluminium. Also with four
wooden legs | Sitzfläche aus
Holz mit Mahagoni- oder Eben-
holzfurnier. Rücken- und Arm-
lehnen aus gebogenem Sper-
rholz. Vordere Stuhlbeine aus
Mahagoni- oder Ebenholz. Hintere Stuhlbeine aus Gußaluminium. Auch erhältlich mit vier
Stuhlbeinen aus Holz | Siège en
bois, finition acajou ou ébène.
Dossier et accoudoirs en contre-
plaqué. Pieds avant en acajou ou
ébène. Pieds arrière aluminium
coulé. Existe également avec
quatre pieds en bois
87 x 55.6 x 54 cm
Driade

Photos: Tom Vack

Toy 1999
Stackable chair | Stapelbarer
Stuhl | Chaise empilable
Polypropylene; available in
ivory, yellow, orange and grey |
Polypropylen; erhältlich in
Elfenbein, Gelb, Orange und
Grau | Polypropylène ; existant
dans les tons : ivoire, jaune,
orange et gris

61.5 x 57.5 x 78 cm
Driade
Photos: Tom Vack

Neoz Kitchen 1999
Kitchen | Küche | Cuisine
Legs of solid, mahogany-coloured cherry wood with die-cast aluminium feet. Worktop of Carrara marble, two sinks of white stoneware and a gas cooker | Tischbeine aus massivem mahagonifarbenem Kirschholz mit Füßen aus Aluminium-Spritzguß. Arbeitsplatte aus Carrara-Marmor, zwei Spülbecken aus weißem Steingut und ein Gaskochfeld | Pieds en cerisier massif teinté acajou avec extrémités en moulage d'aluminium. Plan de travail en marbre de Carrare, deux cuvettes en grès blanc et une cuisinière à gaz
140 x 140 x 94 cm
Driade

Neoz Kitchen 1999
Kitchen | Küche | Cuisine
Cupboard in mahogany-coloured cherry with die-cast aluminium feet . Worktop and back edge of Carrara marble, two sinks of white stoneware and a gas cooker | Unterschrank aus mahagonifarbenem Kirschholz, mit Füßen aus Aluminium-Spritzguß. Arbeitsplatte und rückwärtiger Aufsatz aus Carrara-Marmor, zwei Spülbecken aus weißem Steingut und ein Gaskochfeld | Placard en cerisier teinté acajou, pieds en moulage d'aluminium. Plan de travail et plaque arrière en marbre de Carrare, deux cuvettes en grès blanc et une cuisinière à gaz
214 x 70 x 168 cm
Driade

Neoz 1997
Table at two different heights with chair | Tisch in zwei verschiedenen Höhen mit Stuhl | Table à deux niveaux avec chaise
Legs of mahogany-coloured cherry, on rollers of injection-moulded aluminium. Table top in wood with mahogany-coloured cherry veneer or Carrara marble | Beine aus mahagonifarbenem Kirschholz, auf Rollen aus Aluminium-Spritzguß. Tischplatte aus Holz mit mahagonifarbenem Kirschbaumfurnier oder aus Carrara-Marmor | Pieds en cerisier teinté acajou, roulettes en aluminium moulé par injection. Plan de travail en bois avec plaquage en cerisier teinté acajou ou marbre de Carrare
H: 73 cm, ø: 129 cm,
H: 102 cm, ø: 129 cm,
Driade

Neoz 1997
Two-seater sofa and high-backed sofa | Zweisitziges Sofa und Sofa mit hoher Rückenlehne | Canapé deux places et canapé à dossier haut
Mahogany-coloured cherry, on rollers of injection-moulded aluminium. Cover available in white fifty-per-cent linen and in white or sand-coloured cotton | Mahagonifarbenes Kirschholz, auf Rollen aus Aluminium-Spritzguß. Bezug erhältlich in weißem Halbleinen und in weißer oder sandfarbener Baumwolle | Cerisier teinté acajou, roulettes en aluminium moulé par injection. Housse disponible en toile métis de couleur blanche et en coton blanc ou beige
146 x 82 x 85 cm and
207 x 88 x 156 cm
Driade

Neoz 1997
Bed and bedside table | Bett und Beistelltisch | Lit et table
Legs in mahogany-coloured cherry, on rollers of injection-moulded aluminium | Beine aus mahagonifarbenem Kirschholz, auf Rollen aus Aluminium-Spritzguß | Pieds en cerisier teinté acajou, roulettes en aluminium moulé par injection
Bed: 199 x 205 x 165 cm,
Table: 30 x 30 x 50 cm
Driade

Neoz 1997
Tables | Tische
Legs in mahogany-coloured cherry, castors in die-cast aluminium. Table top in Carrara marble | Beine aus mahagonifarbenem Kirschholz, auf Rollen aus Aluminium-Spritzguß. Tischplatte aus Carrara-Marmor | Pieds en cerisier teinté acajou, roulettes en aluminium moulé par injection. Plateau en marbre de Carrare
Driade

Neoz 1997
Three-seater sofa | Dreisitziges Sofa | Canapé trois places
Mahogany-coloured cherry, on rollers of injection-moulded aluminium. Cover available in white fifty-per-cent linen and in white or sand-coloured cotton | Mahagonifarbenes Kirschholz, auf Rollen aus Aluminium-Spritzguß. Bezug erhältlich in weißem Halbleinen und in weißer oder sandfarbener Baumwolle | Cerisier teinté acajou, roulettes en aluminium moulé par injection. Housse disponible en toile métis de couleur blanche et en coton blanc ou beige
206 x 152 x 85 cm
Driade

Photos: Tom Vack

Drawing by | Zeichnung von | Dessin par Jean-Baptiste Mondino

Hairdressing furniture for L'Oréal | Friseursalonmöbel für L'Oréal | Meubles de salons de coiffure pour L'Oréal 1989

Adjustable wash unit | Verstellbarer Sessel mit Waschbecken | Fauteuil de lavage réglable 1989
Hydraulic system incorporated in the legs. Shaped shower, wash basin in polished fibreglass, arm rest. Plastic | In den Fuß eingelassene Hydraulik. Gestylte Handdusche. Waschschüssel aus poliertem Glas. Armstütze mit Ablage. Kunststoff | Installation hydraulique intégrée dans les piétements. Douchette façonnée. Cuvette en verre poli. Accoudoir avec tablette. Plastique
95 x 53 x 105 cm
Maletti/L'Oréal

Basic 1989
Swivel work chair, assembled on star base | Arbeitsdrehstuhl mit sternförmigem Fuß | Fauteuil de travail pivotant, monté sur piétement en étoile
Metal, plastic, cast aluminium | Metall, Kunststoff, Gußaluminium | Métal, plastique, aluminium coulé
80 x 50 x 50 cm
Maletti/L'Oréal

Stool 1989
Multi-purpose stool on castors, adjustable height. Pump and castors incorporated. Pump lever under the seat | Vielzweckhocker auf Rollen, Höhe verstellbar. Pumpe und Rollen integriert. Pumphebel unter dem Sitz | Tabouret emplois multiples sur roues, hauteur réglable. Pompe et roues intégrées. Levier de la pompe sous le siège
Plastic | Kunststoff | Plastique
H: 40 cm, ø: 40 cm
Maletti/L'Oréal

Techno 1989
Swivel work chair assembled on star base with hydraulic pump | Arbeitsdrehstuhl mit sternförmigem Fuß und hydraulischer Pumpe | Fauteuil de travail pivotant, monté sur piétement en étoile avec pompe hydraulique
Plastic, cast aluminium | Kunststoff, Gußaluminium | Plastique, aluminium coulé
95 x 53 x 105 cm
Maletti/L'Oréal

Ara Starck
Photo: Hervé Bialé

Ara 1985
Stool | Hocker | Tabouret
Plastic | Kunststoff | Plastique
42 x 30 x 30 cm
VIA

Ray Menta (project) 1984
Lamp | Lampe
XO

Photo: Jean-Baptiste Mondino

Dole Melipone 1981
Folding table | Klapptisch | Table pliante
Epoxy, tubular steel, glass | Epoxyd, Stahlrohr, Glas | Epoxy, tube d'acier, verre
H: 73 cm, ø: 120 cm
XO

Dr. Sonderbar 1983
Chair | Stuhl | Chaise
Nickel-plated metal | Metall, vernickelt | Métal, nickelé
63 x 90 x 47 cm
XO
Photo: Tom Vack

Philippe Starck 1999
Photo: Helmut Newton

SUMO table 1999
Folding table, designed exclusively for Helmut Newton's SUMO book | Klappbarer Tisch, exclusiv entworfen für Helmut Newtons SUMO | Table pliante, dessinée exclusivement pour le livre SUMO de Helmut Newton

Helmut Newton and Benedikt Taschen 1999
Photo: Alice Springs

M.T Minimum Table 1998
Table | Tisch
Glass, wood, steel | Glas, Holz, Stahl | Verre, bois, acier
210 x 85 cm, H: 71.5-73 cm
Cassina
Photo: Matthew Donaldson

M.T Minimum Table 1998
Table | Tisch
Glass, wood, steel | Glas, Holz, Stahl | Verre, bois, acier
211 x 85 cm, H: 71.5-73 cm
Cassina
Photos: Matthew Donaldson

Drawing by | Zeichnung von | Dessin par Jean-Baptiste Mondino

Miss C.O.C.O (five pictures of how to use it) 1998
Folding chair | Klappstuhl | Chaise pliante
Aluminium, polypropylene | Aluminium, Polypropylen | Aluminium, polypropylène
41 x 46 x 80 cm
Cassina
Photos: Matthew Donaldson

L.W.S Lazy Working Sofa 1998
Sofa | Sofa | Canapé
Polyurethane and polyester wadding, cloth, aluminium, wood. The sofa can be fitted with side tables and electrical wiring for lamps, computers etc. | Polyurethanschaumstoff, Stoff, Aluminium, Holz. Das Sofa kann mit seitlichen Ablageflächen ausgestattet und verkabelt geliefert werden, so

daß Strom für Lampen, Computer usw. zur Verfügung steht | Polyuréthane, tissu, aluminium, bois. Le canapé peut être munis de plans d'appui latéraux et équipés de systèmes intégrés d'alimentation électrique pour lampes, ordinateurs, etc.
218 x 97 x 83 cm
Cassina
Photo: Matthew Donaldson

L.W.S Lazy Working Sofa (two people relaxing over 16 photos) 1998
Cassina
Photos: Matthew Donaldson

Bubu 1er 1991
Stool | Hocker | Tabouret
Injection-moulded polypropylene | Polypropylen-Spritzguß | Polypropylène injecté
H: 43.5 cm, ø: 33 cm
up to | bis | jusqu'à 1995 OWO
from | ab | depuis 1996 XO

Bubu 1er 1991
in four colours | in vier Farben | en quatre couleurs
Photos: Tom Vack

Bo Boolo 1995
Table, console and bench | Tisch, Konsole und Bank | Table, console et banc
Mahogany-stained beechwood, natural birch trunk | Mahagonifarben gebeiztes Buchenholz mit naturbelassenem Birkenstamm | Hêtre teinté acajou, tronc en bouleau naturel

190 x 90 x 73 cm;
190 x 40 x 82 cm;
170 x 27 x 42 cm
up to | bis | jusqu'à 1995
3 Suisses/O.N.F.
from | ab | depuis 1996 XO
Photo: Jean-Philippe Piter

Slick Slick 1999
Stackable chair | Stapelbarer Stuhl | Chaise empilable
Coloured polypropylene | Farbiges Polypropylen | Polypropylène teinté
44 x 52 x 80 cm
XO
Photo: Tom Vack

Mister Bliss 1982
Stool | Kniehocker | Agenouilloir
Epoxy, tubular steel, material, padding | Epoxyd, Stahlrohr, Stoff, Polsterung | Epoxy, tube d'acier, tissu, rembourrage
50 x 40 x 58 cm
XO

Dr. Sonderbar 1983
Chair | Lehnstuhl | Chaise
Nickel-plated metal | Metall, vernickelt | Métal, nickelé
63 x 90 x 47 cm
XO

Pat Conley II 1986
Armchair | Lehnstuhl | Fauteuil
Frame and seat of epoxy-lacquered sheet metal, in silver or anthracite finish | Rahmen und Sitzfläche aus Metall, mit silber- oder anthrazitfarbenem Epoxydlack überzogen | Structure et assise en tôle laquée époxy, argent ou anthracite
105 x 44 cm
XO

Royalton Bar Stool 1988
Bar stool | Barhocker | Tabouret de bar
Cast aluminium, velvet, padding | Gußaluminium, Samt, Polsterung | Aluminium coulé, velours, rembourrage
H: 77 cm, ø: 37 cm
XO

Peninsula 1995
Chair | Stuhl | Chaise
Mahogany-stained beechwood. Upholstered seat and back with removable cotton covering | Rahmen aus mahagonifarben gebeiztem Buchenholz. Sitz und Rückenlehne gepolstert und mit abziehbarem Baumwollstoff bezogen | Structure en hêtre teinte acajou. Siège et dossier rembourrés. Housse de coton amovible
89 x 46 x 46 cm
XO

Théâtre du Monde 1984
Secretaire | Sekretär | Secrétaire
Polyester, lacquer or anthracite finish, with four shelves and castors | Polyester, klar- oder anthrazitfarben lackiert, ausgestattet mit vier Fächern und Rollen | Polyester laqué ou anthracite équipé de quatre étagères et roulettes
198 x 55 x 55 cm
XO

Lundi Ravioli 1995
Chair | Stuhl | Chaise
Chrome-plated tubular steel frame. White skai seat. Armrest in laminated wood. Wooden back in various finishes | Rahmen aus verchromten Stahlrohr. Gepolsterter Sitz mit weißem Skai-

Bezug. Lehne aus laminiertem Holz in verschiedenen Farbtönen | Structure en tube d'acier chromé. Siège rembourré en skaï blanc. Dossier bois lamellé collé en plusieurs finitions.
81 x 50 x 46 cm
XO

Slick Slick 1999
Stackable chair | Stapelbarer Stuhl | Chaise empilable
Coloured polypropylene | Farbiges Polypropylen | Polypropylène teinté
44 x 52 x 80 cm
XO
Photos: Tom Vack

Lila Hunter 1988
Stackable chair | Stapelbarer Stuhl | Chaise empilable
Metal, wood, leather | Metall, Holz, Leder | Métal, bois, cuir
75 x 51 x 56 cm
XO

Lio Comun 1991
Chair | Stuhl | Chaise
Welded pale grey tubular steel frame and varnished wooden seat and back with crocodile pattern, or welded dark grey tubular frame and pearwood or mahogany seat and back | Rahmen aus verschweißtem hellgrauen Stahlrohr mit lackiertem Sitz und Rückenlehne aus Holz mit »Krokodil«-Muster oder Rahmen aus verschweißtem anthrazitfarbenen Stahlrohr mit lackiertem Sitz und Rückenlehne aus Birnbaumholz oder Mahagoni | Structure en tube acier soudé gris clair avec siège et dossier en bois impression « crocodile » laqué ou structure en tube acier soudé anthracite avec siège et dossier en poirier

ou acajou
88 x 49 x 56 cm
XO

Monsieur X Rocking 1996
Folding rocking chair | Klapp-Schaukelstuhl | Fauteuil pliant
Beech, seat and back in coloured cotton canvas | Buche, Sitzfläche und Rückenlehne aus farbiger Baumwolle | Hêtre clair, assise et dossier en toile de coton
55 x 59 x 88 cm
XO

Os Library 1998
Shelf | Regal | Etagère
Wenge, supporting elements in china | Wenge, Stützelemente aus weißem Porzellan | Wenge, éléments de support en porcelaine blanche
L: 180 cm
XO

Popopo 1993
Vase
Polyester resin, aluminium base | Polyester, Fuß aus Aluminium | Résine de polyester, base en aluminium
H: 158 cm, ø: 40 cm
XO

Monsieur X Chaise longue 1996
Folding chair | Klappsessel | Fauteuil pliant
Beech, seat and back in coloured cotton canvas | Buche, Sitzfläche und Rückenlehne aus farbiger Baumwolle | Hêtre clair, assise et dossier en toile de coton
55 x 115 x 84 cm
XO

Cheap Chic Table 1998
Table | Tisch
Base in epoxy-laquered steel, top in polypropylene | Sockel aus epoxid-harz-lackiertem Stahl, Tischplatte aus Polypropylen | Piétement acier laqué, époxy, plateau en polypropylène
H: 72 cm, ø: 60 cm
XO

Cheap Chic 1997
Stackable chair | Stapelbarer Stuhl | Chaise empilable
Laquered tubular aluminium frame, epoxy resin. Polypropylene shell | Rahmen aus epoxid-harz-lackiertem Aluminiumrohr, Sitzschale aus Polypropylen | Structure en tube d'aluminium laqué, époxy. Coque polypropylène
45 x 49 x 80 cm
XO

Cheap Chic Armchair 1997
Stackable armchair | Stapelbarer Lehnstuhl | Fauteuil empilable
Frame and arms in laquered tubular aluminium, epoxy resin. Polypropylene shell | Rahmen aus epoxid-harz-lackiertem Aluminiumrohr, Sitzschale aus Polypropylen | Structure et bras en tube d'aluminium laqué, époxy. Coque polypropylène
58 x 49 x 80 cm
XO
Photos: Tom Vack

Poaa 1999
Dumb-bells | Hantel | Haltère
Polished die-cast aluminium,
filled with steel | Polierter Alu-
minium-Spritzguß mit Stahl-
kern | Fonte d'aluminium,
noyau en acier
L: 20 cm
XO
Photo: Tom Vack

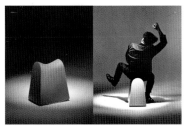

Dadada 1993
Stool | Hocker | Tabouret
Injection-moulded polypropy-
lene stacking chair | Stapel-
hocker aus Polypropylen-
Spritzguß | Siège empilable en
polypropylène injecté
51.8 x 46.5 x 31.2 cm
up to | bis | jusqu'à 1995 OWO
from | ab | depuis 1996 XO

Philippe Starck on Dadada

Photos: Tom Vack

Pax Now

Frieden jetzt

La paix maintenant

Industrial Design
Industriedesign
Design industriel

Faitoo 1996
Diverse kitchen utensils |
Diverses Küchenzubehör |
Divers ustensiles de cuisine
Alessi
Photo: Jean-Baptiste Mondino

Plywood car (project) 1996
Plywood | Sperrholz | Bois
contre-plaqué
Photos: DEIS

Toto la toto car (project) 1996
Photo: Jean-Baptiste Mondino

TeddyBearBand 1998
Children's soft toy | Plüschtier |
Animal en peluche
Bear's head, 3 limbs with
heads of a dog, a goat, and a
rabbit, and one leg with a nor-
mal paw. Cotton covering |
Bärenkopf, drei Gliedmaßen
laufen in verschiedenen Köpfen
aus: Hund, Ziege und Kanin-
chen, die vierte ist als Pfote
gestaltet. Bezug aus Baum-
wolle | Tête d'ours, 3 membres
sont terminés par des têtes
différentes, chien, chèvre,
lapin, membre inférieur droit
en forne d'une patte. Dessus
coton
H: 37 cm
Moulin Roty
*Photos: Michel Lelièvre/Studio
Bleu for GOOD GOODS/
La Redoute*

Drawing by | Zeichnung von |
Dessin par Jean-Baptiste
Mondino

Dr. Life 1991
Floor lamp giving direct light |
Bodenleuchte mit direktem
Licht | Lampadaire à lumière
directe
Cast iron and aluminium base,
aluminium stem, 'Bright eye'
made of moulded etched
glass with continuous colour
change. May be adapted to
wall or ceiling use. Dr. Life's
300-watt halogen beam may
be tinted in many hues thanks
to a multi-coloured filter and
an auxiliary low-voltage halo-
gen bulb | Sockel aus Guß-
eisen und Aluminium, Fuß aus
Aluminium. »Großes Auge«
aus mattglänzendem Relief-
glas mit variierenden Farben.
In Wand- oder Deckenleuchte
umwandelbar. Dank eines
Farbfilters und einer zusätz-
lichen Halogenbirne mit Nied-
rigspannung kann der 300-
Watt-Halogenstrahl von Dr.
Life in den verschiedensten
Farbtönen leuchten | Socle en
fer forgé et aluminium, pied
aluminium, « œil large » en
verre gaufré satiné aux couleurs variables. Adaptable au
mur et au plafond. Le rayon
halogène de 300 watts de Dr.
Life peut être teinté dans de
nombreuses nuances grâce
à un filtre aux couleurs multiples et un bulbe halogène
auxiliaire à bas-voltage
40 x 197 cm
Flos

Rosy Angelis 1994
Floor lamp giving diffused light |
Bodenlampe mit indirektem
Licht | Lampadaire à lumière
diffuse
Carbon fibre legs, special shade
of lightweight fabric. Technopo-
lymer structural support, elec-
tronic dimmer | Beine aus Kar-
bonfaser. Schirm aus besonders
leichtem Stoff. Technopolymer-
Struktur. Elektronischer Dim-
mer | Pieds en fibre de carbone.
Diffuseur en tissu spécial extra
léger. Structure en technopo-
lymère. Variateur d'intensité
électronique
H: 185 cm, ø: 50 cm
Flos

Miss Sissi 1990
Table and wall lamp | Tisch- und
Wandleuchte | Lampe de table
et suspension murale
H: 28.4 cm, ø: 14.3 cm
Flos

Romeo Moon 1995
Pendant lamp | Deckenleuchte |
Plafonnier
Pendant lamp giving diffused
light, supported by three steel
wires. White satin-finished glass
inside, moulded glass outside |
Indirektes Licht spendende, an
drei Stahldrähten aufgehängte
Deckenlampe. Innerer Schirm
aus weißsatiniertem Glas, äuße-
rer Schirm aus Reliefglas | Suspen-
sion à lumière diffuse, re-
tenue par trois fils d'acier. Abat-

jour intérieur en verre blanc satiné, abat-jour extérieur en
verre gaufré
Crown height | Höhe des
Schirms | Hauteur de la cou-
ronne: 22.5 cm
Flos

Light Lite 1992
Lamp | Lampe
Energy-saving lamp of a special plastic material that has
been thermoformed in a vac-
uum and serigraphed, either
hanging from the ceiling or
plugged into the wall socket
and hung from a hook. Available in four metallized colours
with six coloured interchange-
able inserts | Energiesparende
Lampe aus in einem Vakuum
thermogeformten und serigra-
phierten Kunststoff; kann an
der Decke befestigt, an eine
Wandsteckdose angeschlossen
oder an einen Haken gehängt
werden. In vier Metallicfarben
mit sechs auswechselbaren
Farbfiltern erhältlich | Lampe
économisant l'énergie, elle est
faite de plastique thermoformé
au vide et sérigraphié, et peut
être suspendue au plafond,
branchée dans une prise de
courant au mur ou pendue à
un crochet. Elle existe en quatre couleurs métallisées avec
six filtres colorés interchangea-
bles
H: 24 cm, ø: 43 cm
Flos

Walla Walla 1994
Wall fitting providing diffused
light | Wandleuchte mit indirek-
tem Licht | Lampe murale à lu-
mière diffuse
Thermopolymer plastic (clear/
green, grey, terracotta) with an
opaline plastic diffuser and a
set of cloroured filters for
different lighting effects | Ther-
mopolymer-Kunststoff (Trans-
parent/Grün, Grün, terrakottafarben) mit opalem Lichtdiffu-
sor aus Plastik und vier Farb-
filtern für unterschiedliche
Lichteffekte | Plastique thermo-
polymère (transparent/ vert,
gris, terre cuite) avec diffuseur
en plastique opalin et quatres
filtres colorés pour divers effets
de lumière
30 x 37 x 10 cm
Flos

Ara 1988
Table lamp | Tischlampe |
Lampe de table
Chrome-plated metal, halogen |
Verchromtes Metall, Halogen |
Métal chromé, halogène
H: 56.5 cm
Flos

Photos: Jean-Baptiste Mondino

Jean-Baptiste Mondino
Photo: Philippe Starck

Romeo Moon Soft T2 1998
Table lamp | Tischlampe |
Lampe de table
Base in metallic grey, cast alu-
minium. Double lampshade:
white satin-finished glass in-
side, fabric outside | Lampen-
fuß aus metallic-grauem
Gußaluminium. Doppelter
Lampenschirm: innerer
Schirm aus weiß-satiniertem
Glas, äußerer Schirm aus
Stoff | Pied en aluminium
coulé gris métallique. Abat-
jour double : abat-jour in-
térieur en verre blanc satiné,
abat-jour extérieur en tissu
H: 73 cm, ø: 50 cm
Flos

Romeo Moon T2 1998
Table lamp | Tischlampe |
Lampe de table
Base in metallic grey, cast aluminium. Double lampshade:
white satin-finished glass in-
side, moulded glass outside |
Lampenfuß aus metallic-
grauem Gußaluminium. Dop-
pelter Lampenschirm: innerer
Schirm aus weiß-satiniertem
Glas, äußerer Schirm aus Re-
liefglas | Pied en aluminium
coulé gris métallique. Abat-
jour double : abat-jour intérieur en verre blanc satiné,
abat-jour extérieur en verre
gaufré
H: 73 cm, ø: 50 cm
Flos

Photos: Piero Fasanotto

ArchiMoon Tech 1998
An almost dematerialized
version with a halogen bulb |
Eine beinahe entmateriali-
sierte Version mit einer Halo-
genlampe | Une version
presque dématérialisée, avec
ampoule halogène
Low wattage lamp, 35 watt,
grey metallic aluminium body,
yellow polycarbonate filter |
Niedervoltleuchte, 35 Watt,
Korpus Aluminium metallic-
grau, Lampenschirm Polycar-
bonat | Lampe basse tension,
35 watts, corps aluminium
gris métal, diffuseur polycarbonate jaune
H: 44 cm
Flos

ArchiMoon Eco 1998
Low wattage lamp | Nieder-
voltleuchte | Lampe basse
tension
Max 18 watt, grey metallic aluminium body, polycarbonate
filter | Max. 18 Watt, Korpus
Aluminium metallic-grau,
Lampenschirm Polycarbonat |
18 watts maxi, corps alu-
minium gris métal, diffuseur
polycarbonate
H: 56.6 cm
Flos

ArchiMoon Classic 1998
Interpretation of a great clas-
sic, the architect's lamp | In-
terpretation eines großen
Klassikers: der Architekten-

lampe | Interprétation du
grand classique de la lampe
d'architecte
Max 60 watt bulb, metallic
grey aluminium body, polycar-
bonate lampshade | Glüh-
birne max. 60 Watt, Korpus
Aluminium metallic-grau,
Lampenschirm Polycarbonat |
Lampe puissance 60 watts
maxi, corps aluminium gris
métal, abat-jour en polycarbonate
H: 56.6 cm
Flos

ArchiMoon Soft 1998
A work light fitted with a
pleated shade | Ein gefalteter
Schirm über einer Arbeits-
leuchte | Un abat-jour plissé
sur une lampe de travail
Low wattage lamp, 35 watt,
body of metallic grey var-
nished aluminium. Taffeta
and glass shade, white filter |
Niedervoltleuchte, 35 Watt,
Korpus metallic-grau lack-
iertes Aluminium. Lampen-
schirm aus Glas und Taft mit
weißem Filter | Lampe basse
tension, 35 watts, corps gris
metal aluminium verni. Abat-
jour taffetas et verre diffuseur
blanc
H: 44 cm
Flos

*Photos: Michel Lelièvre/Studio
Bleu for GOOD GOODS/
La Redoute*

Miss Yee 1987
Drawing | Zeichnung | Dessin

Miss Yee 1987
Shelf | Regal | Etagère
Chrome-plated sheet steel,
silk cording | Verchromtes
Stahlblech, Seilaufhängung
aus Seide | Tôle d'acier
chromée, cordons en soie
4.3 x 90 x 30 cm
Idée

Oa 1998

Shoe (prototype) 1996
Della Valle

Male model wearing a Starck
mask | Männermodell mit
Starck-Maske | Modèle mas-
culin portant un masque de
Starck
Photo: Jean-Baptiste Mondino

Starck Masks by Ingo Maurer |
Starck-Masken von Ingo
Maurer | Masques de Starck par Ingo
Maurer
Cologne 1998

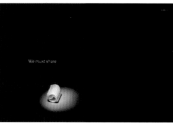

We must share

Wir müssen teilen

Partageons

Mandala 1987
Pasta | Nudel | Pâtes
ø: 5 mm
Panzani
Photo: Hervé Ternisien

Ti Tang 1992
Teapot | Teekanne | Théière
White porcelain, with aluminium coat coloured with epoxy
resins | Weißes Porzellan, Alu-
miniummantel mit farbiger
Epoxydharzbeschichtung |
Porcelaine blanche, gaine aluminium coloré avec résine
époxy
22 x 14 x 18 cm
Alessi

Su Mi Tang 1992
Cream jug | Sahnespender |
Pot à crème
White porcelain | Weißes
Porzellan | Porcelaine blanche
H: 14 cm, ø: 7.5 cm
Alessi

Mister Meumeu 1992
Cheese grater | Käsedose mit
Reibe | Fromagère avec râpe
Stainless steel, polyamide |

Edelstahl, Polyamid | Acier
inoxydable, polyamide
13.5 x 8.5 x 20.5 cm
Alessi

Toothbrush and toothbrush
holder | Zahnbürste und
Behälter | Brosse à dents et
base 1989
H: 19.5 cm
Fluocaril

Philippe Starck

Toothpaste dispenser | Zahn-
pastaspender | Doseur à den-
tifrice 1989
Fluocaril

Toothbrush | Zahnbürste |
Brosse à dents 1989
Fluocaril

Toothbrush and toothbrush

holder | Zahnbürste und
Behälter | Brosse à dents et
base 1989
Fluocaril

Toothbrushes and toothbrush
holder | Zahnbürsten und
Behälter | Brosses à dents et
base 1989
Fluocaril

Dr Skud 1998
Fly swat | Fliegenklatsche |
Tapette à mouches
Polyamide | Polyamid
L: 44 cm
Alessi

Nous n'avons pas
besoin de tuer pour survivre

We do not have to kill to
survive

Wir müssen nicht töten,
um zu überleben

Nous n'avons pas besoin
de tuer pour survivre

Washtub, pump, wash-bowl
(traditional form) | Zuber,
Pumpe, Waschschüssel (Ur-
formen) | Baquet, pompe,
bassine (formes traditionnelles)

Washbasin | Waschbecken |
Lavabo 1994
Sanicryl
85 x 58 x 58 cm
Duravit/Axor/Hoesch

Washbasin mixer | Einarmige
Mischbatterie | Mitigeur d'évier
1994
Chrome | Chrom
Duravit/Axor/Hoesch

Bathtub | Badewanne |
Baignoire 1994
Sanicryl
180 x 90 x 59 cm
Duravit/Axor/Hoesch

Photos: Rudolf Schmutz

Toilet and bidet | Toilette und
Bidet | Toilette et bidet 1998
Ceramic | Keramik |
Céramique
Duravit

Bathtub | Badewanne | Baig-
noire 1998
Sanicryl
Hoesch

Photos: Rudolf Schmutz

Two-handled mixing faucet |
Zweiarmige Mischbatterie |
Mélangeur à deux robinets
1998
Chrome-plated brass | Mes-
sing, verchromt | Laiton
chromé
Axor
Photo: Rudolf Schmutz

Drawing by | Zeichnung von |
Dessin par Jean-Baptiste
Mondino

Shower | Dusche | Douche 1998
Hoesch
Photo: Jean-Baptiste Mondino

Beneteau Collection « First S »
1988–1994

First 41 S5 Voilier L Coque 1989
L: 12.30 m
Beneteau

First 35,7 Voilier L Coque 1992
Interior | Innenausstattung |
Intérieur |
L: 10.55 m
Beneteau

First 35 S5 Voilier L Coque 1988
Detail | Détail
L: 10.60 m
Beneteau

Photos: G. Martin Raget

Ara III
House boat | Hausboot |
Bateau aménagé
Various views | Verschiedene
Ansichten | Vues diverses

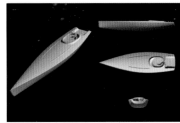

Ara III
House boat | Hausboot |
Bateau aménagé
Various views | Verschiedene
Ansichten | Vues diverses

Virtuelle 1997
Fast sailing boat | Schnell-
segelboot | Voilier rapide
Sloop, carbon kevlar sandwich hull, carbon mast, milar
and carbon sails | Sloop,
Sandwichrumpf aus Kevlar-
Karbon, Karbonmast, Milar-
Karbonsegel | Sloop, coque
sandwich, carbone kevlar, mât
carbone, voile milar/carbone

L: 24,08 m
Ill.: DEIS, Paris

Urgency is back again

Rückkehr der Dringlichkeit

L'urgence est revenue

Motó 6,5 1995
Single-cylinder, four strokes,
with balancing countershaft,
light alloy cylinder, with Gilni-
sil coating. Liquid cooled, one
radiator with separate expan-
sion tank | Einzylinder, Vier-
takter, Vorgelegewelle,
Leichtmetallzylinder mit Gil-
nisil-Beschichtung, wasserge-
kühlt, Kühler mit separatem
Ausdehnungsgefäß | Monocy-

lindre 4 temps à transmission
intermédiaire, cylindre en al-
liage léger à revêtement Gilni-
sil. Refroidissement par liquide, radiateur à vase d'ex-
pansion séparé
213,3 x 80 x 106 cm
Aprilia
Photos: Tom Vack

Motó 6,5 & friends
Bigas Luna
Patricia Bailer
Ivano Beggio + Philippe Starck
Javier Mariscal
Peter Gabriel
Philippe Starck
Florent Pagny
Placido Arango
Jenna de Rosnay
Azucena Caamano

Thierry Gaugain
Jean-Louis Aubert
Photos: Jean-Philippe Piter

Motó 6,5 1995
Detail | Détail
Photo: Tom Vack

Motó 6,5 1995
*Photo: Michel Lelièvre/
Studio Bleu for GOOD GOODS/
La Redoute*

Scooter Lama (prototype) 1992
Vehicle with two wheels for urban transport for one or two persons with a large load capacity. Two-stroke combustion engine with catalyser. Plastic recyclable materials | Zweirad für Stadtverkehr, Zweisitzer, mit großer Ladekapazität. Zweitaktmotor, Katalysator. Recycelbare Kunststoffmaterialien | Un deux-roues pour déplacements urbains, biplace, grande capacité de chargement. Moteur deux temps, pot catalytique. Matières plastiques recyclables
120 x 72 x 173 cm
Aprilia
Photo: Gianni Sabbadin

Philippe Starck, Alberto Meda, Thierry Gaugain 1992

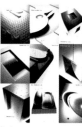

Remote control 1994
Remote control unit | Fernbedienung | Télécommande
ABS plastic | ABS-Kunststoff | Plastique ABS
2.5 x 6 cm, ø: 3 cm
Thomson
Photo: Tom Vack

Alo 1996
Voice command telephone | Durch Zuruf bedienbares Telefon | Téléphone à commande vocale
Soft case made of translucent polymer coloured with natural dyes, revealing an oblong aluminium core protecting the delicate technical components | Der weiche Korpus besteht aus durchsichtigem, mit Naturfarben gefärbtem Polymer-Kunststoff und enthüllt einen rechteckigen Aluminiumkern aus der das empfindliche technische Innenleben enthält | Son corps moelleux en polymère translucide coloré de pigments naturels révèle un noyau oblong en aluminium protégeant ses délicats composants techniques
14 x 6 cm
Thomson
Concept: Philippe Starck
Designer: Jérôme Olivet
Photo: Guido Mocafico

From technology to love

Von der Technologie zur Liebe

De la technologie à l'amour

Plasmaa 1995
Ultra-flat Television set | Ultraflacher Fernseher | Téléviseur ultra-plat
Plasmaa is the result of a dream: an ultra-flat TV visible only as a screen. Plasmaa frees the image from its cathode ray tube: two glass walls, only a hundred or so microns apart, enclose a gaseous mixture that is activated by electrodes. The ultraviolet radiation from this plasma is then converted into the basic colours visible to the human eye. When the power is off, its front layer of glass looks like a mirror reflecting the first artifical image that marked mankind: his own reflection | Plasmaa ist das Ergebnis eines Traums: ein ultraflacher Fernseher, der äußerlich nur aus einem Bildschirm zu bestehen scheint. Plasmaa befreit das Bild von der Kathodenstrahlröhre: Zwei Glaswände, die nur wenige hundert Mikrone auseinanderliegen, enthalten ein Gasgemisch, das von den Elektroden aktiviert wird. Die von diesem Plasma ausgehende ultraviolette Strahlung wird dann umgewandelt in die Spektralfarben, die für das menschliche Auge sichtbar sind. Das Hochpräzisionsbild kommt von einer dünnen Oberfläche. Ausgeschaltet sieht die Vorderseite wie ein Spiegel aus: Sie reflektiert das erste künstliche Bild, das die Menschheit kennzeichnet: die eigene Spiegelung | Plasmaa concrétise un rêve : le téléviseur ultra plat uniquement incarné par la présence magistrale de son écran. Plasmaa libère de son tube cathodique : deux parois de verre distantes d'une centaine de microns renfermant un mélange gazeux activé par des électrodes. Le rayonnement ultraviolet de ce plasma est ensuite traduit en couleurs de base perceptibles par l'homme. Une image d'une grande finesse jaillit alors d'une surface mince. Mis en veille, il devient miroir par un jeu de surface de son verre frontal, proposant la première image artificielle qui ait marqué l'homme : son propre reflet
58 x 47 x 8.8 cm
Thomson
Concept: Philippe Starck
Designer: Bernard Guerrin
Photo: Guido Mocafico

Cub 1996
LCD projector – overhead projector | LCD Projektor – Overheadprojektor | Projecteur LCD – Rétroprojecteur
A diaphanous form containing a core of dense energy emitting a light ray carrying the image. Can be viewed on the opposite side of the cube made of a liquid crystal screen or freed for the projection of a larger image | Eine durchscheinende Form mit einem Energiezentrum, das einen hellen Strahl aussendet und so das Bild trägt: Dieses kann entweder auf die gegenüberliegende Seite des Würfels projiziert werden, der aus einer Kristallwand besteht, oder auch unabhängig davon größer projiziert werden | Une forme diaphane contenant un noyau d'énergie dense d'où s'échappe un rayon lumineux véhiculant l'image. Elle peut être lue sur la surface opposée du cube devenu écran à cristaux liquides ou peut être libérée pour une projection en plus grande dimension
22 x 22 x 22 cm
Thomson
Concept & Design: Matali Crasset
Photo: Didier Griffoulliere/ Edelkoort Conseil

Radio 1995
ABS plastic | ABS-Kunststoff | Plastique ABS
5.7 x 19.8 x 16.6 cm
Thomson

Video recorder 1995
Video recorder | Videorekorder | Lecteur vidéo
ABS plastic | ABS-Kunststoff | Plastique ABS
9 x 39.4 x 43.9 cm
Thomson

Television 14" 1994
Television set | Fernseher | Téléviseur
ABS plastic | ABS-Kunststoff | Plastique ABS
33.7 x 34 x 37.8 cm
Thomson

Speaker 16.9 1995
Speaker | Lautsprecher | Haut-parleur
ABS plastic | ABS-Kunststoff | Plastique ABS
54 x 85.8 x 53.8 cm
Thomson

Don'O 1995
Clock | Uhr | Horloge
ABS plastic | ABS-Kunststoff | Plastique ABS
26 x 16 x 11.5 cm
Thomson

Television 14" 1994

Television 1994
Television set | Fernseher | Téléviseur
ABS plastic | ABS-Kunststoff | Plastique ABS
55.8 x 66.1 x 48.2 cm
Thomson

Aloo Telephone 1995
Voice command telephone | Durch Zuruf bedienbares Telefon | Téléphone à commande vocale
ABS plastic | ABS-Kunststoff | Plastique ABS
55 x 16.3 x 20.5 cm
Thomson

Speaker 1994
Speaker | Lautsprecher | Haut-parleur
ABS plastic | ABS-Kunststoff | Plastique ABS
54 x 95 x 63.8 cm
Thomson

Photos: Guido Mocafico

TV Bicolonne 1996
Television set | Fernseher | Téléviseur
70 cm
Saba

TV Bicolonne M5116F Screen 1995
Screen | Bildschirm | Ecran
51 cm
Saba

TV Bicolonne T7049SLT 1994
Television set | Fernseher | Téléviseur
70 cm
Saba

Photos: Edelkoort Conseil

Zéo TV 1994–1995
Television set | Fernseher | Téléviseur
36 x 36 x 36 cm
Thomson
Photo: Guido Mocafico

Lebanon 1975

Drawing by | Zeichnung von | Dessin par Jean-Baptiste Mondino

Oz 1994
Portable TV set | Tragbarer
Fernseher | Téléviseur porta-
ble
Mahogany, tinted glass |
Mahagoni, getöntes Glas |
Acajou, vitre teintée
136 x 39 x 34.5 cm
Telefunken

Photos: Jean-François Aloisi

Jim Nature 1994
Portable TV | Tragbarer Fern-
seher | Téléviseur portable
High-density wood, plastic |
Preßholz, Kunststoff |
Bois aggloméré, plastique
38.5 x 37 x 37.5 cm
Saba

Remote control unit (M 5107)
1994
Remote control unit | Fernbe-
dienung | Télécommande
Saba

Remote control unit 1995
Remote control unit | Fernbe-
dienung | Télécommande
ABS plastic | ABS-Kunststoff |
Plastique ABS
24 x 3 x 3 cm
Thomson

Remote control unit 1995
Remote control unit | Fernbe-
dienung | Télécommande
ABS plastic | ABS-Kunststoff |
Plastique ABS
4 x 4 x 23 cm
Telefunken

Photos: Tom Vack

Drawing by | Zeichnung von |
Dessin par Jean-Baptiste
Mondino

Torche radio 1996
Radio
Thomson

Ola 1996
Monoblock telephone | Mono-
block-Telefon | Téléphone
monobloc
ABS plastic | ABS-Kunststoff |
plastique ABS
27.5 x 6 x 5.2 cm
Thomson

Moa Moa 1994
Radio
Bakelite | Bakelit | Bakélite
23.2 x 11.6 x 13.4 cm
Saba
Photo: Jean-François Aloisi

PalaPala 1996
Digital telephone-answering
machine | Digitaler Anrufbeant-
worter | Répondeur télépho-
nique digital
17.5 x 17.5 x 3.2 cm
Thomson

*Photos: Michel Lelièvre/
Studio Bleu for GOOD GOODS/
La Redoute*

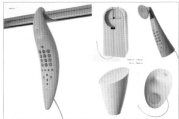

Hook 1996
Telephone | Telefon | Téléphone
ABS plastic | ABS-Kunststoff |
Plastique ABS
26 x 6 x 39 cm
Thomson/Alessi

CooCoo 1996
Radio alarm-clock | Radio-
wecker | Réveil-radio
Analog clock, quartz controlled, made in ABS plastic, terracotta coloured. Alarm on radio or melody, with adjustable
volume. Back lighting | Ana-
loge Quarzuhr aus ABS-
Kunststoff, terrakottafarben.
Alarm und Radiowecker mit
verstellbarer Lautstärke. Be-
leuchtetes Zifferblatt |
Horloge à quartz analogique,
produit en plastique ABS,
couleur terracotta. Réveil par
radio ou sonnerie avec volume réglable. Cadran de
l'horloge éclairable
22 x 10 x 10 cm
Alessi

To yoo 1996
Telephone | Telefon | Téléphone
ABS plastic | ABS-Kunststoff |
Plastique ABS
24 x 6.6 x 7.7 cm
Thomson/Alessi

Poe 1996
Radio
ABS plastic | ABS-Kunststoff |
Plastique ABS
25.5 x 19 cm
Ø: 7.5 cm
Thomson/Alessi

Moosk 1996
Radio
ABS plastic | ABS-Kunststoff |
Plastique ABS
19 x 12 x 10 cm
Alessi

Photos: Hervé Ternisien

Krazy Jacket 1996
Sound-emitting nylon jacket |
Klingende Nylonjacke | Blou-
son en nylon sonore
Saba/Adidas
Concept: Patrick Jouin
Designer: Michael Michalsky

Street Master 1996
FM Radio
17.5 x 20 x 8.2 cm
Saba
Concept: Philippe Starck
Designer: Claude Bressan

Vertigo 1996
TV and video projector | Fern-
seher und Videoprojektor |
Téléviseur et vidéoprojecteur
Projector used like a torch to
project images in phase with
the user's movements. Vertigo
can also be placed on one
of the branches of its bronze
support; the other holds a
glass screen that delivers a
small overhead image | Die-
ser Projektor wird wie eine
Taschenlampe benutzt, die die
Programme in Einklang mit
der Bewegung des Benutzers
bringt. Anschließend legt
man Vertigo auf einen Ast des
bronzenen Ständers; an dem
anderen Ast sitzt ein kleiner
Bildschirm aus Glas, der ein
kleines Overhead-Bild über-
mittelt | Ce projecteur s'utilise
comme une torche, projetant
ses programmes au gré des
mouvements de son manipu-

lateur. Ensuite Vertigo vient
se poser sur l'une des deux
branches d'un support de
bronze, l'autre extrémité
accueillant un petit écran de
verre qui livre une image
intime en rétroprojection
55 x 21 x 41 cm
Saba
Designer: Jean-Michel Policar

Boa 1996
Stereo FM Radio
96 x 9 x 3 cm
Saba
Concept: Philippe Starck
Designer: Claude Bressan

*Photos: Didier Griffouliere/
Edelkoort Conseil*

TV Partoo 1996
Portable TV with integrated
satellite antenna | Tragbarer
Fernseher mit integrierter Sa-
tellitenantenne | Téléviseur
portable avec récepteur sate-
litte
40.8 x 34.8 x 44 cm
Saba
Concept: Philippe Starck
Designer: Claude Bressan
Photo: Edelkoort Conseil

Icipari 1995
AM/FM radio with three mem-
ories and digital tuning | mit
drei Speichern und digitalem
Tuning | avec trois mémoires
et tuner digital
14 x 8 x 9.5 cm
Telefunken
Concept & Design: Matali
Crasset
Photo: Guido Mocafico

Comboo 1995
Combined TV and video disc
player | Kombinierter Fernse-
her und Videorecorder | Télé-
viseur et lecteur DVD com-
biné
Comboo combines the large
format of a 16:9 TV with the
visual and auditory precision
of a digital video disc (SD-
DVD) | Comboo kombiniert
das Großformat eines 16:9
Fernsehers mit der audiovisu-
ellen Präzision einer digitalen
Videokassette (SD-DVD) |
Avide d'images pures, Com-

boo unit le format spectacle
d'un téléviseur 16/9 à la préci-
sion visuelle et sonore d'un
lecteur de vidéo disque
numérique DVD
67.8 x 41 x 43.5 cm
Thomson
Concept: Philippe Starck
Designer: Gérard Vergneau
Photo: Guido Mocafico

Lux Lux 1996
16:9 Pal Plus television set |
Fernseher | Téléviseur
Telefunken
Concept: Philippe Starck
Designer: Mike Davison
Photo: Guido Mocafico

Toccata 1996
Front-loading CD-player. Inte-
grated touch-sensitive keys |
Von vorne bedienbarer CD-
Player. Tastenempfindliche
Bedienung | Lecteur CD à
chargement frontal. Touches
à effleurement intégrées.
Closed | Geschlossen | Fermé:
60 x 40 x 2.5 cm
Open | Geöffnet | Ouvert:
30 x 40 x 5 cm
Telefunken
Concept & Design: Manuela
Simonelli, Andréa Quaglio
Photo: Guido Mocafico

Ego 1996
Video recorder | Videorecorder | Lecteur vidéo
A collective work equipped with a digital video disk (SD-DVD) player and encyclopaedic memory, its sole page is a glass screen controlled by a bookmark across the left-hand side. Fine leather case and silky papers | Ausgestattet mit einem digitalen Videorecorder (SD-DVD) und enzyklopädischem Speicher ist die einzige Seite dieser Kollektivarbeit ein gläserner Bildschirm, der von einem Lesezeichen auf der linken Seite kontrolliert wird. Kasten aus feinem Leder und Seidenpapieren | Ouvrage collectif équipé d'un lecteur de vidéo disque numérique SD à mémoire encyclopédique, sa page unique est un écran de verre sont commandé par un signet. Ecrin de cuir fin et papier de soie
26.7 x 21 x 1.7 cm
Telefunken
Concept: Philippe Starck
Designer: Gérard Vergneau

Perso 1996
Portable visiophone in a Hermès leather case | Tragbares Visiophon im Lederkasten von Hermès | Visiophone portable dans un coffret de cuir Hermès
11.6 x 14.5 x 1.1 cm
Telefunken/Hermès
Concept: Philippe Starck
Designer: Matali Crasset

Fuga 1996
Portable CD player | Tragbarer CD-Player | Lecteur CD portable
Lining of silky fabric | Verkleidung aus Seidenstoff | Capitonnage intérieur de tissu soyeux
46 x 13.3 x 4.1 cm
Telefunken
Concept & Design: Elsa Frances

Photos: Guido Mocafico

Rock'n'Rock 1996
Micro hi-fi system | Mikro Hi-Fi-System | Micro chaîne hi-fi
Amplifier, wireless infrared speakers and CD player, which can also be used separately with headphones. When not used, the units can be stacked together to form a pile of rocks | Verstärker, kabellose Infrarot-Lautsprecher und CD-Player, der auch einzeln als tragbares Gerät mit Kopfhörern genutzt werden kann. Ungenutzt können die einzelnen Teile aufeinander gesteckt werden und bilden so einen Steinhaufen | Amplificateur, haut-parleurs infrarouges sans fil et lecteur CD, qui peut aussi devenir nomade en utilisant un casque. Quand il n'est pas utilisé, les éléments peuvent s'encastrer pour former une pile de pierres
Rocks | Steine | Pierres :
20.8 x 13.5 cm
Telefunken
Concept: Philippe Starck
Designer: Elsa Frances
Photo: Guido Mocafico

Babel 1996
Multimedia column | Multimediaturm | Tour multimédia vidéo
Satellite, cable, digital VCR, digital video disc (SD-DVD), CD-ROM, PC and CDs. Its rectangular column can hold up to 100 + 1 digital discs (SD-DVD), CD-ROM and audio CD) or the equivalent of a home media centre | Satellit, Kabel, digitales VCR, digitale Videokassette (SD-DVD), CD-ROM, PC und Audio-CDs. Die rechteckige Säule kann bis zu 100 und 1 digitale Disketten (SD-DVD, CD-ROM und Audio-CD) oder das Äquivalent eines Heim-Mediencenters aufnehmen | Satellite, réseaux câblés, magnétoscope numérique, vidéo disque numérique DVD, CD-ROM, ordinateur personnel. Sa colonne rectangulaire peut accueillir jusqu'à 100 + 1 disques numériques (DVD, CD-ROM, CD Audio), l'équivalent d'une médiathèque domestique
170 x 42 x 21 cm
Thomson
Concept: Philippe Starck
Designer: Bernard Guerrin
Photo: Edelkoort Conseil

 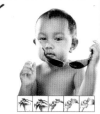

Starck Eyes BIOCITY 1998
Sunglasses | Sonnenbrille | Lunettes de soleil
Black acetate, amber lenses | Schwarzes Acetat, bernsteinfarbene Brillengläser | Acétate noire, verres ambres
Alain Mikli
Photo: Silver Azoulay

Starck Eyes 1996
Advertisement with Dorian Tran, the child of a friend of a friend of Philippe Starck | Werbung mit Dorian Tran, dem Kind eines Freundes eines Freundes von Philippe Starck | Publicité avec Dorian Tran, bébé d'un ami d'un ami de Philippe Starck
Alain Mikli
Photo: Jean-Baptiste Mondino

Philippe Starck with Starck Eyes
Photo: Jean Larivière

Starck Eyes BIOOP.T 1996
Sunglasses | Sonnenbrille | Lunettes de soleil
Matt palladium rims, transparent temples, green lenses | Mattes Palladium, transparente Bügel, grüne Brillengläser | Palladium mat,

branches translucides, verres verts
Alain Mikli
Photo: Michel Lelièvre/ Studio Bleu for GOOD GOODS/ La Redoute

Drawing by | Zeichnung von | Dessin par Jean-Baptiste Mondino

Tomorrow there will be less

Morgen wird es weniger sein

Demain sera moins

Montre sous-cutanée (project) 1976
Watch | Armbanduhr | Montre

Montre digitale (project) 1996
Watch | Armbanduhr | Montre
Computer graphics | Computergrafiken | Infographies: Pascal Cagninacci/DEIS

Low Cost Watch 1998
Watch | Armbanduhr | Montre
Seven Eleven
Ill.: Michel Lelièvre/Studio Bleu

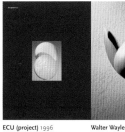

ECU (project) 1996
Photo: Hervé Ternisien

Walter Wayle 1989
Wall clock | Wanduhr | Horloge murale
Thermoplastic resin, grey coloured | Thermoplastisches Harz, grau | Résine thermoplastique, colorée gris
H: 2 cm, ø: 28/11 cm
Alessi

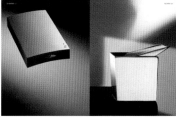

K 1 1991
Hard disk | Festplatte | Disque dur
Plastic | Kunststoff | Plastique
4.4 x 14.5 x 25.4 cm
D2
Photo: Hervé Ternisien

Ray Hollis 1986
Ashtray | Aschenbecher | Cendrier
Polished aluminium | Poliertes Aluminium | Aluminium poli
7.5 x 11.5 x 10 cm
XO
Photo: Tom Vack

Snake (prototype) 1999
4 megapixel digital camera | 4 Megapixel Digitalkamera | Appareil numérique, 4 mega pixels
Aluminium body | Korpus Aluminium | Corps aluminium
Fujifilm

Pour la vie 1990
Vase with flowers | Vase mit Blumen | Vase avec fleurs
Marble and glass | Marmor und Glas | Marbre et verre
72 x 55 cm
up to | bis | jusqu'à 1995
OWO
from | ab | depuis 1996 Alessi

Moondog model 1987
Numbered scale model | Numeriertes Architekturmodell | Maquette d'architecture numérotée
Polished aluminium | Poliertes Aluminium | Aluminium poli
12 x 5.5 x 19 cm
up to | bis | jusqu'à 1995
OWO
from | ab | depuis 1996 Alessi

Pour la vie 1990

Laguiole model 1987
Numbered scale model | Numeriertes Architekturmodell | Maquette d'architecture numérotée
Polished aluminium | Poliertes Aluminium | Aluminium poli
15.3 x 10.5 x 6.5 cm
up to | bis | jusqu'à 1995
OWO
from | ab | depuis 1996 Alessi

Jojo Long Legs 1991
Cheese knife | Käsemesser | Couteau à fromage
Bakelite handle, blade in stainless steel. Available in yellow ocre, red, green and black | Griff aus Bakelit, Klinge aus rostfreiem Stahl. Erhältlich in Ockergelb, Rot, Grün und Schwarz | Manche en bakélite, lame en acier inoxydable. Exisatant dans les tons: ocre jaune, rouge, vert et noir
L: 29.5 cm
up to | bis | jusqu'à 1995
OWO
from | ab | depuis 1996 Alessi

Jojo Long Leg 1991

Laguiole knife 1986
Folding knife | Klappmesser | Couteau pliant
Handle in polished aluminium. Blade in stainless steel | Griff aus poliertem Aluminium. Klinge aus Edelstahl | Manche en aluminium poli. Lame en acier inoxydable
L: 21 cm
up to | bis | jusqu'à 1995
OWO
from | ab | depuis 1996 Alessi

Asahi model 1986
Numbered scale model | Numeriertes Architekturmodell | Maquette d'architecture numérotée
Polished aluminium | Poliertes Aluminium | Aluminium poli
14 x 18 x 19 cm
up to | bis | jusqu'à 1995
OWO
from | ab | depuis 1996 Alessi

Pour la vie 1990

Joe Raspoutine 1987
Wall candle-holder | Wandkerzenhalter | Bougeoir mural
Polished cast aluminium | Aluminium, Muschelguß, glänzend | Aluminium moulé en coquille, brillant
20 x 11 cm
up to | bis | jusqu'à 1995
OWO
from | ab | depuis 1996 Alessi

Photos: Tom Vack

Oa 1996
Table lamp providing diffused light | Tischleuchte mit indirektem Licht | Lampe de table à lumière diffuse
Vase and flower in handcrafted Murano glass. Touch dimmer | Vase und Blume aus mundgeblasenem Murano-Glas. Mit Dimmer | Vase et fleur en verre de Murano. Touche variateur de lumière
59 x 50 x 50 cm
Flos

Berta Youssouf 1987
Table card holder | Platzkartenhalter | Porte-carte
Polished aluminium | Poliertes Aluminium | Aluminium poli
H: 5.3 cm
up to | bis | jusqu'à 1995
OWO
from | ab | depuis 1996 Alessi

Teatriz 1988
Fire screen | Funkenschutz | Ecran de cheminée
Polished aluminium | Poliertes Aluminium | Aluminium poli
86 x 60 cm
up to | bis | jusqu'à 1995
OWO
from | ab | depuis 1996 Alessi

Nani Nani model 1986
Numbered scale model | Numeriertes Architekturmodell | Maquette d'architecture numérotée
Polished aluminium | Poliertes Aluminium | Aluminium poli
15 x 10.5 x 6.5 cm
up to | bis | jusqu'à 1995
OWO
from | ab | depuis 1996 Alessi

Laguiole Set 1986
6 table knives | 6 Tafelmesser | 6 couteaux de table
Stainless steel | Edelstahl | Acier inoxydable
L: 21.5 cm
up to | bis | jusqu'à 1995
OWO
from | ab | depuis 1996 Alessi

O'Kelvin 1989
Table candlestick | Tischkerzenhalter | Bougeoir de table
Base in polished aluminium. Glass lampshade in four colour versions: green, blue, cognac and transparent | Fuß aus gedrechseltem Aluminium, glänzend. Glasschirm in vier Farbversionen: Grün, Blau, Cognac und

Transparent | Pied en aluminium façonné au tour et poli. Abat-jour en quatre versions-couleur: vert, bleu, cognac et transparent
14 x 36 cm
up to | bis | jusqu'à 1995
OWO
from | ab | depuis 1996 Alessi

Paramount IV 1990
Mirror | Spiegel | Miroir
Nickel-plated brass | Vernickeltes Messing | Laiton nickelé
100 x 70 cm
up to | bis | jusqu'à 1995
OWO
from | ab | depuis 1996 Alessi

Miss Zenzen 1986
Numbered scale model | Numeriertes Architekturmodell | Maquette d'architecture numérotée
Polished aluminium | Poliertes Aluminium | Aluminium poli
H: 26 cm
up to | bis | jusqu'à 1995
OWO
from | ab | depuis 1996 Alessi

Paramount II 1990
Mirror | Spiegel | Miroir
Nickel-plated brass | Vernickeltes Messing | Laiton nickelé
205 x 66 cm
up to | bis | jusqu'à 1995
OWO
from | ab | depuis 1996 Alessi

Objets Pointus 1986
Tableware | Besteck | Couverts
Knife | Messer | Couteau : 25 cm
Fork | Gabel | Fourchette : 22.5 cm
Spoon | Löffel | Cuiller : 22 cm
Teaspoon | Teelöffel | Petite cuiller : 15.5 cm
Chopsticks | Eßstäbchen | Baguettes : 24.5 cm
up to | bis | jusqu'à 1995
OWO
from | ab | depuis 1996 Alessi

Photos: Tom Vack

Joe Cactus 1990
Ashtray | Aschenbecher | Cendrier
Bakelite in three colour combinations: ochre and green, red and green, black and green | Bakelit in drei Farbkombinationen: Ocker und Grün, Rot und Grün, Schwarz und Grün | Bakélite en trois versions couleur : ocre et vert, rouge et vert, noir et vert
20.5 x 9 cm
up to | bis | jusqu'à 1995
OWO
from | ab | depuis 1996 Alessi

Miss Donna 1987
Mirror | Spiegel | Miroir
Polished aluminium | Poliertes Aluminium | Aluminium poli
41 x 24 x 1.9 cm
up to | bis | jusqu'à 1995
OWO
from | ab | depuis 1996 Alessi

Luciana Fortyfour 1988
Lantern | Windlicht | Photophore
Polished aluminium, frosted pyrex glass | Poliertes Aluminium, Mattglas | Aluminium poli, pyrex dépoli
H: 25 cm
up to | bis | jusqu'à 1995
OWO
from | ab | depuis 1996 Alessi

Smoki Christiani 1986
Corkscrew | Korkenzieher | Tire-bouchon
Polished cast aluminium. Teflon-coated screw | Poliertes Gußaluminium. Schraube teflonbeschichtet | Aluminium poli, moulé en coquille. Vis revêtue de teflon
H: 27 cm
up to | bis | jusqu'à 1995
OWO
from | ab | depuis 1996 Alessi

Tito Lucifer 1986
Andirons | Kaminböcke | Chenets
Cast iron | Gußeisen | Fonte brute
28.5 x 38.5 x 8 cm
up to | bis | jusqu'à 1995
OWO
from | ab | depuis 1996 Alessi

Joe Cactus 1990
Three colour combinations | Drei Farbkombinationen | Trois versions-couleurs

Picfeu 1986
Poker | Schürhaken | Tisonnier

Chrome steel | Verchromter Stahl | Métal chromé
H: 59 cm
up to | bis | jusqu'à 1995
OWO
from | ab | depuis 1996 Alessi

Mimi Bayou 1987
Handle | Griff | Poignée de placard
Polished aluminium | Poliertes Aluminium | Aluminium poli
Depth | Tiefe | Profondeur : 5 cm
up to | bis | jusqu'à 1995
OWO
from | ab | depuis 1996 Alessi

Chab Wellington 1987
Coat hooks | Kleiderhaken | Patères
Polished aluminium | Poliertes Aluminium | Aluminium poli
20 x 5.3 cm
up to | bis | jusqu'à 1995
OWO
from | ab | depuis 1996 Alessi

Le Moult model 1987
Numbered scale model | Numeriertes Architekturmodell | Maquette d'architecture numérotée
Polished aluminium | Poliertes Aluminium | Aluminium poli
7.5 x 4.5 x 23.5 cm
up to | bis | jusqu'à 1995
OWO
from | ab | depuis 1996 Alessi

Photos: Tom Vack

Dr Kiss 1998
Toothbrush | Zahnbürste | Brosse à dents
Available in orange, pink, violet and yellow. Conical ABS base | Erhältlich in Orange, Rosa, Violett und Gelb. Kegelförmiger Ständer aus ABS-Kunststoff | Existant dans les tons : orange, rose, violet et jaune. Base conique en ABS
H: 20 cm

Alessi

Dr Spoon 1998
Set of four small ear-cleaning spatulas | Set vier kleiner Ohrenreiniger | Lot de 4 petites spatules cure-oreilles
Heat-moulded plastic resin, ABS base | Thermoplastisches Kunstharz, kegelförmiger Ständer aus ABS-Kunststoff | Résine thermo-

plastique avec base en ABS
Alessi

Dr Cheese 1998
Interdental toothbrush | Interdentale Zahnbürste | Brosse interdentaire
Resin, sold with 6 interchangeable heads, ABS base | Thermoplastisches Kunstharz, mit sechs Ersatzbürsten und kegelförmigem Ständer

aus ABS-Kunststoff | Résine thermoplastique livrée avec 6 brossettes interchangeables, base conique en ABS
Alessi

Dr Kleen 1998
Set of six toothpicks | 6er-Satz Zahnstocher | Lot de 6 cure-dents
Polyamide, conical ABS base | Polyamid, kegelförmiger Stän-

der aus ABS-Kunststoff | Polyamide, base conique en ABS
Alessi

Photos: Michel Lelièvre/ Studio Bleu for GOOD GOODS/ La Redoute

Juicy Salif 1990–1991
Drawings | Zeichnungen |
Dessins

Juicy Salif 1990–1991
Lemon squeezer | Zitronen-
presse | Presse-citron
Cast aluminium. Thermo plas-
tic rubber feet | Gußalumi-
nium. Füße aus thermoplasti-
schem Gummi | Fonte
d'aluminium. Pieds en
caoutchouc thermoplastique
H: 29/11.5 cm, ø: 14/5.5 cm
Alessi

**Philippe Starck and | und | et
Juicy Salif** 1990

Max le Chinois 1990–1991
Design drawing | Entwurfs-
zeichnung | Dessin de con-
ception

Max le Chinois 1990–1991
Colander | Abtropfsieb |
Passoire
Stainless steel, brass | Edel-
stahl, Messing | Acier inoxy-
dable, laiton
H: 29 cm, ø: 30 cm
Alessi

Hot Bertaa 1990–1991
Design drawing | Entwurfs-
zeichnung | Dessin de con-
ception

Hot Bertaa 1990–1991
Kettle | Wasserkessel |
Bouilloire
Aluminium, plastic | Alumi-
nium, Kunststoff | Aluminium,
plastique
H: 25 cm
Alessi

Vase Mendini 1990
Vase with lid in white porcelain, and decorated with indeli-
ble transfer and fired at a
temperature of 850 °C |
Deckelvase aus weißem Por-
zellan mit bei 850 °C aufge-
branntem unverwüstlichem
Abziehbilddekor | Ce vase
avec couvercle en porcelaine
blanche décorée avec décal-
comanie appliquée de ma-

nière indélébile par cuisson à
850 °C
H: 38.5 cm, ø: 12.5 cm
Alessi

Olympic Flame for the Winter
Olympics at Albertville |
Olympisches Feuer für die
Winterspiele in Albertville |
Flambeau Olympique pour
les Jeux olympiques d'hiver
d'Albertville 1992
Stainless steel | Edelstahl |
Tôle d'inox
H: 41.4 cm, ø: 8 cm
Photo: Hervé Ternisien

Sesamo 1991
Door handle | Türgriff | Poi-
gnée de porte
Handle reduced to a small
metal wing, without any true
references: looks like a knob,
but works like a handle with-
out a catch mechanism | Der
Griff ist auf eine schmale Flü-
gelform reduziert, ohne ältere
Vorbilder: Er ähnelt einem
Knopf, funktioniert aber wie
ein Griff, ohne Verschlußme-
chanismus | La poignée est
réduite à une étroite aile de
métal, sans références vérita-
bles: elle ressemble à un bou-
ton mais fonctionne comme
une poignée, sans méca-
nisme de fermeture
Aluminium
Rds Kleis

**Door handle (prototype) | Tür-
griff (Prototyp) | Poignée de
porte (prototype)** 1991
Chrome-plated steel | Ver-
chromter Stahl | Acier chromé
14 x 5.5 cm
FSB

Apriti 1991
Door handle | Türgriff | Poi-
gnée de porte
It harks back to the traditional
curved metal handle but with
a special study of the mecha-
nism: one brushes the handle
to open rather than applying
pressure | Rückbezug auf die
traditionelle Griffform, aber

mit einem speziellen Mecha-
nismus: Zum Öffnen der Tür
reicht eine leichte Berührung
des Griffs | Un retour appa-
rent à la poignée en métal
traditionnelle, mais le méca-
nisme est spécialement
étudié: il suffit d'effleurer la
poignée pour ouvrir la porte
Aluminium
Rds Kleis

**PS 1 Door handle | Türgriff |
Poignée de porte** 1991
Matt silver backplate. Polish-
ed lever. Both in high-quality
aluminium | Matt-silberne
Rückenplatte. Polierter Griff.
Beides in hochwertigem Alu-
minium | Face arrière argentée
mate. Poignée polie. Les deux
éléments en aluminium de
haute qualité
FSB

Street Lamp 1992
Street lamp | Straßenlaterne |
Réverbère
Decaux
Ill.: Marc Auger/Decaux

Bus stop 1996
Bus shelter and bench |
Bushäuschen und Sitzbank |
Abribus et banc
Decaux
Ill.: DEIS, Paris

**Computer image of a dustbin |
Computergraphik eines Müll-
eimers | Visualisation infor-
matisée d'une poubelle** 1992
Decaux
Ill.: Pascal Cagninacci/DEIS

**Dustbin | Mülleimer | Pou-
belle** 1992
Decaux

Bench | Bank | Banc 1992
Decaux

**Dustbin | Mülleimer | Pou-
belle** 1992
Decaux

Fence | Zaun | Clôture 1992
Decaux

Fence | Zaun | Clôture 1992
Decaux

Bench | Bank | Banc 1992
Decaux

**Dustbin | Mülleimer | Pou-
belle** 1992
Decaux

**Historic sign | Historisches
Schild | Panneau historique**
1992
Decaux

**Dustbin | Mülleimer | Pou-
belle** 1992
Decaux

Ill.: Marc Auger

**Mineral water bottle | Mine-
ralwasserflasche | Bouteille
d'eau minérale** 1991
Plastic | Kunststoff | Plastique
H: 19 cm, ø: 7 cm
Glacier
Photo: Hervé Ternisien

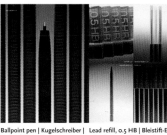

Eau St Georges 1997
Mineral water bottle | Mineral-
wasserflasche | Bouteille d'eau
minérale
PET plastic | PET-Kunststoff |
plastique PET
Eau St Georges, Corse
Photo: Guido Mocafico

Water fountain 1999
Water fountain | Wasser-
spender | Fontaine à eau
ABS body, polycarbonate bot-
tle | ABS-Kunststoff, Flasche
aus Polycarbonat | Corps en
ABS, bouteille en polycarbo-
nate
Château d'Eau
Ill.: DEIS, Paris

Intelligence is feminine

Intelligenz ist weiblich

L'intelligence est féminine

Visionnaire 1999
Plastic box for the magazine
Visionnaire | Kunststoffbox für
die Zeitschrift *Visionnaire* |
Boîtier en plastique pour le
magazine *Visionnaire*
Ill.: DEIS, Paris

**Ballpoint pen | Kugelschreiber |
Stylo à bille** 1998
Polypropylene | Polypropylen |
Polypropylène
Seven Eleven

**Lead refill, 0.5 HB | Bleistift-Er-
satzminen, 0,5 HB | Recharge
de mines, 0,5 HB** 1998
Seven Eleven

**Fluorescent marker pens | Flu-
oreszierende Marker | Mar-
queurs fluorescents** 1998
Polypropylene | Polypropylen |
Polypropylène
Seven Eleven

**Retractable pencil | Druckblei-
stift | Porte-mines** 1998
Polypropylene | Polypropylen |
Polypropylène
Seven Eleven

**Pencils | Bleistifte | Crayons à
papier** 1998
Polypropylene | Polypropylen |
Polypropylène
Seven Eleven

Photos: Yukio Shimizu

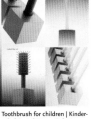

**Toothbrush | Zahnbürste |
Brosse à dents** 1998
Polycarbonate | Polycarbonat
Seven Eleven

**Toothbrush for children | Kinder-
zahnbürste | Brosse à dents
pour enfants** 1998
Polycarbonate | Polycarbonat
Seven Eleven

Hairbrush Blow 1998
Hairbrush | Haarbürste | Brosse
à cheveux
Polypropylene | Polypropylen |
Polypropylène
Seven Eleven
Photos: Yukio Shimizu

X-Acto Knife 1998
Cutter
Stainless steel, polystyrene |
Rostfreier Stahl, Polystyrol |
Acier inoxydable, polystyrène
Seven Eleven

Note Book 1998
B5 Notebook, 40 pages |
Heft, B5, 40 Seiten | Cahier
B 5, 40 pages
Seven Eleven

**Tape dispenser | Tesafilm-
Abroller | Dévidoir de ruban
adhésif** 1998
Polystyrene | Polystyrol | Poly-
styrène
Seven Eleven

**Eraser | Radiergummi |
Gomme** 1998
Seven Eleven

Scissors | Schere | Ciseaux
1998
Stainless steel | Rostfreier
Stahl | Acier inoxydable
Seven Eleven

Photos: Yukio Shimizu

Low Cost Clock 1998
Clock | Wecker | Réveil
ABS plastic, polycarbonate |
ABS-Kunststoff, Polycarbonat |
Plastique ABS, polycarbonate
Seven Eleven

Lighter 1998
Refillable lighter | Nachfüll-
bares Feuerzeug | Briquet
rechargeable
Seven Eleven

*Photos: Michel Lelièvre/Studio
Bleu*

StarckNaked 1998
Seamless tubular garment
with integrated pantihose |
Nahtloses Schlauchkleid mit
integrierter Strumpfhose |
Collants intégrés à un tube,
sans coutures
Wearable as a skirt, or short
to medium-length dress. 80
denier, 92% polyamide and
8% elasthan | Mehrzweck-
kleidungsstück: Tragbar als

Rock und als kurzes oder
mittellanges Kleid. 80-Denier-
Strickstoff, 92% Polyamid,
8% Elastan | Vêtement sus-
ceptible d'être porté aussi
bien comme une jupe, une
robe courte ou moyenne.
Maille 80 deniers, 92% polyamide et 8% élasthane
Wolford
Photos: Jean-Baptiste Mondino

StarckNakedHOT 1999
Multi-purpose garment: Wearable as a skirt, or a short to
medium-length dress. 80 denier stocking-knit, 92% poly-
amide and 8% elasthan | ,
Mehrzweckkleidungsstück:
Tragbar als Rock und als
kurzes oder mittellanges Kleid.
80-Denier-Strickstoff, 92%
Polyamid, 8% Elastan | Vête-
ment susceptible d'être porté

aussi bien comme une jupe,
une robe courte ou moyenne.
Maille 80 deniers, 92% poly-
amide et 8% élasthane
Wolford
Photo: Jean-Baptiste Mondino

**Catalogue Good Goods –
La Redoute**
*Photos: Michel Lelièvre/Studio
Bleu*

Drawing by | Zeichnung von |
Dessin par Jean-Baptiste
Mondino

Starck as Shiva 1998
Catalogue Good Goods – La
Redoute
Photo: Jean-Baptiste Mondino

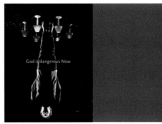

Philippe Starck and | und | et
Miss Sissi

God is dangerous Now

Jetzt ist Gott gefährlich

Dieu est dangereux aujour-
d'hui

Drawing by | Zeichnung von |
Dessin par Jean-Baptiste
Mondino

Philippe Starck 1997
*Photos: Francis
Giacobetti/Turner & Turner*

Paris team 1999
Bénédicte Deverre, Bruno
Borrione, Thierry Gaugain,
Jean-Philippe Hazard and
Patrick Jouin

We just need Love

Wir brauchen nur Liebe

Nous n'avons besoin que
d'amour

Babel 1996 **311, 439**
Badewanne | Baignoire (Hoesch) 1998 **262, 436**
Badewanne | Baignoire (Duravit/ Axor/Hoesch) 1994 **261, 436**
Ballpoint pen (Seven Eleven) 1998 **360, 442**
Banc | Bank (Decaux) 1992 **353, 441**
Basic (Maletti/L'Oréal) 1989 **193, 432**
Bathtub (Duravit/Axor/Hoesch) 1994 **261, 436**
Bathtub (Hoesch) 1998 **262, 436**
Bench (Decaux) 1992 **353, 441**
Berta Youssouf 1987 **331, 440**
Bidet (Duravit) 1998 **262, 436**
Big Nothing 1997 **186, 431**
Bleistifte (Seven Eleven) 1998 **361, 442**
Bleistift-Ersatzminen (Seven Eleven) 1998 **361, 442**
Bo Boolo 1995 **214/215, 433**
Boa 1996 **305, 438**
Bob Dubois 1987 **183, 431**
Boom Rang 1992 **180, 181, 431**
Bouteille d'eau minérale 1991 **354, 441**
Boutique Hugo Boss 1991 **104-107, 427**
Briquet (Seven Eleven) 1998 **367, 442**
Brosse à dents (Seven Eleven) 1998 **362, 442**
Brosse à dents et récipient (Fluocaril) 1989 **255-257, 435/436**
Brosse à dents pour enfants (Seven Eleven) 1998 **363, 442**
Bubu 1er 1991 **212/213, 433**
Bushaltestelle | Bus stop (Decaux) 1996 **351, 441**

Dadada 1993 **224/225, 434**
Delano Hotel 1995 **133-139, 428/429**
Dévidoir de ruban adhésif (Seven Eleven) 1998 **364, 442**
Dick Deck 1989 **183, 431**
Dole Melipone 1981 **198/199, 432**
Don'O 1995 **290, 437**
Douche (Hoesch) 1998 **267, 436**
Dr Cheese 1998 **335, 440**
Dr Kiss 1998 **335, 440**
Dr Kleen 1998 **335, 440**
Dr Skud 1998 **258, 436**
Dr Spoon 1998 **335, 440**
Dr. Glob 1990 **172, 430**
Dr. Life 1991 **236, 434**
Dr. No 1996 **166/167, 430**
Dr. Sonderbar 1983 **198/199, 218, 432, 433**
Druckbleistift (Seven Eleven) 1998 **361, 442**
Dusche (Hoesch) 1998 **267, 436**
Dustbin (Decaux) 1992 **353, 441**

Faitoo 1996 **229, 434**
Faucet, two-handled (Axor) 1998 **265, 436**
Fauteuil de lavage réglable (Maletti/L'Oréal) 1989 **192, 432**
Felix Restaurant in the Peninsula Hotel 1994 **140-143, 429**
Fence (Decaux) 1992 **353, 441**
Fernbedienung (Telefunken) 1995 **299, 438**
Fernbedienung (Thomson) 1994 **286, 437**
Fernbedienung (Thomson) 1995 **299, 438**
Fernbedienung M5107 (Saba) 1994 **299, 438**
Fernseher (Thomson) 1994 **290, 437**
Fernseher 14" (Thomson) 1994 **290, 437**
Feuerzeug (Seven Eleven) 1998 **367, 442**
First 35 S5 Voilier L. Coque 1988 **269, 436**
First 35,7 Voilier L Coque 1992 **269, 436**
First 41 S5 Voilier L Coque 1989 **268, 436**
Flambeau Olympique 1992 **346, 441**
Fluorescent marker pens | Fluoreszierende Marker (Seven Eleven) 1998 **361, 442**
Fontaine à eau (Eau St Georges, Corse) 1999 **357, 442**
Formentera House 1995 **25-27, 423/424**
Fuga 1996 **309, 439**

Hairbrush Blow 1998 **363, 442**
Haut-parleur (Thomson) 1994 **290, 437**
Haut-parleur 16.9 (Thomson) 1995 **290, 437**
Heft (Seven Eleven) 1998 **364, 442**
Historic sign | Historisches Schild (Decaux) 1992 **353, 441**
Hook 1996 **302, 438**
Hot Bertaa 1990-1991 **342/343, 441**
Hotel Mondrian 1996 **92, 94/95, 427**
Hotel St. Martins Lane 1999 **96/97, 427**

J. (Série Lang) Armchair | Lehnstuhl | Fauteuil 1987 **182, 431**
J. (Série Lang) Table | Tisch 1991 **182, 431**
Jim Nature TV 1994 **297, 438**
Joe Cactus 1990 **332, 333, 440**
Joe Raspoutine 1987 **329, 440**
Jojo Long Legs 1991 **329, 440**
Juicy Salif 1990-1991 **336-339, 441**

La Cigale 1988 **124/125, 428**
La Main Bleue 1976 **72/73, 426**
La Marie 1998 **170/171, 430**
Laguiole factory 1987 **46, 425**
Laguiole knife 1986 **329, 440**
Laguiole model 1987 **329, 440**
Laguiole set 1986 **331, 440**
Lama Scooter (prototype) 1992 **284, 437**
Lautsprecher (Thomson) 1994 **290, 437**
Lautsprecher 16.9 (Thomson) 1995 **290, 437**
Lavabo (Duravit/Axor/ Hoesch) 1994 **260, 436**
Le Baron Vert 1992 **20/21, 423**
Le Moult House 1985-1987 **36-39, 424**
Le Moult model 1987 **333, 440**
Le paravent de l'autre 1992 **185, 431**
Lead refill (Seven Eleven) 1998 **361, 442**
Lecteur vidéo (Thomson) 1995 **290, 437**
Les Bains-Douches 1978 **70/71, 426**
Light Lite 1992 **237, 434**
Lighter (Seven Eleven) 1998 **367, 442**
Lila Hunter 1988 **218, 433**
Lio Comun 1991 **218, 433**
Lola Mundo 1988 **174/175, 182, 430, 431**
Lord Yo 1994 **176/177, 430**
Louis XX 1992 **156/157, 429**
Low Cost Clock 1998 **366, 442**
Low Cost Watch 1998 **320/321, 439**
Luciana Fortyfour 1998 **333, 440**
Lundi Ravioli 1995 **218, 433**
Lux Lux 1996 **306, 438**
L.W.S Lazy Working Sofa 1998 **208-211, 433**

A B C D E F G H I J K L M

A
Abribus (Decaux) 1996 **351, 441**
Alo 1996 **287, 437**
Aloo 1995 **290, 437**
Angle (project) 1991 **65, 425**
Apriti 1991 **349, 441**
Ara III **270-273, 436**
Ara Stool 1985 **195, 432**
Ara table lamp 1988 **237, 434**
Arango Jr. House 1996 **34/35, 424**
ArchiMoon Classic 1998 **240, 435**
ArchiMoon Eco 1998 **240, 435**
ArchiMoon Soft 1998 **241, 435**
ArchiMoon Tech 1998 **240, 435**
Asahi Beer Hall 1990 **16-19, 423**
Asahi model 1986 **329, 440**
Asahy 1991 **180, 181, 185, 431**
Asia de Cuba Restaurant 1997 **148/149, 429**
Attila 1999 **169, 430**

C
Café Costes 1984 **69, 76-79, 426**
Café Mystique 1988 **122/123, 428**
Cahier (Seven Eleven) 1998 **364, 442**
Cam El Eon 1999 **187, 431**
Cameleon 1992 **183, 431**
Catalogue Good Goods – La Redoute **372-389, 442**
Ceci n'est pas une brouette 1996 **153, 429**
Chab Wellington 1987 **333, 440**
Chaussure (prototype) 1996 **246/247, 435**
Cheap Chic Armchair 1997 **221, 433**
Cheap Chic Chair 1997 **221, 433**
Cheap Chic Table 1998 **221, 433**
Ciseaux (Seven Eleven) 1998 **365, 442**
Clôture (Decaux) 1992 **353, 441**
Colucci 1986 **182, 431**
Comboo 1995 **306, 438**
Computer image of a dustbin | Computergraphik eines Mülleimers **352, 441**
Condominiums (project) 1992 **65, 425**
CooCoo 1996 **303, 438**
Coppola Salon 1992 **110/111, 427**
Coque 1999 **160, 429**
Costes 1984 **182, 431**
Costes Alluminio 1988 **182, 183, 431**
Crayons à papier (Seven Eleven) 1998 **361, 442**
Cub 1996 **289, 437**

E
Eau St Georges (Eau St Georges, Corse) 1997 **356, 442**
Ecole des Beaux-Arts 1991 **56/57, 425**
ECU (project) 1996 **322, 439**
Ego 1996 **308, 439**
ENSAD (project) 1993 **58/59, 425**
ENSAD (Ecole Nationale Supérieure des Arts décoratifs) 1998 **60-63, 425**
Eraser (Seven Eleven) 1998 **364, 442**

G
Ganesh by | von | par Jean-Baptiste Mondino **7, 423**
Gomme (Seven Eleven) 1998 **364, 442**
Good Goods Catalogue – La Redoute **372-389, 442**
Groningen Museum 1993 **42-45, 424/425**

I
Icipari 1995 **306, 438**

K
K 1 Hard disk | Festplatte | Disque dur 1991 **324, 439**
Kinderzahnbürste (Seven Eleven) 1998 **363, 442**
Krazy Jacket 1996 **304, 438**
Kugelschreiber (Seven Eleven) 1998 **360, 442**

M
Maison de Fran… **52/53, 425**
Mandala 1987 2…
Manin Restaura… **102/103, 427**
Marqueurs fluo… (Seven Eleven) **361, 442**
Max le Chinois **340/341, 441**
Mélangeur à deu… (Axor) 1998 26…
Mendini Vase 19…
Mimi Bayou 19…
Mineral water b… Mineralwasser… (Glacier) 1991
Mischbatterie, z… (Axor) 1998 26…
Mischbatterie (… Hoesch/Axor) **261, 436**
Miss C.O.C.O. … **206/207, 433**
Miss Donna 198…
Miss Sissi 1990… **434, 443**
Miss Trip 1996 …
Miss Yee 1987 2… **435**
Miss Zenzen 19…
Mister Bliss 198…
Mister Meumeu… **253, 435**
Mitigeur monoc… (Duravit/Axor… 1994 **261, 436**
Moa Moa 1994 …
Monsieur X Cha… 1996 **220, 433**
Monsieur X Roc… **220, 433**
Montre digitale … 1996 **318/319,**
Montre sous-cu… (project) 1996
Moondog (proje… **50/51, 425**
Moondog mode… **329, 440**
Moosk 1996 30…
Motó 6,5 1995 2… **436/437**
M.T Minimum … **202-205, 432**
Mülleimer (Dec… **353, 441**

Saint Esprit 1999 **168, 430**
Salon Coppola 1992 **110/111, 427**
Sarapis 1986 **182, 431**
Schere | Scissors (Seven Eleven)
1998 **365, 442**
Schuh (prototype) 1996
246/247, 435
Scooter Lama (prototype) 1992
284, 437
Sesamo 1991 **348, 441**
Shoe (prototype) 1996
246/247, 435
Shower (Hoesch) 1998 **267, 436**
Slick Slick 1999 **216/217, 219,
433**
Smoki Christiani 1986 **333, 440**
Snake (prototype) 1999
326/327, 439
Speaker (Thomson) 1994
290, 437
Speaker 16.9 (Thomson) 1995
290, 437
St. Martins Lane Hotel 1999
96/97, 427
Star's Door 1992 **47, 425**
Starck Club 1982 **98/99, 427**
Starck Eyes BIOCITY 1998
312, 439
Starck Eyes BIOOP.T 1996
314/415, 439
Starck House (3 Suisses) 1994
13, 28-33, 423, 424
Starck House (project) 1991
65, 425
StarckNaked 1998 **368/369, 442**
StarckNakedHOT 1999 **371, 442**
Stool (Maletti/L'Oréal) 1989
193, 432
Straßenlampe | Street lamp
(Decaux) 1992 **350, 441**
Street Master 1996 **305, 438**
Stylo à bille (Seven Eleven) 1998
360, 442
Su Mi Tang 1992 **252, 435**
SUMO table 1999 **200, 432**

Walla Walla 1994 **237, 434**
Walter Wayle 1989 **323, 439**
Waschbecken (Duravit/
Hoesch/Axor) 1994 **260, 436**
Waschtisch, verstellbar | Wash
unit, adjustable (Maletti/
L'Oréal) 1989 **193, 432**
Washbasin (Duravit/
Hoesch/Axor) 1994 **260, 436**
Washbasin mixer (Duravit/
Hoesch/Axor) 1994 **261, 436**
Wasserspender (Chateau d'Eau)
1999 **357, 442**
Water fountain (Chateau d'Eau)
1999 **357, 442**
W.W. Stool 1990 **155, 429**

O P Q R S T U V W X Y Z

ani 1989 **22/23, 423**
ani model 1986 **331, 440**
on 1999 **168, 430**
97-1999 **190/191, 432**
ok (Seven Eleven) 1998
2

Palais de l'Elysée 1983-1984
74/75, 426
PalaPala 1996 **301, 438**
Panneau historique (Decaux)
1992 **353, 441**
Paramount Armchair 1991 **180,
185, 431**
Paramount Hotel 1990
86-89, 426
Paramount II 1990 **331, 440**
Paramount IV 1990 **331, 440**
Pat Conley II 1986 **218, 433**
Pencils (Seven Eleven) 1998
361, 442
Peninsula 1995 **218, 433**
Peninsula Hotel 1994
140-147, 429
Perso 1996 **309, 439**
Picfeu 1986 **333, 440**
Placide of the Wood 1989
183, 431
Placido Arango Jr. House 1996
34/35, 424
Plasmaa 1995 **288, 437**
Plywood car (project) 1996
230/231, 434
Poaa 1999 **222/223, 434**
Poe 1996 **303, 438**
Poignée de porte (FSB) 1991
348, 441
Pointus 1986 **331, 440**
Popopo 1993 **220, 433**
Porte-mines (Seven Eleven)
1998 **361, 442**
Poubelle (Decaux) 1992 **353, 441**
Pour la vie 1990 **328, 329, 440**
Pratfall 1985 **182, 431**
Président M. 1984 **158/159, 429**
Prince Aha 1996 **165, 430**
PS 1 Door handle | Türgriff |
Poignée de porte 1991 **349, 441**
Puzzle 1987 **108/109, 427**

Radiergummi (Seven Eleven)
1998 **364, 442**
Radio (Thomson) 1995 **290, 437**
Ray Hollis 1986 **325, 439**
Ray Menta (project) 1984 **196,
432**
Recharge de mines (Seven Ele-
ven) 1998 **361, 442**
Remote Control (Thomson)
1994 **286, 437**
Remote Control Unit (Telefun-
ken) 1995 **299, 438**
Remote Control Unit (Thomson)
1995 **299, 438**
Remote Control Unit M 5107
(Saba) 1994 **299, 438**
Retractable pencil (Seven Ele-
ven) 1998 **361, 442**
Réverbère (Decaux) 1992 **350,
441**
Richard III 1985 **162, 430**
Rock'n'Rock 1996 **310, 439**
Romantica 1987 **183, 431**
Romeo Moon 1995 **236, 434**
Romeo Moon Soft T2 1998 **238,
435**
Romeo Moon T2 1998 **239, 435**
Rosy Angelis 1994 **236, 434**
Royalton Armchair 1991 **184, 431**
Royalton Bar Stool 1988 **218, 433**
Royalton Bed 1992 **185, 431**
Royalton Chair 1988 **185, 431**
Royalton Chair and bench 1991
181, 431
Royalton Couch 1991 **184, 431**
Royalton Hotel 1988 **81-85, 426**
Royalton Long Chair 1991 **184,
431**
Rue Starck (project) 1991 **64,
425**

Tape Dispenser (Seven Eleven)
1998 **364, 442**
Teatriz 1988 **331, 440**
Teatriz Restaurant 1990
114-121, 428
Techno (Maletti/L'Oréal) 1989
193, 432
TeddyBearBand 1998 **234, 434**
Télécommande (Telefunken)
1995 **299, 438**
Télécommande (Thomson) 1994
286, 437
Télécommande (Thomson) 1995
299, 438
Télécommande M5107 (Saba)
1994 **299, 438**
Téléviseur | Television
(Thomson) 1994 **290, 437**
Téléviseur | Television 14"
(Thomson) 1994 **290, 437**
Tesafilm-Abroller (Seven Eleven)
1998 **364, 442**
Tessa Nature 1989 **183, 431**
Tesa 1988 **331, 440**
Théâtre du Monde 1984 **218, 433**
Theatron Restaurant 1985
127-131, 428
Ti Tang 1992 **252, 435**
Tippy Jackson 1985 **182, 431**
Tito Lucifer 1986 **333, 440**
Titos Apostos 1985 **182, 183, 431**
To yoo 1996 **303, 438**
Toccata 1996 **307, 438**
Toilet | Toilette (Duravit) 1998
262, 436
Toothbrush (Seven Eleven) 1998
362, 442
Toothbrush and toothbrush hol-
der (Fluocaril) 1989 **255-257,
435/436**
Toothbrush for Children (Seven
Eleven) 1998 **363, 442**
Torche radio 1996 **300, 438**
Toto la toto car (project) 1996
232/233, 434
Tour de Contrôle 1993 **49, 425**
Toy 1999 **188/189, 431**
Türgriff (FSB) 1991 **348, 441**
TV Bicolonne 1996 **292, 437**
TV Bicolonne M5116F Screen
1995 **293, 437**
TV Bicolonne T7049SLT 1994
293, 437
TV Partoo 1996 **306, 438**

Vase Mendini 1990 **344/345, 441**
Vertigo 1996 **305, 438**
Vicieuse 1992 **180, 431**
Videorekorder | Video recorder
(Thomson) 1995 **290, 437**
Virtuelle 1997 **274/275, 436**
Visionnaire 1999 **358, 442**
Visualisation informatisée d'une
poubelle 1992 **352, 441**
Vitry 2001 **54/55, 425**
Von Vogelsang 1985 **182, 431**

X-Acto Knife 1998 **364, 442**

Zahnbürste (Seven
Eleven) 1998 **362, 442**
Zahnbürste und Behälter
(Fluocaril) 1989
255-257, 435/436
Zaun (Decaux) 1992
353, 441
Zéo TV 1994-1995
294, 437

We just need Love

for thinking for us
der für uns das Denken übernimmt
pour réfléchir pour nous

for being an elegant American
den eleganten Amerikaner
pour être un Américain élégant

for protecting us 'fro
die uns vor »from wh
pour nous protéger ‹

Shiro Kuramata   **Alessandro Mendini**   Afra, Carlo & Tobia **Scarpa**   **Charles Eames**   **Jean-Luc Godard**   **Jenny Holzer**

pour avoir parlé de l'invisible
der Worte für das Unsichtbare fand
for having spoken of the invisible

pour avoir prouvé que Dieu est dans le détail
die bewiesen haben, daß Gott im Detail steckt
for having proved that God is in the details

pour nous avoir réappris à écouter
der uns lehrte, wieder zuzuhören
for having taught us to listen again